THE HISTORY OF DYESS AIR FORCE BASE

LT. COL. GEORGE A. LARSON, USAF (RET.)

Schiffer Publishing Ltd
4880 Lower Valley Road • Atglen, PA 19310

Wooden highway sign marking the way to Camp Barkeley from Abilene, Texas. *Courtesy 12th Armored Division Museum, Abilene, Texas*

Published by Schiffer Publishing, Ltd.
4880 Lower Valley Road
Atglen, PA 19310
Phone: (610) 593-1777; Fax: (610) 593-2002
E-mail: Info@schifferbooks.com
Web: www.schifferbooks.com

Library of Congress Control Number: 2015956637

Designed by RoS
Cover design by Danielle Farmer
Type set in NewsGoth BT/Sabon
ISBN: 978-0-7643-4822-8
Printed in China

CONTENTS

PREFACE

After my book *Thunder Over Dakota*, Dyess Air Force Base inquired about the possibility of a similar book on the history of Dyess Air Force Base. There is always a start to telling a story, and this begins with the US military buildup prior to WWII and subsequent training on the base during the war. WWII veterans who served at the base were eager to tell their stories and provide the history of the military facility. These rapidly disappearing WWII veterans want to leave a piece of history for relatives telling the story of what NBC's Tom Brokaw refers to as the Greatest Generation. With the Cold War, Dyess again jumped to the forefront of another military buildup, with Nike-Hercules SAMs and Atlas F ICBMs. In the 1950s, the US military viewed the long-range bomber threat of the Russian Air Force seriously enough to push significant funds to deploy surface to air missiles around Strategic Air Command bomber (SAC) bases. SAC evolved as a command at Dyess with the Boeing B-47 Stratojet and KC-97G Stratofreighter (tanker) supported by a special cargo squadron equipped with the Douglas C-124C Globemaster. This allowed the short-range B-47 bombers and CK-97G tankers to forward deploy around the perimeter of the Soviet Union. SAC transitioned to the long-range and more capable Boeing B-52 Stratofortress, supported by the turbojet Boeing KC-135A Stratotanker. SAC and Dyess AFB were on nuclear alert to launch within fifteen minutes in response to a threat or impending Soviet ICBM, SLBM, or bomber attack. Chapter 11 explains the function of the base's special weapons storage area (WSA), built during the Cold War to support B-47s, Atlas ICBMs, Nike-Hercules SAMs, B-52s, and B-1B, and critical to handling and storing nuclear and conventional weapons. Dyess AFB now has an important troop carrier and airlift group flying the Lockheed C-130 Hercules, with the current variant (C-130J) assigned to the base.

The transition from the B-52 to the B-1B, along with President George Bush ending the standing nuclear alert, eventually switched the B-1B's primary role from nuclear to a conventional mission bomber crucial in supporting US and coalition forces in Southwest Asia. Dyess B-1Bs are an important support function for America's war on terrorism around the world. Dyess ties its WWII heritage to the present with an on-base airpark displaying thirty aircraft. It is a tribute from the past to the present and to the future. A photo tour of the base is provided, indicating the breadth of base operations and the significance of the mission. The base went from SAC control to Air Combat Command (ACC) and in 2015, under Air Force Global Strike Command to better respond to changing threats around the world and refinement of its bomber support missions. Dyess is a historic military base and is an indispensable part of the nation's defense against external threats to security.

WORLD WAR II TRAINING CAMP BARKELEY and ABILENE ARMY AIRFIELD

US Army photo of Pvt. David B. Barkley. *Courtesy West Texas Historical Society*

WWII not only changed Texas society and its economy, but its landscape. The state's moderate climate and expansive available (sparsely populated) land made it perfect for year-round military training. Planning and construction of training and command facilities reached unprecedented levels. Texas became the wartime home to 175 military installations, along with numerous minor training and support facilities. Texas was site to sixty-five Army Air Force airfields, thirty-five Army forts and camps, and seven naval stations and bases. There were also more than sixty main and branch/satellite prisoner of war (POW) camps—more than any other state—and three internment camps for the detention of individuals—mostly Axis nationalities—suspected of being US national security risks.[1]

Early in 1940, the Abilene Chamber of Commerce dedicated itself, supported by the City of Abilene's elected officials, to the coming war effort. They offered the War Department a site for training purposes adjacent to the city. Many briefs were filed in Washington, DC, with the War Department, stating the natural advantages of conducting military training operations in west Texas. Approximately 2,200 acres would be needed for the proposed training camp and supporting field training areas. The city had to raise funds to purchase land required for the training site cantonment area. The land was offered under lease agreement to the US government for one dollar per year for a period—extended at the government's option—for a maximum of twenty-five years. The adjoining tract of approximately 68,000 acres would also be leased from its owners in the name of the government at one dollar per acre per year. Preliminary estimates and initial negotiations with the owners of the 2,200 acre tract indicated it would cost $125,000. The Chamber of Commerce Military Affairs Committee began raising funds.

The pedigree of Dyess Air Force Base (AFB) came out of WWII military construction projects near Abilene, Texas. Camp Barkeley (a clerical error in spelling David B. Barkley) was eleven miles southwest of Abilene, in Taylor County. It was originally planned as a temporary camp to train infantry and supply troops. During the war it became one of the state's largest military installations.[2] The camp was named after David B. Barkley, a native Texan who was awarded the Medal of Honor for service in WWI.[3]

David Bennes Barkley was born in 1899 to Josef and Antonia (Cantu) Barkley in Laredo, Texas. Barkley enlisted in the US Army when the United States entered WWI. He was assigned to Company A, 356th Infantry, 89th Division. In France, he was assigned the mission of swimming the Meuse River near Pouilly to infiltrate German lines and gather information about the strength and deployment of troop formations. While returning with the collected information, Barkley developed cramps in the cold river water and drowned on November 9, 1918, two days before the Armistice. His sacrifice earned praise from Gen. John J. Pershing, Commander American Expeditionary Force. Barkley was one of three Texans awarded the nation's highest military honor during WWI. He was also awarded the French *Croix de Guerre* and the Italian *Croce Merito*. On January 10, 1941, the War Department named Camp Barkeley for the Texas WWI hero.[4]

Construction of the camp started in December 1940 (before Pearl Harbor as part of the United States preparations and buildup to the Axis military threat in Europe and the Empire of Japan's growing ambitions in Asia and the Pacific), with the Federal government leasing 70,229 acres, along with the option to purchase a small portion to accommodate the facility and maneuvering grounds.[5] While the camp was under construction, every day before dawn there was a line of car and truck lights moving workers on Highway 277 toward the base.[6] Although the cost of construction was originally estimated at four million dollars, when completed in July 1941 it had escalated to seven million dollars.[7]

Practically all of the post's activities were housed in "Theater of Operations" or hutment type construction, with the exception of the hospital; this was a more permanent wood frame construction, with individual wards and clinics interconnected by walled and roofed corridors and arcades. Camp Barkeley was provided with sufficient mobilization barracks to accommodate 4,000 men, based on eighty square feet of floor space per man. The remainder of the training cadre and all trainees were housed in four to eight man pyramid tents with poured concrete floors and four-foot high wooden plank side walls.[8]

Subsequent expansion and conversions from a temporary tent camp to a cantonment of hutments increased construction costs to twenty-five million dollars. The first major expansion in August 1941 was contracts for building new facilities. Approximately 50,000 men were trained at the camp during its peak of operations, including a 4,000 man Medical Replacement Training Center (MRTC). Construction was completed on December 1, 1941.

The first unit to occupy the camp was the 45th Infantry Division, consisting of 19,000 men under the command of US Army Maj. Gen. William S. Key. The division occupied the unfinished camp. The *45th Divisional News* was published at Camp Barkeley. A member of the newspaper named William Mauldin became a famous WWII cartoonist. After these troops arrived and began training, downtown Abilene was always crowded with soldiers who wanted to get away from the military training camp and its plain surroundings for a few hours. The town's theaters had long lines, and cafés could not accommodate the hungry soldiers at the same time, resulting in long waiting lines.

Other units that trained at Camp Barkeley or were based at the camp included:

Camp Barkeley headquarters of the 12th Armored Division. *Courtesy 12th Armored Division, Abilene, Texas*

90th Infantry Division
11th Armored Division
12th Armored Division
Medical Replacement Training Center
Medical Administrative Officer Candidate School
1846 Unit Prisoner of War (POW) camp (for captured German prisoners)[9]

Another expansion took place in 1942, with the construction of facilities for the Medical Administrative Corps' Officer Candidate School (OCS), activated in May. The OCS was the only school of its kind operated by the Medical Administrative Corps. Commanding the MRTC was US Army Brig. Gen. Roy C. Heflebower, a veteran Army medical officer. From a description of the training at the MRTC in 1942, the rigors of training are apparent:

Camp Barkeley was the site of the US Army Officer Candidate School (OCS) for the Medical Administration Corps. Candidates are in formation, marching to class. Many period cars are visible in the parking lot, along with rows of wood barracks and classrooms in the background. *Courtesy West Texas Historical Society*

The modern medical soldier must be rugged and in tip top physical condition. He must be able to assimilate and retain the techniques of his instructors. He must be a tactician, able to think and act on the split second that maybe the difference between life and death for both himself and his patient. The medic must be fearless, with the courage to go out on the field of battle unarmed and give medical service without regard to his own life in the tradition of the Army Medical Department. It is in striving towards these and many other ends that the trainee spends his time in class and out in the field at the MRTC. The accent is on physical conditioning, with rigorous road marches of the "Commando Training" type, daily exercises to develop muscles for medical care activities in combat. This is besides the classes that include such subjects as military courtesy, chemical warfare, anatomy and physiology, organization of the Army, communications, map reading, sanitation, logistics and first aid treatment. All these and more are woven into the program, and at the same time, the trainee is kept in touch with what is going on in the world through lectures and sound training films on current events and actual war scenes. He has at least one hour of drill each day, at least four or five marches each week. These marches started at a distance of four miles in two hours, increasing to four miles in 45-minutes (including halts) and nine miles in two hours, 16 miles in four hours and 25 miles in eight hours. That's the schedule and they do it with packs weighing up to 45 pounds.

There are night problems, setting up and camouflaging medical installations at night, seeking out and then treating and transporting patients by litter in the dark, under simulated combat conditions. There are two exacting obstacle courses, one negotiated on foot with a full pack and the second by litter teams carrying patients through a maze of barriers, and a hasty entrenchment area where the trainee learns to increase his speed in diving into a trench, foxhole or other cover from air to ground attacks. Trainees are given a rigid course in "hand to hand combat" to protect themselves in case of personal attack and their patients. They become accustomed to gun fire by negotiating the infiltration course by crawling 120 yards on their stomachs with .30 caliber machine gun bullets fired over their heads.

The acid test for the trainee, besides the academic tests he has received and been graded on in his daily classroom and field work, is the bivouac near the end of his training. Equipped with full packs, the trainees hike 16 miles out to the bivouac area, live and operate under simulated battle conditions. They sleep under camouflage, walk under camouflage and set up their medical installations under camouflage. Here, every phase of their basic training is brought into play in a mock battle.

During the time the MRTC was operating (May 1942 until the end of the war) it graduated 12,500 Medical Officer Candidates.[10]

As Camp Barkeley reached its peak training capacity it became a city within itself, with every facility essential to a modern army camp (at that time). It had a 230-bed hospital, adequate warehouses, two large cold storage plants, a bakery, bank, four large theaters, two enlisted men's service clubs, eleven chapels, and thirty-five Post Exchange buildings. All military personnel were housed in hutments except for 4,000 men in sixty-four-man barracks.[11]

On February 1, 1944, the 1846th Unit POW Camp was activated under the command of US Army Lt. Col. Harry Slaughter. At its maximum occupancy in March 1945, the POW compound at Camp Barkeley held 840 German prisoners. Two months after the POW camp opened twelve prisoners escaped, but were recaptured in one week.[12]

The primary difference between POW camps in the United States and stateside Army installations were the guard watch towers along the double barbed wire fence enclosure, floodlights, and armed guards. Guards were kept to a minimum and were usually recruited from personnel that for health, lack of military training, education, or psychological makeup were classified unsuited (qualified)

Camp Barkeley in 1944. US Army trainees going through the obstacle course. *Courtesy West Texas Historical Society*

for overseas combat. Discipline among the German prisoners was rigidly enforced by the camp's officers and sergeants. However uncomfortable, Texas residents considered the treatment of POWs in their state too good, given their own sacrifices while living in a wartime economy and worrying about loved ones overseas.

This was not reality. From 1943—when the POWs began arriving in Texas in large numbers—until the end of the war in 1945, these prisoners worked hard. They picked peaches and other citrus fruits, harvested rice, cut wood, bailed hay, threshed grain, gathered pecans, and baled record amounts of cotton. Many Texas farmers remembered their POW workers with admiration for hard work completed.

Daily POW life was basically the same as at military installation camps, main camps, and smaller satellite camps to a lesser level set up where agricultural labor was needed. Reveille was at 5:45 a.m. with lights out at 10 p.m. Between these times prisoners worked, took care of their personal needs, and entertained themselves with a variety of handicraft and educational opportunities. Every camp usually had a selection of prisoner-taught courses, ranging from English to engineering; an orchestra; a theater group; a camp newspaper; and a soccer team. Some prisoners were allowed to take correspondence courses from local colleges and universities. Most of these US academic credits were accepted by German universities after the prisoners returned home.

Camp Barkeley at peak capacity in 1944, at which time wood barracks, hutments, and tents could hold 60,000 troops. *Courtesy West Texas Historical Society*

Beginning in November 1945, after the fall harvest in the United States, German POWs held in the United States were returned to Europe at the rate of 50,000 a month. Unfortunately, they were not permitted to travel directly to Germany. Most were detained in England and France for forced labor projects. Many became embittered over their treatment in England and France after their release from POW camps in the United States, where they had been well treated. As the POWs left Texas the POW camps were closed.[13]

On April 30, 1945, Camp Barkeley was deactivated, although the war in Europe and the Pacific continued. The camp was closed in September 1945 and dismantled. The War Department estimated its construction, land acquisition, and operational costs from December 1940 to September 1945 at $27,332.00. At the time Camp Barkeley closed, the military reservation encompassed one-ninth of Taylor County (approximately 77,436 acres), of which the government owned 18,976 acres. After Camp Barkeley was abandoned leased land reverted to its previous owners. The military installation had a long term impact on nearby Abilene. Construction and US Army payrolls helped the local economy pull out of the terrible downslide of the Depression, providing jobs and hopes for a better tomorrow even during the war. Abilene's ability to maintain satisfactory relations with a large military population (Camp Barkeley and Tye Army Air Base—during construction, later renamed Abilene Army Airfield) was a factor in the 1950s Department of Defense's locating Dyess AFB there.[14]

Today, few structures remain of Camp Barkeley. The Texas National Guard retained 993 acres of the former military facility as a firing range from 1945 to 1999. This facility was used as a training range for US Army troops preparing for deployment to peacekeeping activities in Bosnia, learning how to defuse land mines. All that remains of the old firing range area is a concrete and earthen berm from which targets were raised and lowered.[15] Later, in 1960 to 1961, part of Camp Barkeley once again became an important military installation as the US Army began constructing two Nike-Hercules surface to air anti-aircraft missile defense sites to protect Dyess AFB. One of these sites was constructed and operated in a corner of the former WWII Army training facility.

During WWII, the most obvious changes in Texas were demographic and economic. Because of wartime demands people migrated to the state in large numbers, as many as 450,000 in less than four years. Since industrial jobs were plentiful in or near the large cities, these areas saw rapid urbanization, along with accompanying benefits and disadvantages. Oil became the dominant resource and economic commodity in the state and cotton and cattle no longer remained the primary economic power, with the petrochemical industry along the Gulf Coast stimulating the state's economy. Advances in agriculture in west Texas—from El Paso to the Pecos River to the Panhandle—used irrigation and advanced agricultural methods for greater and diverse production. In east Texas, many became dairy farmers and cattle ranchers while maintaining a vibrant lumber industry. The area from Brownsville to Laredo (the Rio Grande Valley) continued development as a truck farming and citrus production region. With the expansion of rural electrification and 600,000 veterans returning home in anticipation of enjoying greater freedoms and benefits after a victorious war, Texas became a more diversified and urban population.[16]

During WWII, the US Army Air Force (USAAF) built Tye Army Airfield to the north-northeast of Camp Barkeley, the current site of Dyess AFB. On December 18, 1942, the airfield was opened—due to its initial construction being authorized and started prior to Pearl Harbor—and was renamed Abilene Army Air Base and then Abilene Army Airfield.[17] Tye, Texas—also referred to earlier as Tebo and Hines—is at the intersection of the Missouri Pacific Line railroad, State Highway 84, and Farm Road 707, and is eight miles west of Abilene in Taylor County. By 1914, Tye included two general stores, a lumberyard, grocery store, and a drug store. This dramatically changed during WWII with the construction and operation of the airfield.[18]

In 1941, the Air Corps operated 156 airfields in the United States. By 1943, this number had increased to 783 for the USAAF. This aspect of expansion, like aircraft production and training, was impacted by a lack of time and frequently increased national defense objectives. The new military installations should have been constructed prior to the expanded training program. The government made arrangements to take over or share commercial and municipal airport facilities. Meanwhile, it was necessary to acquire new sites and build new installations. As the Air Corps grew, new airfields appeared throughout the country. Each new airfield involved a basic decision regarding temporary or permanent construction. The pressure of time to complete these facilities generally followed trends toward less permanent wood construction, with buildings as rough covered shells. The large complex of fields around San Antonio, Texas, for example, includes every possible combination of facilities, ranging from the modern architecture of Randolph Field to the heat baked tar-paper hutments of the Aviation Cadet Center; from the huge shops and concrete ramps of Duncan Field to the cow pasture sod of auxiliary landing strips, such as the two used at Camp Barkeley for L-5 Sentinel light/liaison, single-engine aircraft. Also included were the three sod runways at Abilene Air Terminal, one of which was 2,500 feet long and ran northwest to southeast.

At Kelly Field, living quarters included modernistic duplexes, permanent barracks, and shacks built during WWI to temporary canvas tent encampments. The general trend was toward less substantial construction, as the Air Corps grew beyond any imagined peacetime size and it became increasingly obvious that national labor and construction materials and resources were not limitless.[19]

The field's name was changed on April 8, 1943, to Abilene Army Airfield. The initial airfield host unit operating at the airfield was the 474th Base Headquarters and Airbase Squadron on December 18, 1942, assisting with construction of the field and starting training operations. The airfield was initially assigned to the Second Air Force, with its primary mission as a flying training center for air cadets.[20]

It took a lot to authorize Abilene Army Airfield. Earlier, on July 3, 1942, the War Department transmitted its initial approval for a "Proposed Air Support Command Base, Camp Barkeley, Abilene, Texas," which started as Tye Army Air Base during construction. The Army Corps of Engineers, Engineering Branch, War Construction Section stated:

1. It is considered economically feasible to construct the proposed installation at this site meeting minimum requirements for military airports.
2. Attention is invited to telephone conversation between this office and the San Antonio District Office concerning the following:
   a. The site is the only one available.
   b. Poor soil is to be gi[illegible]n.
   c. The 4.1 mile pipeli[illegible] serious problem.
   d. Railroad facilities v[illegible]
   e. Drainage toward th[illegible]h line west of the flying field.
3. Approval of this is re[illegible]

Al[illegible]

Size	1,516 acres
Runways	[illegible]0 feet by 150 feet) asphalt
	[illegible]0 feet by 150 feet) asphalt
	[illegible]0 feet by 150 feet) asphalt
Hangar	[illegible]ood (213 feet by 162 feet)
Available fuel storage	[illegible]ge tanks (187,000 gallons)
Service units	(11)
Communications	[illegible]ne, telegraph, and teletype
Shops	For major repairs
Buildings	Wood and tent[22]

Construction work on Abilene Army Air Base. *Courtesy Abilene Library Digital Archives*

The following units trained at Abilene Army Airfield during WWII:

1. 77th Tactical Reconnaissance Group (April 6, 1943, to September 13, 1943). The group was disbanded at Birmingham Army Airfield, Alabama, on November 30, 1953.*
2. 69th Tactical Reconnaissance Group (September 10, 1943, to November 12, 1943)*
3. 408th Fighter-Bomber Group (November 10, 1943, to April 1, 1944). The group was disbanded on April 8, 1944, at Klamath Falls Municipal Airport. Trained with A-24, A-26, P-40, and P-47 aircraft.
4. 261st Army Air Base Unit (March 25, 1944, to April 1, 1946).[23]

The USAAF activated Abilene Air Base on December 12, 1942, as the 474th Base Headquarters and Air Base Squadron. The authority to activate the airfield was in General Order Number 180, Second Air Force, Fort George, Wright, Washington, dated December 18, 1942. Personnel were drawn from the 96th Headquarters and Air Base Squadron, Elser Field, Louisiana. The first personnel to arrive consisted of eleven officers and twenty-two enlisted men during the construction phase of the field. During construction facilities for the 96th were limited. The 96th grew to eventually include:

908th Quartermaster Company
Finance Department Third Air Force
853rd Signal Service Company
3rd Weather Squadron
206th Ordnance Company Aviation
Medical detachment
3rd Airways Communications Squadron

US Army Stinson L-5 Sentinel, a two-seat liaison and observation aircraft from Abilene Army Air Base, adjacent to Camp Barkeley. The L-5 pilot is flying low and slow to engage a line marked with flags (visible behind and below the aircraft) on it to pick up a message from the troops on the ground. L-5s were used to fly over advancing troops to drop messages on enemy troop positions. *Courtesy 12th Armored Division Museum, Abilene, Texas*

Dedication of the base was on June 3, 1943. On March 31, 1944, the first class graduated from the Replacement Training Unit (RTU) Program. Thirty P-47 pilots trained in navigation, aerial gunnery, enemy aircraft recognition, and aircraft maintenance; they completed their last hour of flying and attended their final ground school class. Throughout the operation of the field there were training accidents, though not as publicized as deaths in combat operations. The official USAAF history for the field (April 1 to 28, 1943) provides a snapshot of what could happen at stateside training bases while preparing pilots for the dangers and rigors of overseas combat. During this time there were five accidents. One was the result of a P-47 sustaining a full flight collision with power lines. One landing accident on April 9 was the result of a trainee pilot attempting to land his P-47 too closely behind the aircraft preceding him on the approach. He was caught in the slipstream of the aircraft in front of him, causing him to lose control of his own aircraft. The plane struck the ground out of control, cartwheeling before coming to a stop. The aircraft was heavily damaged but the pilot escaped injury.

Class AB 5-15 was the second group of P-47 pilots trained under the Combat Crew Training School (CCTS) and departed from the field on May 17, 1944. These sixty pilots transferred to Harding Field, Louisiana, to await their combat assignments. This class completed all its training on schedule without a single fatal accident. In August 1944, Class AB 7-29's curriculum expanded, including an additional seventy hours and adding thirty days to the training schedule (total class training, excluding air time, was 145 hours of ground training and forty-five hours of combat intelligence training).

As training increased additional aircraft parking was needed. To provide additional parking space, constructing 180,000 square feet of parking apron was authorized. This increased available aircraft parking by thirty-five percent. The apron was constructed under the supervision of the post engineer by L.H. Lucy Company of Dallas, Texas, for $67,000. The parking apron was added to the south end of the existing apron and was 300 feet wide and 720 feet long, oriented north-south. The concrete was

* Both reconnaissance groups trained reconnaissance pilots, aircrews, and personnel who fought overseas.

placed on a twelve-inch compacted select material base eight inches thick. Fire hydrants were placed 200 feet apart. Aircraft tie downs were in alternate rows spaced on twenty-foot centers. All work was completed by November 15, 1944.

Douglas A-24 at the National Museum of the United States Air Force at Wright-Patterson Air Force Base, Dayton, Ohio. *Author*

In December 1944, a complete P-47 mock up divided into eleven sections arrived from Peterson Field, Colorado Springs, Colorado. The mock up was set up in one of the empty training buildings to provide detailed instruction, enabling trainee pilots to study the sections of a P-47 and see how each part functioned. Construction also began on December 3 to install a permanent night landing system at a cost of $40,500, replacing Kerosene filled light pots to reduce night taxiing and take-off and landing accidents. To increase P-47 pilot production, in January 1945 the field acquired Avenger Field at Sweetwater—forty miles to the west—under satellite operations. Prior to January, the mission of Avenger Field was to train women pilots to ferry all types of aircraft for the USAAF, augmenting the Ferrying and Transport Service of the USAAF and releasing male pilots for combat duty. Under the new training operation Avenger Field turned out P-47 pilots.

In March 1945, for the first time Abilene AAF failed to meet its allocation of trained pilots sent to the staging area for overseas assignment: it furnished sixty, with the shortfall of two made up from other air force command fields.

As with those fields operating in tornado alley, high winds, hail, and heavy rain were always a danger. On March 14, winds tore into the base at eighty-five miles per hour, damaging buildings (destroying two) and aircraft (seven with major damage and twelve with minor damage). Most of the aircraft damage was on external surfaces. The wind ripped aircraft from their moorings, causing several aircraft to bounce crazily and collide. Several were struck by flying debris. Two aircraft had their wings completely changed, with others requiring new rudders, elevators, and vertical and horizontal stabilizers. The closing of Camp Barkeley in April created problems with hospital services, rations, and commissary facilities.

During this time Abilene Municipal Airport—which had been on lease to the USAAF since the early days of the war—was declared federal surplus. Its runways were too short for safe P-47 operations and handling large transient aircraft, and operations at Abilene AAF and Avenger Field were sufficient to handle military aircraft numbers. If necessary, release of the contract would allow the City of Abilene to negotiate its use by a civilian agency—probably American Airlines Inc., which had a terminal there. The introduction of rocket firing into the flying training program took place in December. The gunnery program included ground and air gunnery, bombing, and rocket firing. Trainees were required to fire twenty-four rockets during advanced training.

During May 1945, the announcement of the end of the war in Europe (V-E Day) affected Abilene AAF; a large number of pilots who had completed their training returned from their ports of embarkation and staging areas for further training. This sudden regrouping placed additional administrative burdens on the P-47 training field and on Avenger Field, finding the training facilities with almost twice as many pilot trainees as normally assigned. Approximately 250 were at Abilene AAF and 175 at Avenger Field, the largest number in training at these two fields since the CCTS was organized in February 1944. Further confusion resulted when pilot trainees from Dalhart AAF were transferred from the closed base to Abilene AAF at about the same time as pilots returned from ports of embarkation and staging areas. Personnel stationed at Abilene Municipal Airport were released and created manpower shortages. The release of almost 200 African Americans created a large manpower gap at the field that was partially filled by German prisoners from Camp Barkeley working in the officer's mess, consolidated mess, motor

Douglas A-26C Invader at the National Museum of the United States Air Force at Wright-Patterson Air Force Base, Dayton, Ohio. *Author*

pool, and in various non-direct war support functions at the field. German prisoners filled similar manpower shortages at Avenger Field. These prisoners were trucked from Camp Barkeley to the two fields in the morning and back at the end of the work day. By the end of the month 140 German prisoners were working at both fields.

Within several days after V-E Day, twenty-five men (nine officers and sixteen enlisted men) were ordered to separation centers in various service commands to be discharged under the point system. (Points were only one of the factors considered when officers on flying status indicated a desire to be relieved from service.) In June 1945, eight Turkish Air Force pilots arrived at Abilene AAF for P-47 fighter pilot training under arrangement between the Turkish and United States governments.

Work on the runways and taxiways at Avenger Field was begun in June to materially aid the training program. Engineers measuring the heading of the runways found that each was ten degrees off and required correction. The runway and taxiway strips were marked with a yellow stripe down the center to aid pilots during take-offs, landings, and taxiing. For the third consecutive time Abilene AAF won the Second Air Force Flying Schedule Campaign in June, establishing itself as the leading Second Air Force installation as the fifth flying campaign closed out. This did not stop P-47 training accidents. On June 4, five farmers from Snyder, Texas, rescued 2nd Lt. Hardin G. Calvert of Dallas, Texas—a trainee at Avenger Field—when his P-47 crashed and burned near Snyder. The plane crashed on Charles Lyons's farm. The five local farmers used a wrench to break open the canopy and used a knife to cut the young pilot from his harness. Less than a minute after they removed him to safety the plane exploded. The pilot was transported to Snyder Hospital.

In August, Abilene AAF and Avenger Field comprised the 261st AAF Base Unit. Abilene AAF was designated Squadron A and Avenger Field was Squadron L. Abilene Municipal Field—leased as an auxiliary field—was returned to the City of Abilene on August 1, 1945, terminating a contract dated June 1941.

On August 26, 1945, an inactivation announcement was made by Headquarters Second Air Force at Colorado Springs, Colorado, that Abilene AAF would be placed on temporary inactive status by December 31, 1945. With the war in Europe and the Pacific over, Abilene AAF was crowded with 256 aircraft (three C-45s, two B-25s, two C-47s, twelve AT-6s, and P-47s) and Avenger Field added another seventy-one programmed to fly to Abilene AAF. Aircraft from Galveston Gunnery School, Brownsville Gunnery School, and Fort Summer Field, New Mexico, were divided between Abilene AAF and La Junta AAF, Colorado, for final 65-2 inspection and ferrying to Reconstruction Finance Corporation (RFC) stations for the disposal of P-47s (except P-47Ns). Twenty-five P-47s were ferried to RFC stations Walnut Ridge, Arkansas; Altus, Oklahoma; and Kingman, Arizona, during the month.

A gradual cutback in flying time was made at the end of September and continued to October 23. At this time Abilene AAF commander Col. Allison cancelled all flying training and support activities, including overnight cross-country flights. At the end of the month all flying was to secure flying time, with some pilots having difficulty obtaining their four earns to maintain flight pay status.

On December 1, 1945, there were 150 aircraft remaining at Abilene AAF; the majority were P-47s, but it did include three C-45s, two B-25s, and two C-47s. One hundred five excess P-47s were transferred to the RFC depot at Independence, Kansas. Only P-47Ns were retained in active flying status and Abilene AAF had thirty. The movement of all supplies from Avenger Field except those required to maintain standby status was to be complete by December 15. The primary mission of Abilene AAF—the training of qualified fighter pilots—was actually completed, although a number of officers were still listed as trainees. The final tabulation shows 642 pilots completed their final stage of training at the field.

For Avenger Field, the Sweetwater City Commission advised the city manager to question and receive an answer to the signed terms of the lease agreement by the Defense Plant Corporation and the City of Sweetwater—originally for a ten year period—on why it was not now satisfactory for the War Department. The City of Sweetwater seeked to obtain the property at the airport through the Civil Aeronautics Administration (CAA) after Washington reported earlier that installations at the field—which had been used by the 72nd Fighter Wing, Second Air Force as a training field for fighter pilots—had been declared and placed on the Federal Surplus Property List. Texas Congressman Sam Russell advised the City of Sweetwater's manager that the property had not been listed earlier in the week with the Surplus Property Board. The City of Sweetwater filed an application with the federal government for the transfer of all buildings, maintenance equipment, and fire and fuel trucks without any exchange of funds to the City of Sweetwater. The City of Sweetwater also requested immediate use of the facilities pending final disposal of the property.

The official deactivation of Abilene AAF was scheduled for December 31, 1946, but was moved up in November 1945 to December 31, 1945. Beginning December 1, Abilene AAF received orders for deactivation and the primary mission of the field became deactivation. There were regular deactivation progress meetings under supervision of the commander Abilene AAF. Sections no longer necessary for the reduction mission were rendered inactive. The first chapter of Dyess AFB had ended.[24]

Republic P-47D Thunderbolt at the National Museum of the United States Air Force at Wright-Patterson Air Force Base, Dayton, Ohio. *Author*

Curtiss P-40E Warhawk at the National Museum of the United States Air Force at Wright-Patterson Air Force Base, Dayton, Ohio. *Author*

ABILENE AIR FORCE BASE and INTRODUCTION to DYESS AIR FORCE BASE

The Korean War erupted on June 25, 1950 (June 24 in the United States east of the International Date Line) after the North Korean People's Army (NKPA) and its Border Constabulary Force crossed the 38th parallel into the Republic of South Korea. The United States again went to war only five years after the end of WWII. President Harry Truman called it a "Police Action."[1]

The City of Abilene's leaders called for the re-establishment of an active military installation at the site of the WWII Abilene Army Airfield. They believed the airfield's 1,500 acres was the perfect site for an Air Force base. The City of Abilene's leaders traveled to the Pentagon to make a formal request. The city leaders showed their determination for a new air base by raising $893,000 to purchase 3,500 acres adjacent to the WWII airfield. They were able to get the assistance of Texas US Senator Lyndon B. Johnson, who had the political strength to persuade Pentagon officials to consider reactivating the airfield near Abilene.[2]

On March 12, 1952, the US House of Representatives held budget appropriation meetings for the operations of the Air Force, including the Strategic Air Command's (SAC) expansion of additional bases. Col. J.C. Jensen, directorate of operations (DO), deputy chief of staff (DCS)/ operations, stated:

> For major repairs and minor construction…The funds in Project 459, which amount to $80,000,000, provide for non-current type work which are beyond the scope of regularly assigned maintenance personnel. The estimate of $80,000,000 is based on Air Force program of installations for Fiscal Year 1953 (FY 53) and encompasses: restoration of reactivated installations and facilities of original design or construction standard for utilization consistent with assigned missions; work which is required at existing installations and facilities to restore damaged, or deteriorated real property to an economically usable condition; and modification of existing facilities when essential to the accomplishment of the mission. The policy of maximum utilization of existing installations requires adaption of operational support installations from WWII standards to meet saturated troop occupancy conditions and modern aircraft operational requirements. Use of newly designed jet and conventional aircraft requires major changes in aircraft fuel storage and dispensing systems, aircraft maintenance facilities and airfield pavements. Minor additional security and provisions, including exterior lighting and fencing, have also become necessary. Due to the use of substandard materials and emergency expedients during the course of original construction, considerable rehabilitation and major repair work is necessary.[3]

Lt. Col. C.M. Turner, director of installations (DI), DCS/Operations, commented: "Typical projects covered in the major repairs category would be on such as Tye Field, Abilene, Texas, is $48,600. These are repairs to existing sewage-treatment plant. This type of work is being done by contract. It is beyond the capabilities of the maintenance staff at the base."[4]

Representative Mahon, chairman house appropriations committee, noted during discussion of the request for funds for bases not yet authorized, "Let us take as an example a major repair or maintenance base, such as Tye Air Force base, and you made reference to that in your formal statement, Colonel."

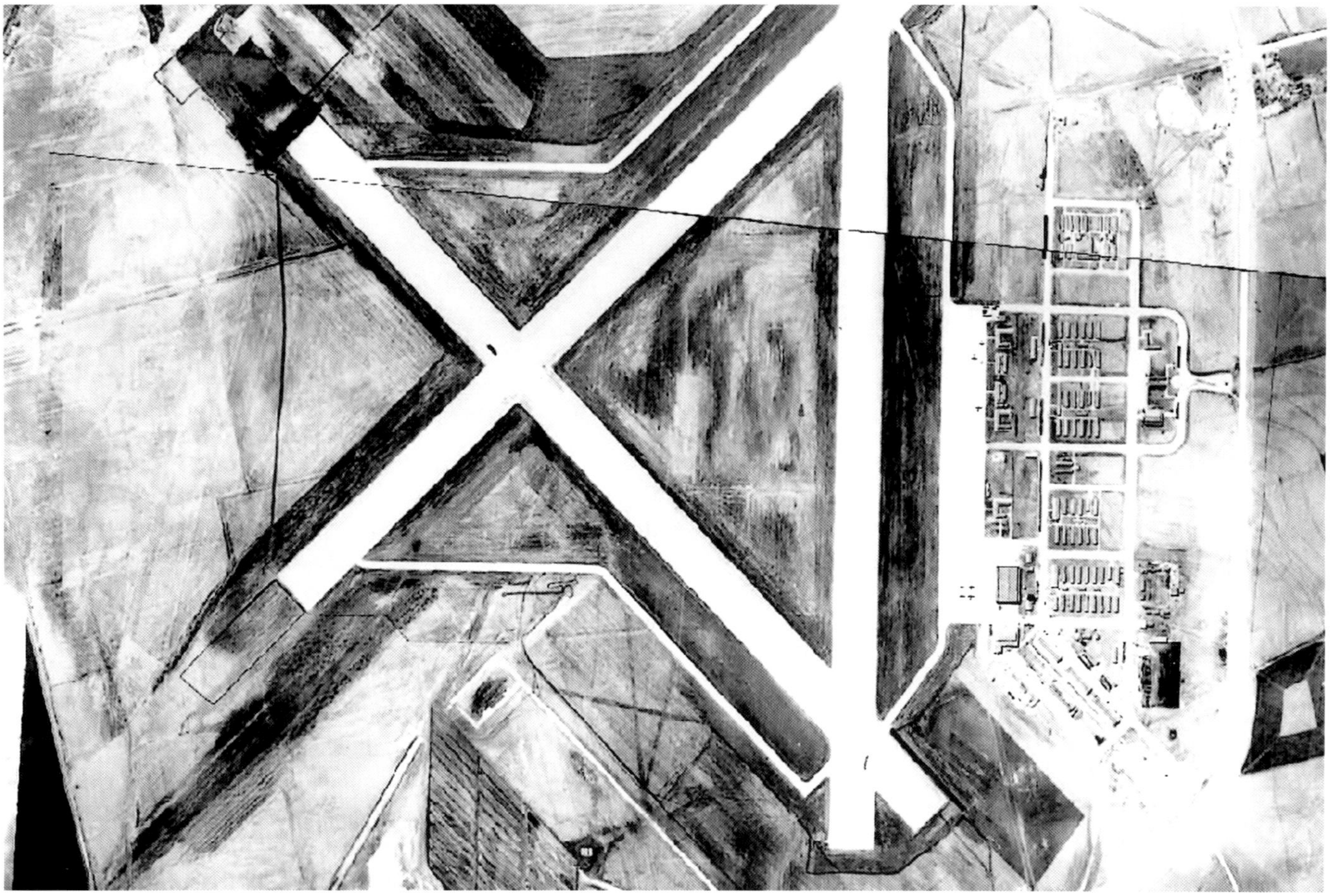

Aerial photo of Abilene Army Airfield during World War II and prior to postwar construction of the base, at which time it became Abilene Air Force Base. *Courtesy Abilene Public Library Digital Archives*

Colonel Jensen, "Yes."

Mahon, "Tye Air Force Base has not been reactivated. It is looked upon favorably by the Strategic Air Command as a base for the B-47, but Congress has not authorized the reactivation of that base, nor has it authorized the reactivation of a number of other bases which are being seriously considered for reactivation. What have you done in this budget toward requesting funds for base maintenance and at bases whose reactivation has not yet been approved by Congress or even considered by Congress?"[5]

Eventually, the committee's questions were answered during testimonies and on July 14, 1952, Public Law 534 was passed by congress "To authorize certain construction at military and naval installations, and for other purposes." Which, under "Title III, Section III, Continental United States, Strategic Air Command. Tye Field, Abilene, Texas: airfield pavements, liquid-fuel storage and dispensing facilities, communications, navigation aids and airfield lighting facilities, operational facilities, aircraft maintenance facilities, troop housing facilities, administrative and community facilities, storage facilities and shops, $23,472.000."[6]

Total appropriations (spending) for the construction project at Abilene Army Airfield reached thirty-two million dollars. During construction the facility was named Abilene Air Force Base (AFB). Ground breaking ceremonies were held on September 24, 1953, beginning extensive construction activities. The red brick ranch-style architecture boasted a definite Texas influence throughout the base. A unique feature of building construction was the buildings were primarily permanent structures. Construction workers rehabilitated the three runways and taxiway system to support planned SAC bombardment air and air refueling missions, construction of a permanent hospital in September 1956, and a 1,000-unit Capehart housing area that remained occupied until 1968.[7]

Dyess Air Force Base fire station. The runway control tower is visible behind and to the right of the three-bay doors of the fire station. A World War II jeep is parked in front. *Courtesy Abilene Public Library Digital Archives*

Construction workers upgraded the 1,200-foot wide and 9,900-foot long concrete parking apron along the east side of the runway to support Boeing B-47 Stratojet and Boeing KC-97L Stratotanker operations, and later the heavier and larger Boeing B-52 Stratofortress supported by the Boeing KC-135 Stratotanker. In December 1963, the runways, taxiways, and parking aprons were rehabilitated. A tri-service landing mat asphalt runway was part of the update. In December 1966, additional hangars and concrete areas to accommodate more B-52s were completed.[9]

Abilene AFB was controlled by SAC and was dedicated by City of Abilene officials on their city's diamond jubilee on April 15, 1956. On December 6, the base was renamed Dyess AFB in honor of Lt. Col. William Edwin Dyess.

Other construction projects at Dyess AFB included the Special Weapons Storage Area (nuclear), two Nike-Hercules surface to air missile sites, and twelve Atlas F surface to surface (SSM—Intercontinental Ballistic Missiles or ICBMs) in hardened underground silos. Later, after the Capehart housing became obsolete, they were demolished and replacement units were built. Dyess currently has 674 family housing units in seven complexes: Eagle Heights, Freedom Run, Patriot Acres, and Liberty Crossing (326 three- and four-bedroom, two-story duplex and single family

Capehart Housing at Dyess Air Force Base. The car in the carport is from 1957 and has distinctive tail fins. *Courtesy Abilene Public Library Digital Archives*

Capehart housing has an interesting history. Wherry and Capehart housing programs represented the government's solution to military housing shortages after WWII. The two programs attempted to involve the private sector in meeting the housing demand. Private developers were used to design and construct the housing. These two building programs led to one of the federal government's largest residential construction projects. Capehart buildings were designed as two-story, two- and three-bedroom duplexes. These wood frame rectangular buildings were constructed on reinforced concrete and brick-pier foundations. Exterior walls were clad in brick veneer and vinyl siding and garden roofs were covered with asphalt shingles. Building entrances were accentuated by flat-roof canopies supported on steel-pipe columns, shielded by masonry screens three feet tall. Each unit included a prefabricated chimney that projected from the rear slope of the roof. Minor variations to the exterior were used to identify the four different building types. Distinguishing exterior features included different brick veneer and siding patterns, the width of the entrance, and the materials used for the porch screen. Porch materials varied from brick to stone, or one of two types of concrete block. Beginning with early construction, the housing units used exterior lap or board-and-batten wall siding and wood shingles for gable ends. The original exterior doors were solid wood with a multi-light transom, and the original windows were two-light with a movable double-sash.[8]

Main gate entrance to Dyess Air Force Base, 1950s. *Courtesy Abilene Public Library Digital Archives*

WWII P-40 pilot William Dyess. *Dyess Air Force Base, 5th Bomb Wing Public Affairs*

Dyess was born on August 9, 1916, and became an officer in the United States Army Air Forces during WWII. He was captured after US and Philippine troops were defeated during the Battle of Bataan. He was among thousands of US and Philippine soldiers forced to march to POW camps under the brutal and barbaric actions of Japanese troops on the long march to the POW camps known as the "Bataan Death March." After one year in captivity he escaped, successfully evading Japanese patrols for three months prior to evacuation by a US Navy submarine. His evacuation was arranged with the assistance of local guerrilla forces. Once back in the United States, Maj. Dyess told his story of capture and prison treatment by the Japanese. His eye-witness account of Japanese brutality during the death march was vivid and verified what happened after the US and Philippine troops surrendered to the Japanese. This information was classified and not released to the public at this time. He was promoted to lieutenant colonel and assigned to fly the Lockheed P-38 Lightning. On December 27, 1943, during a training mission over Burbank, California, his aircraft caught fire. He did not bail out, remaining in the burning P-38 and flying it into the ground in a vacant lot, saving the lives of countless civilians.[10]

homes built in 2007-2008); Lonestair Trails (eighty-five two- and three-bedroom single family homes); Hunter Mesa (173 two- and three-story bedroom duplex and single family homes built in 1995-1996; and Frontier Meadows (ninety two-, three-, and four-bedroom two story single family homes built in 2009). Housing amenities include washer and dryer hook ups, refrigerators, dishwashers, central heating and air conditioning, attached garages, and fenced yards. There are numerous tot-lots throughout the housing areas, as well as basketball courts and baseball fields. The Base Youth Center is centrally located in the housing area. There is a self-help store in the housing area that carries numerous items.[11] Dyess AFB housing is now under Department of Defense Housing Privatization for operations under a private company. In 2012, approximately two-thirds of Dyess military families lived in non-privatization housing on the local housing market (purchase, lease, and rentals).[12]

Dyess AFB unaccompanied housing (UH) is provided for airmen ranks E-1 to E-3 and E-4s with less than three years of service. Each airman is provided a private sleeping room, furnishings, bed linens, and supplies for a comfortable living area. The permanent party campus on Dyess AFB consists of two areas with eleven buildings totaling 744 unaccompanied housing rooms. There are four buildings configured as 1 + 1 rooms with a shared bathroom and kitchen. There are four buildings configured as 2 + 2 rooms with a shared bathroom without a kitchen. There are three buildings with private bedrooms and no kitchens. The buildings have between sixty-four to seventy-four individual rooms. Amenities include laundry rooms, day rooms, pool tables, and large screen flat panel televisions.[13] Dyess AFB provides 160 visitor (including thirty-nine temporary) housing units. The base personnel force consists of 13,000 military (4,666) and civilian personnel. The base operates a medium-size commissary, a small Army and Air Force Exchange Service (AAEFS), a mall, and one shoppette. Recreation provided on base consists of an arts and crafts facility, bowling alley, library, auto hobby shop, recreation center, theater, gym, tennis courts, swimming pool, and outdoor activities including camping, fishing, and horse riding stables.[14]

Dyess Air Force Base privatized two-story duplex housing. *Courtesy Dyess Air Force Base.*

The operational part of the base consists of:

Runway 162/342, asphalt surface: 3,500 feet long and 60 feet wide.

Runway 16/34, PEM surface: 13,500 feet long and 300 feet wide.

Runway 161/341, gravel surface—used as a C-130 assault strip: 3,500 feet long and 60 feet wide.

Parking Apron (along the east side of the main runway—concrete), 9,900 feet long and 1,200 feet wide.[15]

Dyess AFB is three miles west-southwest of Abilene, Texas. The base is the area's largest single employer, operating over 200 facilities on the base. Dyess AFB has a yearly impact of 310 million dollars on local economies.[16] Dependent students in the housing areas (grades K-5) attend Dyess Elementary School outside the Delaware gate, which is accessed through a walking gate. Students in grades six to eight are bused to Clack Middle School, with students grades nine through twelve bused to Cooper High School.[17]

1950s aerial photo of Dyess Air Force Base. *Courtesy Abilene Public Library Digital Archives*

Dyess Air Force Information

Tye Army Air Base (during WWII construction), September 1942.................. (Major command)
Second Air Force (October 13, 1942)
Abilene Army Air Base, December 18, 1942.. (Major command)
Third Air Force (March 2, 1943) ....(Base operating unit)
474th Headquarters and Air Base Squadron (December 18, 1942)...........................(Major unit)
69th Tactical Reconnaissance Group (September 10, 1943, to November 12, 1943)
Abilene Army Airfield, April 8, 1943, to January 1947 .... (Major command)
Second Air Force (November 15, 1943)
Continental Air Force (April 16, 1945, to January 31, 1946).......................(Base operating unit)
261st Army Air Force Base Unit (April 1, 1944)
233rd Army Air Force Unit (Detachment) (March 1946–January 1947) ....(Major unit)
77th Reconnaissance Group (April 6, 1943, to September 12, 1943)
408th Fighter-Bomber Group (November 10, 1943, to January 1944)
Abilene AFB, October 1, 1953, to December 1, 1956...................................... (Major command)
Strategic Air Command (October 1, 1953, to December 1, 1956)...............(Base operating unit)
4021st Air Base Squadron (January 1, 1955)
341st Air Base Group (September 1, 1955)
819th Air Base Group (June 15, 1956, to December 1, 1956) ....(Major unit)
341st Bombardment Wing (September 1, 1955, to December 1, 1956)
Boeing B-47E Stratojet (45 aircraft—15 per squadron; not all four squadrons operational at same time)
337th Bombardment Squadron
338th Bombardment Squadron
339th Bombardment Squadron
413th Bombardment Squadron
Dyess AFB, December 1, 1956, to the present ....(Major command)
Strategic Air Command (December 1, 1956, to May 31, 1992).......... (Major unit)
341st Bombardment Wing (December 1, 1956, to June 25, 1961) Boeing B-47E Stratojet
11th Air Refueling Squadron (1956 to 1959) Boeing KC-97G Stratotanker (20 to 22 aircraft assigned)
819th Air Division (February 1, 1956, to July 1966)
96th Bombardment Wing (September 8, 1957, to October 1993—under ACC for a short time)
Boeing B-47E Stratojet (45 assigned to three squadrons to 1962)
Boeing B-52E Stratofortress (33 aircraft assigned 1963 to 1969)
Boeing B-52D Stratofortress (16 aircraft assigned 1971 to 1981)
Boeing B-52C Stratofortress (six aircraft assigned, used in a training role 1969 to 1971)
Boeing B-52H Stratofortress (18 aircraft assigned 1982 to 1985)
917th Air Refueling Squadron
Boeing KC-135A Stratotanker (20 aircraft assigned 1965 to 1993)
4th Strategic Support Squadron (4th SSS, June 17, 1957, to March 15, 1961)
Lockheed C-124 Globemaster II (12 aircraft assigned to the squadron)
578th Strategic Missile Squadron
Construction of 12 Atlas F Intercontinental Ballistic Missile launch silo complexes (June 7, 1960)
Squadron activated (July 1, 1961)
Operational (1962)

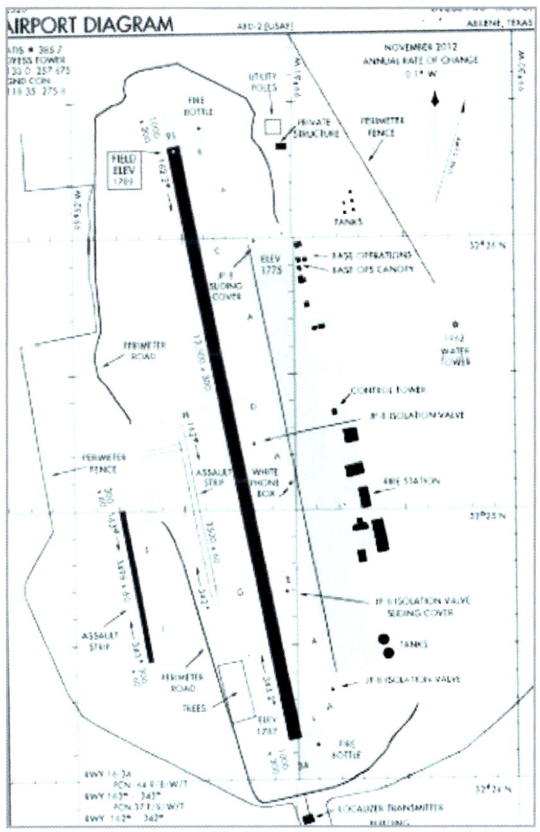

Airport diagram of Dyess Air Force Base. *Courtesy Dyess Air Force Base, 7th Bomb Wing Public Affairs*

Deactivated (March 25, 1965)
Headquarters Battery, 5th Missile Battery, 517th Artillery of the US Army Defense Command
Nike-Hercules Surface to Air Missile system (November 19 1959 to June 1966)
Launch Site DF-10 with 12 launchers (October 1960 to June 1966)
Launch Site DF-50 with 12 launchers (October 1960 to June 1966)
64th Troop Carrier Wing (February 8, 1961, to January 1, 1963)
516th Troop Carrier Wing (January 1, 1963, to 1972)
463rd Tactical Airlift Wing (1972 to 1974)
12th Air Division (September 30, 1967, to July 1988)
Air Combat Command (June 1, 1992, to the present) .... (Base operating unit)
819th Air Base Group (December 1, 1956, to November 1, 1958)......... Redesignated the 819th Combat Support Group on November 1, 1958
96th Combat Support Group (June 25, 1961)
7th Bomb Wing (October 1, 1993, to the present)
Groups
7th Operations Group
436th Training Squadron
28th Bomb Squadron (22 B-1B Lancers, blue/white Chex tail marking)
9th Bomb Squadron (14 B-1B lancers, black tail stripe marking)
7th Mission Support Group
7th Civil Engineering Squadron
7th Contracting Squadron
7th Communications Squadron
7th Logistics Readiness Squadron
7th Security Forces Squadron
7th Force Support Squadron
7th Maintenance Group
7th Aircraft Maintenance Squadron
7th Component Maintenance Squadron
7th Equipment Maintenance Squadron
7th Maintenance Operations Squadron
7th Munitions Squadron (conventional special weapons storage area) Prior to stand down of nuclear alert status the storage area held nuclear weapons
7th Medical Group
7th Medical Support Squadron
7th Aeromedical Operations Squadron
317th Airlift Group (April 1, 1997, to present, authorized strength 23 C-130Js)
Squadrons
39th Airlift Squadron (red tail stripe marking)
40th Airlift Squadron (blue tail stripe marking)
317th Operations Support Squadron
317th Aircraft Maintenance Squadron
317th Maintenance Squadron
317th Maintenance Operations Squadron
Tenant Units
Air Combat Command (ACC) Training Support Squadron (C-130 Hercules)
29th Training systems Squadron
337th Test and Evaluation Squadron
77th Weapons Squadron
7th Bomb Wing Honor Guard
7th Bomb wing Chapel
Air Force Office of Special Investigations (AFOSI), Detachment 222[18]

THE BOEING B-47E STRATOJET and the 341st BOMBARDMENT WING (MEDIUM)

The 341st Bombardment Wing (BW), medium, was activated on September 1, 1955, at Abilene AFB. On December 6, 1956, the later renamed Dyess AFB was activated as a Strategic Air Command (SAC) base.[1] The 341st BW consisted of:

337th Bomb Squadron (BS)
November 18, 1953, to March 15, 1963
Non-operational: September 15, 1963, to December 22, 1963
Non-operational: June 22, 1970, to September 19, 1970
Non- operational: April 8, 1972, to October 28, 1973
Flew B-47E from December 1963 to 1970
338th BS
November 18, 1953, to March 15, 1963
Non-operational: November 18, 1953, to March 13, 1955
339th BS
November 18, 1953, to March 15, 1963
Non-operational: November 18, 1953, to April 29, 1955
413th BS
November 1, 1958, to January 1, 1962
Non-operational: October 1, 1961, to January 1, 1962[2]

SAC shield carried on aircraft and missiles. *Courtesy Strategic Air Command, Offutt Air Force Base, Omaha, Nebraska, January 1990*

The 341st BW flew B-47Es from 1956 to 1962. The wing's SAC aircraft authorization was forty-five, with operational numbers fluctuating between forty and forty-nine.[3] The wing's bombers carried the SAC shield. The command emblem is on sky-blue over two clouds: one in the upper left and one in the lower right, extending to the edges of the shield, white shaded blue-gray, and a cubit armor issuing from the lower left and extending toward the upper part of the shield, the hand grasping an olive branch green, and three lightning flashes red. The shield is azure. The blue sky represents Air Force operations. The arm and armor signify strength, power, and loyalty and represent science and the art of employing far reaching advantages in securing objectives of war. The olive branch—a symbol of peace—and the lighting flashes—symbolic of speed and power— are qualities underlying SAC's mission.[4]

The B-47, although capable of carrying conventional munitions, was primarily SAC's medium atomic and thermonuclear bomber. The B-47E's bomb load capacity made it a versatile weapons system.

Even though the B-47E had a limited range, SAC placed these bombers on stateside nuclear alert status armed with four MK-28 thermonuclear weapons. SAC's standard alert package consisted of ten B-47Es and five KC-97Gs. They were set to an alert standard to begin takeoffs within thirty minutes of receipt of the launch order and sounding of the Klaxon alarm from SAC Headquarters. At Dyess, alert bombers and tankers were positioned at the south end of the large concrete parking apron. Dyess did not have a dedicated, separate "Christmas Tree" alert area near the end of the runway. SAC reorganized to support its one-third alert status facility for bombers and tankers, the majority of which were now B-47Es. A deputy commander for operations was authorized to assist the wing commander, replacing the Directorate System in operation since 1951. Within each B-47 wing a fourth bomb squadron was activated to assist alert operations that fell into a four-cycle rotation: ground alert, flight planning, flying training, and a day off. To bring similar functions under singular control, organizational maintenance squadrons were organized to replace periodic maintenance squadrons and absorbed maintenance functions performed by tactical squadrons.

While the ground alert force rapidly approached its one-third objective, SAC was taking other actions to ensure a survivable and responsible bomber force. During the tremendous expansion of the early and mid-1950s SAC bases had become overcrowded, with some double wings assigned ninety B-47Es and forty KC-97Gs. Dyess AFB was classified as a single bomber wing.[5]

In 1957, the 96th BW was assigned to Dyess AFB, operating in conjunction with the 341st BW, which was activated earlier on June 25, 1991. The 96th BW was made up of four squadrons (337th, 338th, 339th, and 413th) and the 96th Air Refueling Squadron (ARS) with KC-97Gs. The Stratofreighter was an improvement over the KB-29, but because it was a piston-powered aircraft, during air refueling operations the KC-97G and B-47E had to conduct a unique maneuver because the Stratofreighter was not as fast as the B-47E. The B-47E's pilot throttled back and lowered wing flaps and rear landing trucks while the KC-97G began a shallow dive to increase air speed.

B-47E and KC-97G alerts on Dyess AFB were part of SAC's "Quick Strike Program." The B-47E was fully loaded with fuel, loaded with nuclear weapons (primarily four MK-28s), and all systems were set so alert mechanics would only have to start the aircraft's external ground power unit and wait until the flight crew members were nearly in their seats before throwing the power switch on the generator. This started the B-47E's number four engine turning before the pilot sat down and buckled into his seat. The other five engines were started as quickly as they could. The wheel chocks were pulled and the pilot started taxiing to the end of the runway, holding short of turning onto the runway until receiving final take-off authorization.[6]

Boeing XB-47 prototype on the parking apron in front of Boeing Aircraft Company's Seattle, Washington, production plant. *Boeing Aircraft Archives to author*

B-47 production line, Boeing Aircraft Company, Seattle, Washington. This was the final and largest production run of massed bombers since the end of World War II, when the Boeing Company built the B-29 Superfortress. At the end of production, Boing had built 2,041 (all models of the B-47E: 931 built by Boeing-Wichita, 274 by Douglas-Tulsa, and 385 by Lockheed-Martin). *Boeing Aircraft Archives to author*

Traditional military supply difficulties were encountered while procuring the quality and type of furnishings desired for the SAC alert force at Dyess AFB. Initially, living space for 100 alert personnel was provided in wood airmen's barracks near the aircraft alert area. Issued dormitory furniture was plentifully available, but the monotonous regimentation of gray steel furniture, regardless of its comfort, had to be avoided while furnishing these facilities. The Abilene Chamber of Commerce obtained $5,000 worth of comfortable, colorful furnishings and included the services of a professional interior decorator.[7]

Because of the limited range of the B-47E, SAC needed congressional funding approval to deploy them and KC-97Gs to overseas staging air bases. Col. Jensen, Headquarters SAC, in testimony before the US House of Military Appropriations Subcommittee on March 12, 1952, indicated:

> Within the category of SAC and aircraft rotational movements are a response to the present world situation demands that strategic air forces be capable to deployment at full operational effectiveness to troubled areas of the world on a short notice. In order to maintain this capability, it is essential that SAC units gain operational experience under various circumstances and conditions in all parts of the world through a continuous process of unit rotation. Due to the requirement for all of these units to be in a constant of readiness, it is mandatory that aircraft and flight crews not be separated from their maintenance personnel and ground equipment over extended periods of time. This demand makes it necessary to use C-124s to move personnel and cargo to and from the rotational area as required.[8]

96th BW B-47Es forward deployed as part of SAC's rotational movement to overseas forward locations. The stationing of SAC bombers at British RAF air bases—from where targets inside the Soviet Union were within range—offered a certain degree of support to SAC nuclear war planning operations. The Pentagon's strategy was based on the concept of "Massive Retaliation" against the Soviet Union if that country attacked the United States with thermonuclear weapons via bombers flying over the North Pole. This plan, nicknamed "Trojan," meant SAC went to nuclear war with the Soviet Union. "Trojan" initially relied on the use of early model B-47s, but was greatly enhanced as B-47Es became the backbone of SAC's medium bomber force. Temporary Duty (TDYs) to overseas bases involved one B-47 wing of forty-five aircraft and twenty KC-97Gs. These aircraft remained for ninety days until relieved by another wing at the same location or at another air base, preventing a tempting target destroyable by a single Soviet nuclear weapon. These deployments were not only supported by SAC's 4th Special Airlift Squadron (C-124s), but also by Military Air Transport Service (MATS) C-124s. These aircraft transported thousands of military personnel and hundreds of tons of material to and from the United States in a few days supporting SAC's rotational movements. The 96th BW deployed to RAF Upper Heyford. This method of B-47E/KC-97 rotations continued until 1965.[9]

A three-man B-47 crew running from a nearby parked Air Force sedan—used by alert crews at SAC bases before going to the larger blue crew-cab trucks used later by B-52 alert crews—to a cocked nuclear bomb-loaded aircraft. The pilot climbing into the cockpit via the lowered, integral crew ladder through the open hatch is wearing a side arm, indicating this is a staged photo. On nuclear cocked B47s, side arms were inside the aircraft. *Courtesy Strategic Air Command, historian Office, Offutt Air Force Base, Omaha, Nebraska, January 1990*

The ADVON of the 341st BW's first overseas deployment arrived at Andersen AFB, Guam, on New Year's Day 1958. Within a few days, approximately 1,400 personnel and 250 tons of cargo were in place to support sustained training operations and to maintain an around-the-clock alert force on this remote site along the US western frontier. The 341st was in business, supported by six KC-97Gs assigned to the 320th ARS from March AFB, California, and the 819th Air Base Group (ABG). A positive response from aircrews and support personnel was produced by the success enjoyed by the wing throughout the TDY. Later in April, on Easter Sunday at 4:21 p.m. (Central Standard Time at Dyess AFB, Texas), a 341st BW B-47E completed a nonstop flight from Andersen AFB to Dyess AFB. The aircraft was commanded by Colonel George M. Lochhard, wing director of operations, who completed the 7,350-mile flight in thirteen hours and twenty-one minutes. The Stratojet refueled after takeoff from Andersen AFB, taking on a full fuel load from a KC-97G, then was refueled a second time north of the Hawaiian Islands by a KC-97G from Hickam AFB. The bomber flight demonstrated the long-range capability of SAC bombers and crews and established another first (record) for the 341st BW.[10]

The 341st BW also flew training missions and participated in SAC exercises and deployments to Morocco and other forward operating air bases. On a stateside training mission on November 4, 1958, a B-47E ATO assisted takeoff turned into a spectacular disaster. As the ATO bottles ignited, instead of the normal contained rocket flame exhaust from each bottle, individual flames merged into a single large flame approximately two-thirds toward the rear of the accelerating aircraft on the left ATO rack. Capt. Don E. Youngmark (aircraft commander) continued the takeoff roll down the runway, passing the 4,000 foot (4) markers on either side of the runway. The fire spread forward to a point just aft of the rear wheel well and advanced toward the tail section. Flames trailed thirty to forty feet from the aircraft's tail in the slipstream. ATO bottles were now flying off the aircraft at irregular intervals. Capt. Youngmark continued the aircraft's takeoff, lifting off the runway with the aircraft in flames and sections now falling off the disintegrating fuselage. The ATO rack and bottles fell off due to the extreme heat. The burning bomber shredded its brake chute, 20mm tail gun ammunition cans, parts of the onboard camera department, entire sections, doors, and miscellaneous parts from the battery compartment, the gun safe switch, and

B-47 using ATO assisted rocket thrust augmentation. *Boeing Aircraft Archives to author*

parts of bulkhead 861 from the 8,000 foot (8) runway marker to the end of the 13,500 foot runway. Capt. John M. Gerding (copilot) finally discovered something was terribly wrong upon reaching 200 feet. The fire had knocked out radio transmissions from the control tower and the ground safety officer. Capt. Youngmark decided to try to climb to 1,500 feet to allow Capt. John Dowling (navigator) and the extra onboard crewman (the aircraft's crew chief) sufficient altitude to safely eject and manually bail out (the crew chief was in an ejection seat). Capts. Youngmark, Gerding, and Dowling successfully ejected from the burning aircraft, parachuting safely to the ground to the right of the runway centerline extension, approximately 3,000 feet from the end of the runway. Tragically, the crew chief, Staff Sgt. Robert E. Schneider, refused to bail out into the flames that were engulfing the aircraft below the navigator's compartment and the open hatch from the ejection by the navigator and died in the crash. The aircraft crashed five miles south of the runway on the former WWII Camp Barkeley area then owned by Mr. Edgar Davis. After plowing into the ground the flaming bomber broke into small fragments scattered over an approximately one-half square mile area. The aircraft was loaded with a thermonuclear weapon (no official confirmation of the type). The only official press release was that the bomb's high-explosive charge did not spread any radioactive material outside the immediate aircraft crash site. However, protocol required Air Force personnel from the Dyess AFB Special Weapons Storage Area (munitions squadron personnel) conduct an immediate radioactive scan to be certain no personnel entering the crash site became contaminated or any debris removed was contaminated to the point it could not safely be transported to Dyess AFB. The crash site was immediately secured to keep unauthorized personnel from disturbing aircraft debris, to determine the cause of the crash, and to prevent any possible contamination.[11]

In 2010, the Air Force made extensive tests of the 1958 B-47E crash site at Camp Barkeley. Dr. Steven E. Rademacher, chief of radioactive materials licensing and safety of the Air Force Safety Center stated this nuclear weapon contained radioactive uranium—meaning it was probably a boosted fission bomb—and lead, and as a result of the explosive action these two contaminants were spread to the

Front nose section crew area. The pilot/copilot sit underneath a clear bubble canopy. The navigator sits below and in front of the pilot in the enclosed nose, above the radar visible on the lower nose position. The forward dual-landing gear truck is visible, with the landing gear doors open to either side. *Aircraft at the Strategic Air Command Museum, Ashland, Nebraska. Author, August 1999*

Both dual in-line landing gear trucks with the bomb bay open between them. *Aircraft at the Strategic Air Command Museum, Ashland, Nebraska. Author, August 1999*

environment. The investigating team made a prudent effort from a precautionary standpoint to remove additional contamination, making the former crash site acceptable for any future private use. The team completed the removal of approximately seventeen cubic yards of contaminated soil sealed in EPA marked and inventoried certified barrels containing unspecified amounts of uranium and lead; final laboratory analysis indicated only grams of the materials. These levels were far below EPA recommended contamination with no hazard to the safety of human health.[12]

By 1957, SAC had refined its bomber dispersal (medium and heavy) plan, increasing the command's survivability if attacked by Soviet nuclear weapons. On May 21, SAC produced a status report on alert and dispersal of its bomber forces. This looked ahead to when its medium bombers (B-47s) would be replaced by the more capable heavy B-52.

"Alert through Dispersal" was a hot topic during the late 1950s and before the Cuban Missile Crisis, as SAC was given the responsibility of protecting its nuclear deterrent forces from Soviet nuclear attack, initially by long-range manned strategic bombers and followed by Russian Strategic Rocket Forces ICBM and Russian Navy SLBMs. The chief of staff of the United States Air Force was given directions to research and move forward with a viable nuclear-survivable aircraft dispersal plan/program:[13]

> Alert Parking. This facility should be sited near the end of the runway, with direct connection to the runway and should provide a segregated area for alert bomber and tanker force isolated from all other aircraft. This is necessary to rigidly control access to these aircraft on a strict need basis. The area should be of sufficient size to permit safe parking of both bomber and tanker aircraft and should be so designated that one burning aircraft in any position will not block the remainder of the alert force from takeoff.[14]

Military and civilian airfields were to be used in raised DEFCONs to spread out SAC's bomber force, increasing the survivability of a Soviet nuclear attack.

In July 1957, "Reflex Action" commenced, with four Second Air Force Wings—including Dyess AFB—sending five B-47Es each to Sidi Slimane AB, Morocco. This new system of SAC bomber operations was based on the premise that a few crews and aircraft on grouped alert at overseas air bases would be more effective than maintaining an entire wing at each air base on a ninety-day rotational training assignment. SAC planned to replace the ninety-day rotational program at all overseas air bases with "Reflex Action," with aircraft (bombers and tankers) frequently rotated from bases in the United States. This would cost less than massed aircraft rotational assignments while presenting a less tempting first strike target to Russian Long Range Aviation bombers and ICBMs, as well as later SLBMs. On October 1, 1957, "Reflex Action" bombers at Sidi Slimane were placed on ground nuclear alert, supported by stateside SAC alert forces. The success of the stateside ground alert program and "Reflex Action" prompted SAC to discontinue the ninety-day Rotational Training Program that had characterized B-47E operations since 1953. The 100th BW—the last B-47E wing to achieve operational nuclear alert status—was the last wing to perform the ninety-day rotational assignment. This assignment was conducted at Brize Norton RAF Station from early January to early April 1958. With the departure of the 100th BW from Brize Norton, SAC replaced the ninety-day rotation with "Reflex Action" alerts, even though this had commenced in early January 1958 at RAF stations Greenham Common and Fairford.[15]

On April 28, 1958, a 341st BW B-47E took off from Dyess AFB on a routine training flight. The B-47E carried a three-man crew plus a navigator/instructor. Approximately three hours after takeoff there was an explosion in one of the engines and the aircraft commander gave the proper order to bail out of the aircraft. He ejected upward and the navigator ejected downward, both safely floating to the ground under their parachutes. As copilot 1st Lt. James E. Obenauf prepared to eject upward, following the pilot, his ejection seat failed to fire. He unstrapped from the ejection seat, heading for the lower escape hatch through which the navigator had ejected downward. At this point he noticed Maj. Joseph Maxwell (the onboard instructor/navigator) was unconscious. Unable to revive Maj. Maxwell, Lt. Obenauf climbed back into his copilot seat and remained in the damaged aircraft. Lt. Obenauf flew the damaged B-47E back to Dyess AFB from his back seat copilot's position, successfully landing on the long runway. He was presented the Cheney Award, Aviator's Valor Award, Korean Kolligan Trophy, and the Air Force Distinguished Flying Cross for his actions in saving the aircraft and Maj. Maxwell's life.[16]

The 341st BW's history report for the month of April 1961 provided a review of the manning level for the wing. During this time in the Cold War with the Soviet Union, the number of personnel assigned to any SAC or US military unit was classified. Soviet intelligence officers and agents were always attempting to determine the manning of not only US military units overseas but those in the United States, especially those assigned to SAC bomb wings. These agents were officially designated cultural affairs officers or economic officers, or were assigned Soviet Embassy and official diplomatic posts throughout the United States, with a high number of personnel compared to what Soviet officials allowed the United States to man in its Moscow embassy. This was the game, with the FBI watching Soviet personnel in the United States assigned to the Soviet embassy, trade offices, and to the United Nations. The Soviets in turn followed all US personnel assigned to Moscow via the GRU, KGB, and specially assigned officers.

UNITS ASSIGNED	ASSIGNED OFFICERS	ASSIGNED ENLISTED	AUTHORIZED OFFICERS	AUTHORIZED ENLISTED
Hq. Sq. 96th BW	79	266	60	188
337th BS	57	3	68	2
338th BS	57	3	70	3
339th BS	57	3	70	2
413th BS	57	3	63	2
96th OMS	9	339	9	290
96th FMS	7	330	9	293
96th A&E	9	281	6	279
TOTALS	332	1,228	305	1,056

The wing had seventy-six B-47E combat aircrews. During April, these aircrews completed 251 sorties, flying a total of 1,836 hours.[17]

The wing's history for the month of May is interesting, in that it references nuclear responsibilities on the base:

> The 42nd Maintenance Munitions Squadron (MMS) will have the capability to maintain, store, and assume custody of the re-entry vehicles for 13 Atlas SM-65F ICBMS (12 in operational silos and one stored in an operational readiness replacement status) and W-38 Thermonuclear warheads (12 mated to the operational missiles and one as a ready replacement). The Air Force Munitions Account of the 42nd MMS will provide warhead supply support for the 578th Strategic Missile Squadron (SMS). The warheads (W-38 thermonuclear) will be received from either an Operational Storage Site (OSS) or National Stockpile (NS), along with the re-entry vehicle for the missile which will include inspect, maintain, modify, and store as required. Warheads will be returned to the Atomic Energy Commission (AEC) for major maintenance and quality assurance re-cycling.

As conditions continued to worsen with the Soviet Union prior to the Cuban Missile Crisis, SAC was working to implement a fifty percent alert capability by July 1, 1961, under SAC Manual (SACM) 136-4. Meanwhile, SAC had to work and implement an effective aircraft (bombers and tankers) plan at its bomber and dispersal bases (non-SAC bomber bases, Air Force bases, and civilian airfields in time of a national crisis where a nuclear attack was imminent from the Soviet Union). This was initially stated in Annex I to SACM 136-4, dated March 31, 1961:

> ...that explosive quantity distances do not apply between the explosive loaded aircraft [unclassified and implied reference to a thermonuclear armed bomber on a SAC base] and alert facilities in the alert area [early in SAC alert bomber operations, as with the B-47E at Dyess AFB, a barracks close to the south end of the runway was converted into a separate and secured alert crew area] [B-47E, KC-97G, security, maintenance, and support personnel] to meet SAC specified alert reaction time, inhabited building distance criteria need not be applied to alert facilities.

This was critical due to the threat of possible nuclear attack from the Soviet Union, and there were no allocated congressional funds for immediate construction of alert facilities at all SAC bases at the same time. This was for support of the twelve Atlas F ICBMs around Dyess AFN with the 578th SMS.[18]

The wing's history for the month of July indicated aircrew status, which SAC required on a daily basis to determine its ability to conduct its national mission of nuclear deterrence to prevent or respond to a nuclear attack from or against the Soviet Union. The wing operated forty-seven

B-47Es (fifteen per three squadrons, with two maintenance spares) and ninety-two B-47E aircrews (pilot, copilot, and navigator/bombardier), of which seventy-five were reported combat ready (SIOP/EWO qualified to complete the wing's assigned nuclear deterrence SAC mission) and three were non-combat (undergoing training to complete SIOP/EWO qualifications by wing intelligence personnel and standard aircrew training officers), with fourteen aircrews not complete (newly assigned personnel not meeting the three officer aircrew authorization for B-47E operations). With only forty-seven B-47Es assigned, the above numbers allowed the wing to complete its assigned SIOP/EWO mission.[19]

The American public slowly became aware that SAC was flying training missions with B-47s—and later B-52s—loaded with thermonuclear weapons. Although not armed, they required presidential or surviving national command authority to release SAC for its nuclear deterrence mission in response to a nuclear attack by the Soviet Union. SAC war planners and safety officers were always concerned about an airborne accident with a bomber carrying nuclear weapons, which did happen with great consequences for SAC (cleanup of radioactive materials, public affairs damage control, and dealing with allied territories over which the bombers flew). But even with crashes of nuclear armed SAC bombers, the weapons' safety systems prevented any nuclear detonation. In August 1961, SAC released a top secret message (because of its reference to and acknowledgment of SAC bombers carrying thermonuclear weapons while flying in the United States) to its bomb wings on the importance of flying safety while carrying thermonuclear weapons:

1. Any abnormal situation, ground or air, involving an aircraft carrying nuclear weapons must be reported immediately by the pilot [aircraft commander] to the Unit Command Post [in this case, the 96th BW Command Post] and by the Unit to the 15th AF Command Post.
2. Routine operation with nuclear weapons on board must be conducted to avoid completely any eventuality that, through the loss of sound supervision or judgment, could result in an accident and the attendant unfavorable publicity for SAC, USAF, and the United States.[20]

There were checklists and training of all aircrew personnel to meet strict SAC SIOP/EWO certification and reoccurring training and testing (100 percent required SIOP/EWO testing for aircrews to maintain combat crew certification). Wing intelligence personnel were heavily involved in constant aircrew SIOP/EWO crew training and testing. At this time, SAC did not allow any test failures and crews were always under extreme stress to pass these tests and Standboard certifications. All SIOP/EWO personnel were under the same stress. When a SAC ORI (no-notice inspection) arrived at the base, if one did not pass the tests and required performance careers were ended. SAC was always in a thermonuclear war posture.

On July 25, 1961, with the United States and the Soviet Union seemingly headed for a possible nuclear exchange over the right of the Western powers to control West Berlin, President John Kennedy delayed his previous decision directing SAC's acceleration of the phasing out of B-47Es to improve the US' defense posture and immediate nuclear striking power. Six B-47E bomb wings and six air refueling squadrons remained on active duty, ready to respond to a presidential order to attack the Soviet Union with thermonuclear bombs if Russian personnel in Cuba launched intermediate-range ballistic missiles (IRBMs) and medium-range ballistic missiles (MRBMs) at any target in the Americas. Any such missile strike would constitute a direct attack on the United States and cause a direct response with the full nuclear arsenal against the Soviet Union.[21]

The wing's history for the month of September indicated an operational change for SAC, in that the word "airborne alert" was classified by the 15th AF on September 28, 1961. This reflected the reality of SAC's confirmation of its airborne alert operations protecting the United States. One section of the report updated the wing's personnel strength.

UNITS ASSIGNED	ASSIGNED OFFICERS	ASSIGNED ENLISTED
Hq. Sq. 96th BW	94	317
578th SMS	61	157
337th BS	71	3
338th BS	71	3
339th BS	71	3
413th BS	76	3
96th OMS	10	48
96th FMS	7	381
96th A&E	8	288
42nd MMS	6	113
TOTAL	475	1,675

Even though SAC was operating the six turbojet B-47E Stratojet with the 96th BW, it also flew other aircraft performing its mission: four twin-engine piston-powered Douglas C-47 Skytrain transports for aerial resupply operations for the wing and movement of wing personnel as required; five Lockheed T-33 T-birds for pilot hours and transition training into the B-47E; two Sikorsky H-19 helicopters (transferred from the US Army to the Air Force); and one Air Force SH-19 search and rescue helicopter. The helicopters were used to support search and rescue operations around Dyess AFB, as well as air support for the twelve Atlas F ICBM launch sites around Dyess.[22]

SAC was evolving its Positive Control (PC) launch and EWO execution procedures for its aircrews. On December 19, 1961, deputy commander for operations, 96th BW, received a message from the 15th AF at March AFB, California, concerning Positive Control Launch and Execution procedures. The message stated that "the requirement for crew and controllers to properly authenticate and react to Fast Reaction Messages (FRMs) providing command interview programs is being established to employ the vital necessity for crews and controllers to receive, decode, authenticate, and implement without error the instructions contained in this message pertaining to their jobs." This was the delivery of thermonuclear weapons on an enemy target anywhere in the world.

Alert crews were required to perform under stress during a SAC ORI as if getting ready to fight a thermonuclear war with the Soviet Union. SAC spelled out what was expected and required for SIOP/EWO certified combat crews to perform their assigned nuclear deterrence mission:

> Alert crews will be notified of the ORI examination so as to not interfere with crew rest. (Even during an ORI there was always the possibility that SAC would have to implement its war plan, bringing the wing under inspection back to combat ready condition to conduct its nuclear attack mission profile.) Crews will be prepared to answer verbal questions on their alert sortie. They will also be prepared to take a closed book examination (100 percent required on the closed book examination) on: SAC Tactical Doctrine, Positive Control and special weapons procedures (thermonuclear weapons). The examination with be given by the SAC Inspector General (I.G.) as soon as possible after "A" hour so it does not interfere with crew rest. After the exam, a briefing on "Fine Line Hotel" (alert facility procedures), given in the alert facility, with current ground rules apply and explained. Navigators will accomplish refresher target study and crews will accomplish route study and complete clearance forms (provided by wing intelligence personnel, under constant surveillance by SAC IG personnel, marking correct procedures and training presentations). Only schedule preflight will be performed on alert aircraft prior to "A" plus 12 (hours). Any maintenance required as a result of this preflight must be cleared with the SAC I.G. At "A" Plus 21, pre-take off briefing on the first four crews in the alert building. All clearance forms will be completed prior to this briefing. Pre-take off briefings will be

Right side of a B-47E, showing the thirty-five degree sweep of the wing and three engines and an auxiliary fuel tank. The outrigger landing gear used during ground taxi operations is also visible. *Aircraft at the Strategic Air Command Museum, Ashland, Nebraska. Author, August 1999*

> given at hourly intervals to four crews. This will include weather, other special information and late changes to the ORI, and issuance of KAC folders (alert procedures folders) and Communication Bags (contains communications flimsy information for the flying of airborne SAC IG sorties, prior to the scoring of the electronic bomb releases). At "A" plus 22, the first four crews will proceed to aircraft for pre-flight. No maintenance can be performed on the aircraft after "A" plus 12 unless decided otherwise. Start engines will be 20-minutes prior to scheduled takeoff time and taxi as soon as possible. At "A" plus 24, the first two alert crews launch, with subsequent aircraft will launch in two ship formations at 30 minute intervals. You must takeoff within -0 to plus five (5) minutes of scheduled takeoff time or you are non-effective. In the event of an abort is eminent before the start of takeoff roll, call the Command Post for permission to abort takeoff and return to the parking apron.[23]

The Cuban Missile Crisis (October 14 to 28, 1962) brought the US and Soviet Union to the brink of nuclear war. On October 16, SAC dispersed from home bases to widely separated military and civilian airfields in reaction to President Kennedy's announcement (a television speech to the American people and a diplomatic message to Chairman Nikita Khrushchev in Moscow) of an arms embargo quarantine against sea transport shipments from the Soviet Union destined for Cuban ports and demanding Khrushchev remove already in-country IRBMs, MRBMs, and bombers (IL-28 twin-engine Beagles). Under SIOP-63, a standard nuclear weapons package of four MK-28s was loaded into alert ("cocked") B-47Es. On October 22, under EWO-44/SIOP 50-63, 183 B-47Es from seventeen bomb wings began dispersal operations. SAC also placed the new B-52s and KC-135As on alert. The 96th BW dispersed to Tinker AFB and Tulsa Airport (both in Oklahoma). Alert bombers at these two locations were in segregated parking areas roped off and posted with applicable "Restricted Area" Signs.[24]

On July 14, 1962, at 6:15 p.m., a tornado hit Dyess AFB. The tornado's path went directly down the flight line from south to north, passing over the B-47Es parked in rows on the parking apron. The whirling storm touched down in the midst of the 64th Tactical Wing's Lockheed C-130s, damaging nine and injuring thirty-eight personnel, with four requiring hospitalization. It was fortunate the storm did not touch down in the dense bomber parking area.[25]

During 1963, SAC continued transition from a purely manned bomber force to a mixed strategic force with bombers and ICBMs. As ICBMs became more predominate B-47Es were phased out. On March 15, 1963, the 96th BW's B-47Es were inactivated. The B-47Es were flown from Dyess AFB to Davis-Monthan AFB, Arizona, for storage in the dry desert air. By the end of December, SAC retained twelve B-47E bomb wings, two of which were equipped with sophisticated electronic countermeasures (ECM). The 96th BW replaced its B-47Es with B-52Es (some B-52Cs were assigned to Dyess as transition training aircraft). Earlier, in June 1960, the wing replaced its KC-97G Stratofreighters with the turbojet powered Boeing KC-135A Stratotanker. In 1965 "Project Fast Fly"—the B-47E and KC-97G phase out program—was accelerated. SAC terminated its B-47E ground alerts. SAC's remaining five B-47E wings and six KC-97G air refueling squadrons were phased out on December 31, 1965.[26]

Tail with radar for aircraft warning and remote-controlled aiming of the two 20mm cannons below in the tail turret. *Aircraft at the Strategic Air Command Museum, Ashland, Nebraska. Author, August 1999*

BOEING KC-97G STRATOFREIGHTER and the 11th AERIAL REFUELING SQUADRON

Boeing C-97A Stratofreighters at Boeing Aircraft Company's parking apron outside its Seattle, Washington, production facility. These are the pure cargo version, without a flying boom or additional fuel tanks to modify the aircraft into a tanker. *Boeing Aircraft Archives to Author*

Boeing KC-97G taking off from Boeing Aircraft Company's production facility. The aircraft is now equipped with the flying boom, two under wing auxiliary fuel tanks, internal fuel tanks for jet fuel, and below nose mounted radar. *Boeing Aircraft Archives to Author*

The 11th Aerial Refueling Squadron (11th ARS) was activated at Abilene AFB, Texas, in 1955. The squadron was equipped with "factory fresh production" Boeing KC-97G Stratofreighters (tankers) in February 1956. The squadron completed a vigorous training program during five months of hard work to reach SAC combat readiness status.[1]

The KC-97G looked similar to the Boeing B-50 piston-powered medium bomber (a sixty percent new version of the WWII B-29 Superfortress) replacement for the B-29, giving SAC an improved, long-range, medium atomic bomber until the Convair B-36 heavy bomber was available, along with the B-47 in sufficient numbers to provide the mission capable bomber force to meet America's nuclear deterrence mission. The KC-97G had the same wings, tail, and engines as the B-50, but with a distinctive whale-like, double bubble fuselage. The aircraft was outfitted with the Boeing Aircraft Company's flying boom refueling probe developed and tested on the Boeing KB-29 tanker (a modification of the B-29 Superfortress tested in combat operations with the Far East Air Force [FEAF] during the Korean War).

Its four piston engines provided barely sufficient airborne cruising speed to allow the KC-97G to fly as fast in level flight as the B-47's slowest pre-stall speed. As noted, the B-47 pilot lowered the wing flaps and dropped the rear twin landing gear trucks to sufficiently slow the bomber down and allow a successful tanker contact. The tanker pilot pushed the nose of the KC-97G down into a slight descent from refueling interception or contact altitude, increasing airspeed to 220 to 240 knots. The higher speed was needed to compensate for the weight of jet fuel for the B-47 (receiving aircraft). Complicating fuel transfer amount availability or offload, the KC-97G used aviation fuel from separate tanks than those with jet fuel. This meant the KC-97G had two separate and independent fuel systems.

During SAC deployments of B-47Es, including those assigned to Dyess AFB, to forward overseas rotational deployment air bases, the KC-97G also transported cargo and/or personnel to and from the United States. Its upper deck was capable of handling oversize cargo accessed (loaded and unloaded) through a large, left-fuselage cargo door forward of the wing's leading edge. It could also haul personnel because the upper cargo deck compartment and lower fuselage fuel tank areas were heated and pressurized. The heated compartments were an operational necessity because of altitudes up to 30,000 feet and lower altitudes of 20,000 feet with a receiving bomber hooked to the tanker via the flying boom. The KC-97G deployed to cold operating locations such as Alaska and Thule Air Base, Greenland.[2]

KC-97G (right side) with its cargo door open and one engine visible, with the crew compartment on top at the front of the nose and the nose mounted radar below. *Aircraft at the Strategic Air Command Museum, Ashland, Nebraska. Author, July 13, 2009*

The 11th ARS, shortly after becoming combat ready in 1956, deployed twelve KC-97Gs to Alaska in December. During the same month, another squadron of KC-97Gs deployed to Andersen AFB, Guam, on a ninety-day TDY. Later in the month, the Alaskan tankers flew to Clark Air Base, Philippines, where they participated in SAC's Operation Power Flight. Twelve KC-97Gs, flight crews, and maintenance and support personnel were secretly positioned halfway around the world in the Western Pacific to support SAC's preparations for a January 1957 round-the-world nuclear power demonstration.[3]

From January 16 to 18, 1957, Operation Power Flight saw three B-52Bs assigned to the 93rd BW, Castle AFB, California, complete a nonstop, round-the-world flight. The B-52Bs were commanded by Maj. Gen. Archie J. Old Jr., 15th Air Force commander. The general was flying in the lead B-52B nicknamed "Lucky Lady III" (aircraft number 53-0394), with the aircraft commanded by Lt. Col. James H. Morris.*

* Lt. Col. Morris flew as "Lucky Lady II's" copilot on the B-50 round-the-world flight on March 3, 1949. This aircraft was assigned to the 43rd BG, Carswell AFB, Texas. Aerial refueling was provided by KB-29s.

Five B-52Bs, including two spares, took off from Castle AFB. One B-52B was unable to take on fuel at the initial aerial refueling rendezvous from a KC-97G, forcing it to abort and land at Goose Bay AB, Labrador. The second airborne spare continued on with the three primary mission Stratofortresses until after completing the second aerial refueling rendezvous with KC-97Gs over Casablanca, Morocco. At this point the remaining airborne spare broke formation, landing at RAF Brize Norton Station, England, according to the pre-planned mission profile. With the completion of three more aerial refuelings, including one provided by the twelve 111th ARS operating out of Clark AB (with 11th ARS KC-97Gs at Andersen AFB, Guam, on alert for an emergency call from the three B-52Bs), "Lucky Lady III" and its two companion B-52Bs reached California without incident. However, because of heavy fog in the valley where Castle AFB was located the runway was closed.

The author was assigned to the 43rd SW from 1976 to 1978 as wing intelligence and SIOP officer. Under an additional duty, during periods of heavy fog THAT closed training operations he assisted in the satellite bed down of the base's B-52s and KC-135s. This had no impact on the bomber and tanker alert force parked in the Christmas tree alert area. These aircraft would take off regardless of weather conditions as part of the SIOP/EWO deterrence package.

KC-97G's tail section, with a view of the Boeing flying boom retracted against the lower fuselage tail section during flight and non-aerial refueling. The bulge behind the flying boom allowed the boom operator to look through the Plexiglas window at the approaching aircraft so he could fly the boom into the aircraft's refueling receptacle. *Aircraft at the Strategic Air Command Museum, Ashland, Nebraska. Author, July 13, 2009*

The three airborne B-52Bs turned south, flying to March AFB and landing there. The three B-52Bs, with the assistance of pre-positioned KC-97Gs, completed the 24,325 mile round-the-world flight in forty-five hours and nineteen minutes—less than half the time required by "Lucky Lady II." The highly publicized flight visibly demonstrated SAC's capability with its new long-range, heavy, strategic B-52 bomber to deliver thermonuclear weapons at any range and on any target.[4]

For its furtherance of SAC's demonstrated nuclear deterrence capabilities, the 11th ARS received the first of its three Air Force Outstanding Unit Awards (AFOUA) during the period 1955 to 1965. In July 1958, the squadron deployed to Alaska and Guam for a ninety-day TDY. Beginning in November 1958, the squadron mission changed to "Reflex Action," resulting in a period of continued operational rotation of a portion of the squadron to Alaska supporting SAC bombers in their attack profile from northern tier bomber bases, refueling them over the Arctic before penetrating Soviet air space to the west in Siberia or over the North Pole to targets in central Russia.[5] At the time, "Reflex Action" was a new SAC operation for its B-47Es and KC-97Gs based on the premise that a few aircrews and aircraft on ground alert at overseas rotational air bases would be more effective than maintaining entire wings on ninety-day TDYs. The reduced number of B-47Es and KC-97Gs was a lesser tempting first strike target for Soviet bombers and later, ICBMs.[6]

The Dyess Linear Air Park has a KC-97L Stratofreighter on display with two J-47-GE-23 turbojet engines each mounted under the wing outboard of the piston engines. This increased the tanker's speed for improved offload to SAC bombers and Tactical Air Command (TAC) turbojet fighters. It still had to carry two separate fuel loads like the KC-97G.[7]

KC-97G refueling a B-47E. *Courtesy Strategic Command historian, Offutt Air Force Base, Nebraska, to author, August 1990*

KC-97G assigned to the 307th BW, 305th Air Refueling Squadron, 1960. *Courtesy Lincoln Air National Guard Archives, Lincoln, Nebraska, to author June 1990*

KC-97Gs removed from active SAC inventory that were not assigned to an Air National Guard air refueling squadron or upgraded to a KC-97L were flown to Davis-Monthan Air Force Base, Arizona, for storage and eventual disposal. *Courtesy 309th Aerospace Maintenance and Regeneration Group to Author, August 1995*

578th STRATEGIC MISSILE SQUADRON and the ATLAS F INTERCONTINENTAL BALLISTIC MISSILE

In September 1959, a joint decision was made by Headquarters Strategic Air Command (SAC), Ballistic Missile Division, and Headquarters United States Air Force (USAF) to investigate if Dyess AFB would be suitable as a support base for one of the nine planned Atlas F Intercontinental Ballistic Missile (ICBM) squadrons. A preliminary selection process and initial investigations of possible launching sites around Dyess AFB began in October 1959. Reports of preliminary sub-surface investigations (core samplings) were provided by Mason-Johnson & Associates to the US Army Corps of Engineers, Fort Worth District Office, in January 1960. Collected information on site investigations including topography, soils exploration by deep core sampling, seismic surveys to determine site location vulnerability to nuclear ground detonation shock waves, and water studies were forwarded by the US Army Corps of Engineers, Fort Worth District Office to the Bechtel Corporation, which completed the final site evaluation reports on March 30, 1960.[1] In January 1960, the Site Activation Task Force received approval for the establishment of an Atlas F ICBM squadron in the vicinity of Abilene, Texas, with silos to be constructed in a circle around Dyess AFB totaling nine launch sites (silo or launch facility and adjacent launch command center).[2]

The architectural engineering firm Black and Veatch was selected to design the facilities for the Atlas squadron's launch site complexes following the standard facility silo design prepared by the Bechtel Corporation. Early in April 1960, direction was sent to the US Army Corps of Engineers to expand to three additional launch sites. Below-grade soil sample investigations were prepared using core drilling samples starting on April 12, 1960. Design drawings and specifications for these sites were completed, reviewed, and approved prior to the previously scheduled bid opening.[3] Construction release for the Dyess Atlas F missile complex was issued by the Air Force Ballistic Missile Division on April 15, 1960, with a statement for a larger silo complex of twelve launch sites instead of nine as originally planned. A pre-bid conference was conducted at Dyess AFB on May 11, 1960, with construction bids opening May 26, 1960.[4]

Notification to proceed with construction was given on May 27, 1960, with the construction contract awarded to H.B. Zachry Company of San Antonio, Texas, and Brown and Root Incorporated of Houston, Texas.[5] The amount of the contract was $20,075,000, with primary construction work starting on June 6, 1960. A large percentage of hired construction workers were procured through the Abilene office of the Texas Employment Commission. The Air Force Ballistic Missile Division field office was activated at Dyess AFB on April 15, 1960, and was charged with executive management responsibilities for the construction, installation, and final operational testing of technical equipment. The weapons system validation demonstrations and the final delivery of a complete facility to the strategic missile squadron concurrently activating as an independent military action to provide trained personnel and operation became its final goal.[6]

A joint tenancy agreement was negotiated with the senior SAC officer at Dyess AFB to provide the Site Activation Task Force with buildings, work spaces, security, administrative services, communications, logistic support, and general housekeeping services. On July 11, 1960, the Air Force Ballistic Mission Division field office began operating as a Detachment Site Activation Task Force.[7] The Detachment was divided into the Technical Design Group and the Weapons System Engineering Group. The major problems encountered with construction schedule deadlines were

Atlas launch at Cape Canaveral, Florida, on February 20, 1958. *Air Force News Service, "100 Years of Air Power"*

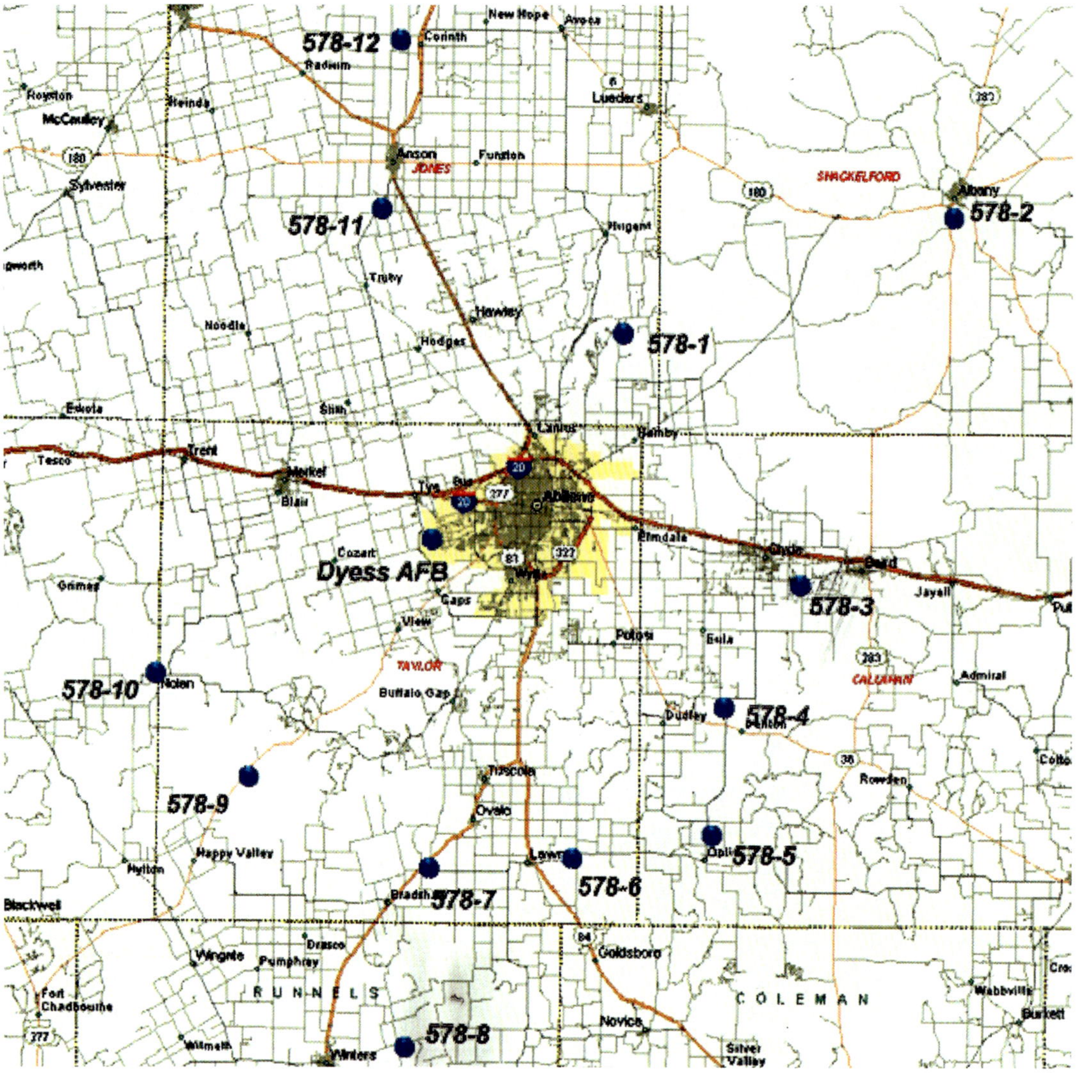

578th SMS Atlas F missile launch sites around Dyess Air Force Base. *Courtesy Association of Air Force Missileers*

completion of excavation, installation of reinforcing steel rebar inside the silo, and concrete pouring. More equipment was added by the contractors, a larger construction work force, and around-the-clock construction work shifts.

There was difficulty building the cryogenic tanks to meet engineering specifications for the propellant loading system, which delayed delivery, placing this part of the construction project six months behind schedule, but the system was completed and met the final timeline for the initial operations of the twelve missile silos.

The 578th SMS, 96th SAW, was activated at Dyess AFB on July 1, 1961, to manage and operate the twelve Atlas F launch sites. Each launch site was self-contained, with its own independent water, sewer, and electrical generation facilities. Each launch site was paved with a flat circular slab of concrete at the top of the launching silo surrounding the silo doors. A concrete surface level entrance vestibule led into the Launch Control Center (LCC), buried below ground level to absorb and survive the ground pressure waves and overpressure shock waves from a nearby thermonuclear detonation (airburst or contact detonation) of a multi-megaton warhead delivered by a Russian Strategic Rocket Forces ICBM. The LCC was a circular room forty feet in diameter with a two-story steel structure called a crib. The crib was suspended from the LCC's ceiling by an air-cushioned steel cable suspension system to absorb ground shock waves. The crib's lower floor contained communications equipment and the launch control console (LCC). The upper floor contained crew and security force living facilities. Emergency stocks of food, medicine, and safety equipment were stored in the LCC. All this was to allow the crew to operate in a thermonuclear war environment for an extended period independent of outside, vulnerable above-ground support facilities at Dyess AFB. A fifty foot personnel tunnel connected the LCC to the launch silo, containing plumbing and electrical cables connecting the LCC to the Atlas F ICBM inside the silo.

The launching silo was a concrete-lined cylinder fifty-two feet in diameter and 174 feet deep. The silo contained an octagonal steel crib structure. Engineers designed a space between the suspended Atlas F and the silo's walls to allow the missile to move side to side, absorbing ground vibrations from a thermonuclear detonation; this was referred to as "rattle space." The silo area was divided into eight levels to which were mounted the various systems required to launch the Atlas F. Inside the silo pipes, cables, and duct works provided electrical power, heat, ventilation, air conditioning, and liquids and gases essential to the Atlas F's operation. An elevator served all crib levels and there was a backup spiral stairway. Above the crib, two concrete silo doors were operated by heavy duty hydraulic cylinders protected by a massive concrete capstone.[8]

The Atlas F was the final variant of this ICBM to be operationally deployed. It was stored vertically inside a reinforced concrete silo. The missile's liquid kerosene could be stored in the fuel tank with its liquid oxidizer fuel tank filled after the missile was raised on an elevator to the surface. It took approximately ten minutes to fuel the raised missile with liquid oxidizer. This gave the Atlas F a narrow launch window once an alert warning of an incoming Soviet IBM attack reached the launch crew. The warning came from the Ballistic Missile Early Warning System (BMEWS), which became operational in 1962, during the Cuban Missile Crisis.[9]

Dyess Air Force Base liquid oxygen (LOX) plant. *Bruce Townsley, Atlas F Museum, Clyde, Texas, to author, October 16, 2012*

The US Army Corps of Engineers Fort Worth District Office was responsible for the nationwide procurement of the Atlas F propellant loading system. With the formation of the US Army Corps of Engineers Ballistic Missile Construction Office (CEBMCO) in 1960, the Fort Worth district office was relieved of silo construction oversight. Due to the increasing intensity of the Cold War, the low bid $20 million construction cost was authorized, with work beginning on June 7, 1960.[10]

The Atlas F sites around Dyess AFB assigned to the 578th SMS were:

SITE NUMBER 1 (578-1): The site was one and a half miles southwest of Lake Fort Phantom Hill, Texas, at 32 degrees 36 minutes 36.09 seconds north and 99 degrees 38 minutes 59 seconds west.

Site 578-1 with its doors open; the entrance to the LCC is through the concrete portal (angled entrance in the center of the photograph). Both Quonsets are completed and the sewage pond is in the foreground. Construction continued at this time. *Bruce Townsley, Atlas F Museum, Clyde, Texas, to author, October 16, 2012*

Site 578-1. Steel rebar was used for construction of the silo, LCC, and associated underground facilities. *Bruce Townsley, Atlas F Museum, Clyde, Texas, to author, October 16, 2012*

SITE NUMBER 2 (578-2): The site was one and a half miles south of Albany, Texas, at 32 degrees 42 minutes 23 seconds north and 99 degrees 17 minutes 51 seconds west.

Site 578-2. One of the LOX tanks installed at the bottom of the silo used to fill the missile fuel tanks after it was raised to the surface in preparation for launch orders. *Bruce Townsley, Atlas F Museum, Clyde, Texas, to author, October 16, 2012*

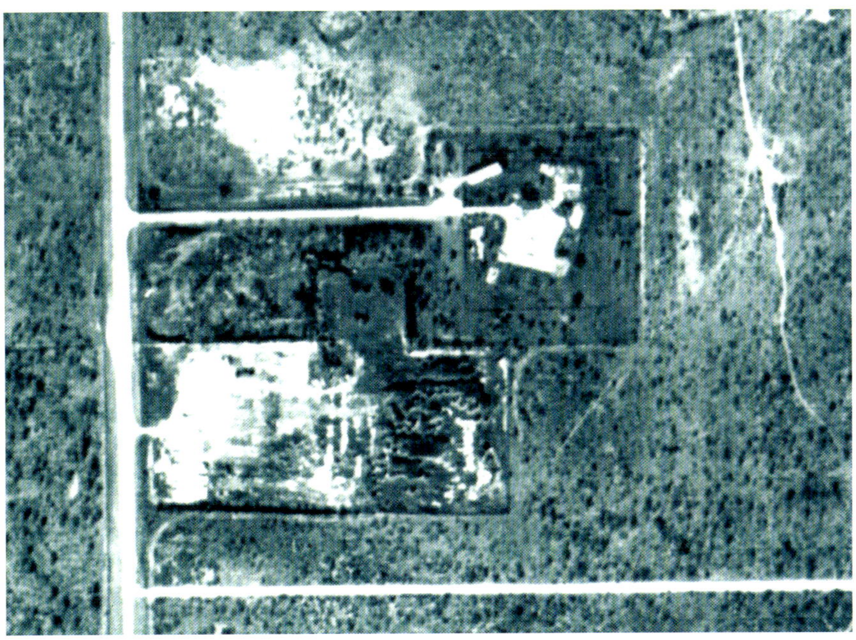

Overhead photo of Site 578-2, providing current view of the signatures of the former Atlas F ICBM launch site (2012). *Courtesy United States Geological Survey.*

SITE NUMBER 3 (578-3): The site was twenty-two and a half miles southeast of Clyde, Texas, at 32 degrees 22 minutes 54 seconds north and 99 degrees 27 minutes 37 seconds west.

Site 578-3. Rebar in the silo walls before concrete is poured in wood forms, creating the desired thickness and shape. *Bruce Townsley, Atlas F Museum, Clyde, Texas, to author, October 16, 2012*

Site 578-3. Wood forms in place over rebars to reinforce the poured concrete and vibrated to create a hardened missile silo. *Bruce Townsley, Atlas F Museum, Clyde, Texas, to author, October 16, 2012*

Site 578-3. LCC is to the left, with the missile silo in the background. The excavation at this point is completely finished, with dirt piled around the open cut that will eventually be back filled to level the surface grade. Bruce Townsley, Atlas F Museum, Clyde, Texas, to author, October 16, 2012

SITE NUMBER 4 (578-4): The site was 9.6 miles south-southwest of Clyde, Texas, at 32 degrees 16 minutes 25 seconds north and 99 degrees 32 minutes 28 seconds west.

Site 578-4. Shock absorbers on which the Atlas F missile elevator/launch platform rests inside the silo to absorb ground and over pressure shock waves. *Bruce Townsley, Atlas F Museum, Clyde, Texas, to author, October 16, 2012*

SITE NUMBER 5 (578-5): The site was one and a half miles southeast of Lake Coleman, Texas (also referred to as Oplin), at 32 degrees 9 minutes 42 seconds north and 99 degrees 33 minutes 10 seconds west.

Site 578-5. Entrance to the LCC. The zigzag corridor prevents direct blast effects from a nearby thermonuclear weapon detonation. *Bruce Townsley, Atlas F Museum, Clyde, Texas, to author, October 16, 2012*

Site 578-5. View of the huge volume of earth removed during excavation to the sub grade for beginning silo and LCC construction (bottom to top). The photo shows the required width of the excavation, as well as the trench required for the service road used for movement of construction equipment, supplies, and workers down to the LCC and silo. *Bruce Townsley, Atlas F Museum, Clyde, Texas, to author, October 16, 2012*

Site 578-5. An Atlas F being raised from its transporter/erecter onto the launch platform on top of the elevator from inside the silo. No warhead has been mated to the missile at this time. The raising of the delicate missile is a precise process constantly monitored by a full complement of military technicians and contractors. *Bruce Townsley, Atlas F Museum, Clyde, Texas, to author, October 16, 2012*

Site 578-5. Atlas F positioned on its raised elevator, with both reinforced concrete missile silo doors open. *Bruce Townsley, Atlas F Museum, Clyde, Texas, to author, October 16, 2012*

SITE NUMBER 6 (578-6): The site was 2.7 miles east of Lawn, Texas, at 32 degrees 8 minutes 25 seconds north and 99 degrees 42 minutes 12 seconds west.

Site 578-6. Concrete work on the LCC. At bottom right is the connection (tunnel) from the LCC to the silo, which is not constructed at this time, although preparation construction work on tunnel supports next to the silo under construction have begun. *Bruce Townsley, Atlas F Museum, Clyde, Texas, to author, October 16, 2012*

Missile site construction locations were considered top secret and off limits to Russian diplomatic or cultural affairs officers. However, this did not stop casual drive-by inspections by intelligence agents, as they were always monitoring SAC bomber bases, as well as major US military installations at the height of the Cold War. The FBI was constantly looking for communist agents operating inside the United States. FBI Director J. Edgar Hoover played this game very well, increasing the power of the FBI and the importance of his position.

SITE NUMBER 7 (578-7): The site was 3.4 miles northeast of Bradshaw, Texas, at 32 degrees 7 minutes 51 seconds and 99 degrees 51 minutes 18 seconds west.

Site 578-7. Missile elevator inside the silo under construction. *Bruce Townsley, Atlas F Museum, Clyde, Texas, to author, October 16, 2012*

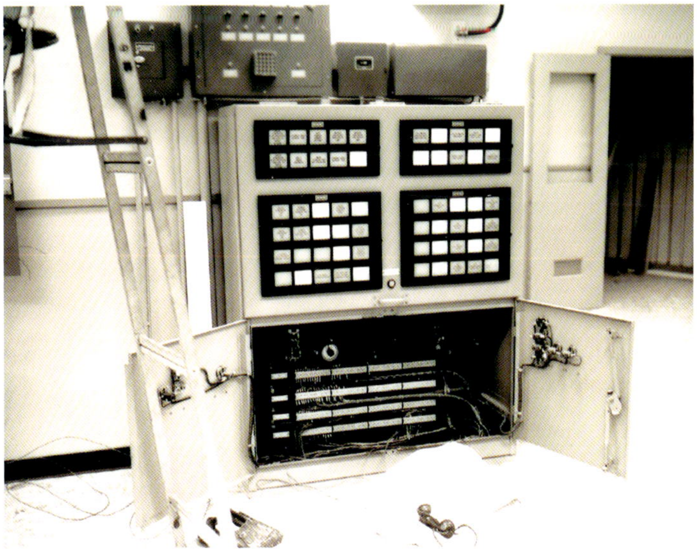

Site 578-7. Interior of the LCC with early 1960s, state-of-the-art vacuum tube electronics. The cabinets containing the electronics were by their nature large and required ventilation to remove the hot air from around the electronics, keeping them functioning. *Bruce Townsley, Atlas F Museum, Clyde, Texas, to author, October 16, 2012*

Site 578-8. One of three blast doors in the concrete corridor between the LCC and the missile silo to maintain blast integrity and seal the LCC off from the silo. *Bruce Townsley, Atlas F Museum, Clyde, Texas, to author, October 16, 2012*

SITE NUMBER 8 (578-8): The site was 4.9 miles northeast of Winters, Texas, at 31 degrees 58 minutes 24 seconds north and 99 degrees 52 minutes 48 seconds west.

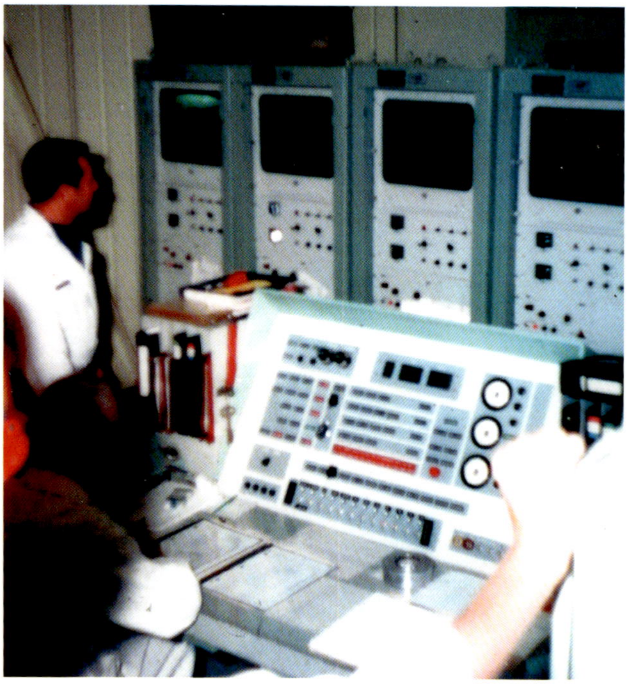

Site 578-8. MCCC console inside the LCC with associated electronics that were constantly monitored by missile alert crew technicians, noting the health of the missile inside the adjacent silo. The electronic equipment in the LCC is undergoing test and evaluation by 578th SMS missile personnel and contractors prior to certifying the systems ready for SAC nuclear alert operations. *Bruce Townsley, Atlas F Museum, Clyde, Texas, to author, October 16, 2012*

Site 578-8. One of the two missile silo blast doors open with construction workers testing fit and operations. The blast doors provided over pressure protection to approximately 200 pounds per square inch, protecting the missile below if not launched prior to the impact of a Soviet ICBM. *Bruce Townsley, Atlas F Museum, Clyde, Texas, to author, October 16, 2012*

SITE NUMBER 9 (578-9): The site was 11.9 miles northwest of Bradshaw, Texas, at 32 degrees 12 minutes 37 seconds and 100 degrees 3 minutes 3 seconds west.

Site 578-9. Final construction grading work on the road leading to the launch site. The majority of backfilling around the silo and LCC is complete at this time, with electrical power to the site provided by offsite commercial power lines, with on-site power as backup during raised DEFCONs or thermonuclear disruption. The Atlas ICBM sites provided a distinctive photo signature from aerial reconnaissance. *Bruce Townsley, Atlas F Museum, Clyde, Texas, to author, October 16, 2012*

SITE NUMBER 10 (578-10): The site was 13.1 miles south of Trent, Texas, at 32 degrees 18 minutes 5 seconds north and 100 degrees 9 minutes 11 seconds west.

Site 578-10. The area inside the silo was filled with plumbing, electrical connections, hydraulics, ventilation, and missile support equipment. Note the sharp edges on the pipes throughout: the silo was designed for missile support and utility, regardless of current safety regulations for construction. *Bruce Townsley, Atlas F Museum, Clyde, Texas, to author, October 16, 2012*

SITE NUMBER 11 (578-11): The site was 3.2 miles south-southwest of Anson, Texas, at 32 degrees 42 minutes 40 seconds north and 99 degrees 54 minutes 34 seconds west.

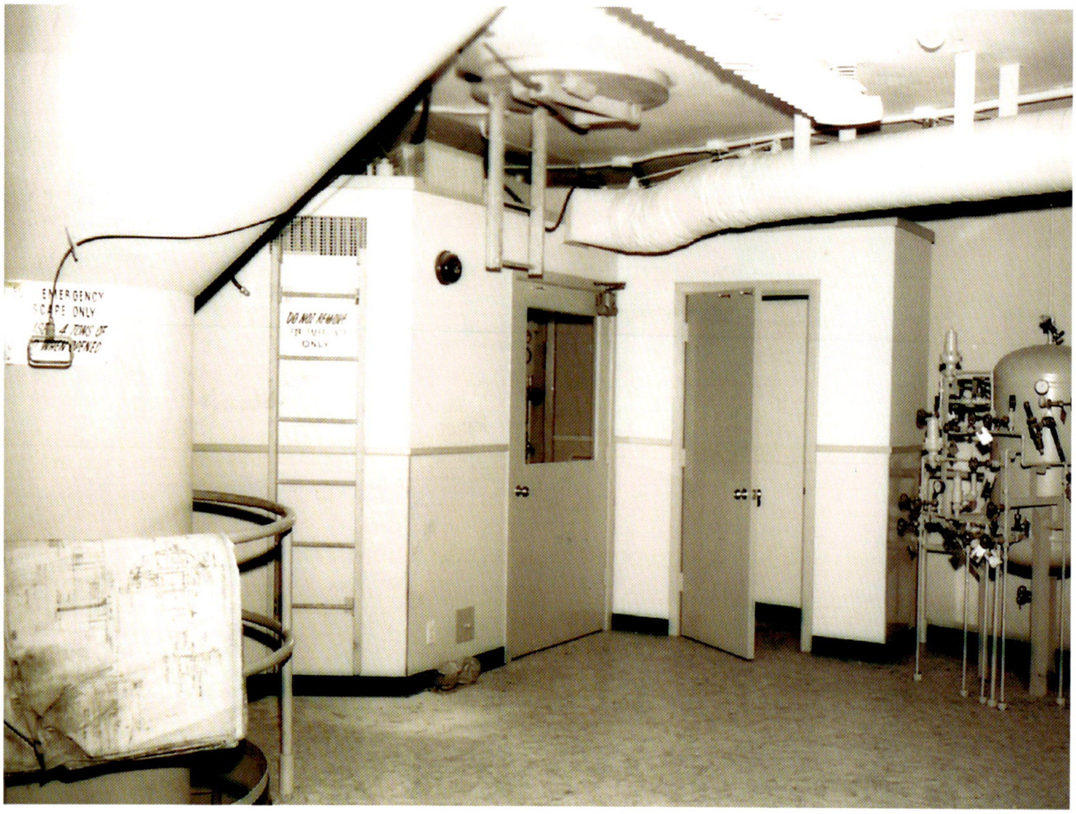

Site 578-11. Upper level of the LCC after cleaning of construction debris. The LCC is still under construction, as noted by contractor blueprints draped over the steel rails (left). The LCC escape hatch is in the top, with the short access ladder hanging part way down. When the hatch was opened, sand inside the escape tunnel to the surface fell to the floor of the LCC. *Bruce Townsley, Atlas F Museum, Clyde, Texas, to author, October 16, 2012*

SITE NUMBER 12 (578-12): The site was 1.4 miles west-northwest of Corinth, Texas, at 32 degrees 51 minutes 37 seconds north and 99 degrees 53 minutes 29 seconds west.[11]

Site 578-12. Initial excavation work by heavy equipment at the construction site to go from ground level to the proper sub-level for construction. *Bruce Townsley, Atlas F Museum, Clyde, Texas, to author, October 16, 2012*

An underground tunnel connected the missile silo to the LCC. The tunnel was protected by three blast doors. The LCC was built of reinforced concrete, positioned fifty feet from the hardened missile silo, and was twenty-seven feet high and forty feet in diameter. The concrete silo and LCC were protected to an over pressure of 200 pounds per square inch from up to a five megaton thermonuclear detonation within four miles of the launch site.[12]

Inside the LCC there was an emergency escape hatch for the crew. The Atlas LCC was manned by a five man missile alert crew:

1. Missile Combat Crew Commander (MCCC): In command of the launch crew and responsible for one of two keys required to launch the Atlas F ICBM.
2. Deputy Missile Combat Crew Commander (DMCC): As with the MCC, an officer second in command of the launch crew responsible for the second of two keys required to launch the Atlas F ICBM.
3. Ballistic Missile Analyst Technician (MBAT): An enlisted person in charge of the various electronic systems involved with the missile, such as the logic cabinets, electrical wiring, sensors, and the remaining equipment necessary to launch the missile.
4. Missile Facilities Technician (MFT): An enlisted person in charge of the various physical systems involved, such as hydraulics, liquid oxygen (LOX) and RPI (high grade kerosene) propellants, air conditioning, and other equipment.
5. Electrical Power Production Technician (EPPT): An enlisted person in charge of the on-site power production equipment, including the diesel generators.[13]

Atlas F sites were set on approximately ten to twenty acres for construction and operational security. The inside secured area consisted of five acres surrounded by a chain link fence eight feet high and topped with barbed wire. The Quonset hut above ground support buildings were a key identifying feature of an Atlas F ICBM site. These two Quonsets—each 4,000 square feet—were forty feet wide and 100 feet long and built on a concrete pad. They contained additional support equipment and personnel areas. The site's secure communications were provided by a hardened antenna silo eight feet in diameter and twenty-nine feet deep.[14] According to construction records, work on the Dyess Atlas F launch sites and on-base missile support facilities was completed on time and on budget. The report indicated there were no labor strikes, but three workers were killed and thirty-three were injured. During construction, the US Army Corps of Engineers set up an office at Dyess AFB to provide supervision of the Atlas missile sites and support facilities. Supervision was under command of Lt. Col. Albert M. Antonelli. This office shared space with the field offices of Air Material Command, which was in charge of supply operations for the missile construction project. These offices employed over 300 men. Construction workers only had fourteen months to complete the twelve missile launch sites.[15]

Construction work on the missile silo began with a shaft 174 feet deep and fifty-two feet in diameter. When the silo was complete, it extended eight feet above ground. A total of twenty-eight shoring ribs five feet in width were installed inside the shaft. What made the silo vulnerable was the location of the LCC buried adjacent to the silo, with access between the silo and LCC via a concrete and steel reinforced tunnel. Each silo and LCC was positioned separate from another site, protecting the missiles from a single Soviet ICBM warhead. In 1962, the ICBM threat of the Soviet Union's Strategic Rocket Forces (SRF) consisted of 200 SS-7 Saddler SSMs. The Saddler was a storable liquid fuel missile with a range of 6,900 miles and was able to be launched from its site to a target in the United States with a Circular Error Probable (CEP, accuracy) of one mile of its desired impact target circle coordinates. The separation of US missile launch sites would make it necessary for Soviet missileers to fire one missile at each site, plus additional missiles to ensure area coverage and destruction of US missile fields. This was the early years of missile technology with accuracy measured in miles, not under ten feet (or less) as with current precision guidance computers, INS/GPS, and continuous course corrections from launch to the point of desired impact. Atlas F sites remained operational until February 10, 1965. By this time, Soviet

SFR forces included the SS-8 Sasin with the same range and CEP of the SS-7, but only nineteen to twenty were deployed with a five megaton thermonuclear warhead.[16]

On June 21, 1961—thirteen months after the general contract was signed—Site 578-5 was the first of the Dyess silos completed. The Atlas F ICBM made its operational debut at the Oplin site during the last week of June 1962 and the missile was lowered into its hardened concrete silo. This was not a classified installation operation.

The missile convoy left the Dyess AFB Missile Assembly Building at 6:30 a.m. with an Atlas F named "Spirit of Oplin" on its transporter/erector, with the name painted on the side of the missile. This started phase three of the Air Force's and General Dynamics' urgent installation operations of the missile complexes surrounding Dyess AFB. At this time, Dyess AFB was the fourth base in the United States bringing Atlas F silos "on line" (Shilling AFB, Kansas; Lincoln AFB, Nebraska; and Altus AFB, Oklahoma). The convoy took ninety minutes to drive from Dyess AFB to the launch site. Prior to mating the W-38 warhead to an operational missile in the silo, missile personnel conducted a Propellant Load Exercise (PLX). This was a maintenance test of the entire missile site to verify that all systems were working properly and that the missile could be launched if necessary. The missile would be fueled with RP-1, raised to its firing position, and fueled with liquid oxygen. If this was successful, the LOX would be off-loaded from the missile, its fuel tank charged with inert nitrogen, and the missile lowered back into the silo.

The warhead was mated to the top of the missile in its shield re-entry cone. At this point, the missile was ready to be sealed inside its silo, with all non-alert personnel removed from the site. Once the site was secured and all checks were completed by the launch crew, it was certified by the squadron command post through Headquarters SAC to be placed on nuclear alert. This procedure was duplicated at the remaining Atlas F launch sites until the entire squadron was on nuclear alert. From this time on the missile was constantly monitored for launch readiness from the LCC. Crews replaced each other on alert and the missiles were "cocked," waiting for launch orders in retaliation of a Soviet ICBM attack on the United States.[17]

Missile assembly building at Dyess Air Force Base. *Bruce Townsley, Atlas F Museum, Clyde, Texas, to author, October 16, 2012*

Overhead crane under installation (construction) inside the missile assembly building. *Bruce Townsley, Atlas F Museum, Clyde, Texas, to author, October 16, 2012*

First Atlas F delivered to Dyess Air Force Base on its transporter/erecter in front of the missile assembly building. *Bruce Townsley, Atlas F Museum, Clyde, Texas, to author, October 16, 2012*

The 578th SMS and the Cuban Missile Crisis

The Cuban Missile Crisis between the United States and the Soviet Union resulted from the Soviet Union's secret shipment and attempted construction of offensive missile sites on the island of Cuba. This initially consisted of six Medium Range Ballistic Missile (SS-4 Sandal MRBM) launch sites, each with four surface prepared launch pads. The SS-4 had a range of 1,200 miles with a one megaton thermonuclear warhead. Three Intermediate Range Ballistic Missile (SS-5 Skean IRBM) launch sites were being built, each with four launch pads. The SS-5 had a range of 2,300 miles with a one megaton thermonuclear warhead. SAC shifted peacetime operations to a war footing prior to President John Kennedy's television speech from the White House Oval Office that the Soviet Union had introduced offensive missiles on Cuba—only ninety miles from Miami, Florida, with over one-half of the United States in range. On October 22, 1962, President Kennedy announced an arms quarantine (embargo) against Soviet shipments to Cuba by sea, demanding Premier Nikita Khrushchev remove the offensive missiles from Cuba identified by SAC U-2 aerial reconnaissance flights over the island. SAC ordered its battle staffs on twenty-four-hour nuclear alert, all personnel were called back from leave, and Air Force reserve personnel were recalled to active duty with SAC and supporting Air Force combat units in preparation for an air assault against Cuba and defense of the United States from possible Soviet attack, especially in Europe (Berlin). SAC B-47s were dispersed to pre-war planned civilian and military airfields for survivability of the bomber force. B-52s went on twenty-four-hour airborne nuclear alert to ensure that a substantial thermonuclear capability remained if the missiles in Cuba were launched against SAC bomber and missile bases; when their launch was detected it gave less than a five-minute warning of a thermonuclear strike. SAC brought its 207 ICBMs on high alert: twenty-seven Atlas E, seventy-two Atlas F, fifty-four Titan I, and the upgraded fifty-four Titan II.[18]

Lucuis A. Morgan, 578th SMS, EPPT, provides a look at the Cuban Missile Crisis as an Atlas F alert crew member:

> I joined the Air Force on July 12, 1961, schooling at Sheppard AFB, Texas, in December 1961, and assigned to 578th SMS launch crew R-39, under Major Truman Grady, the MCCC. Our crew was on nuclear alert at a combat-ready Atlas F launch site when the Cuban Missile Crisis came to a showdown. Of course, we knew the climax was getting close before we ever reached the site. When we reached DEFCON 2, Major Grady told me to start number two generator and put it on line.[19]

United States nuclear forces operated under the following Defense Conditions (DEFCONs), from peacetime to nuclear war:

DEFCON 5: Lowest state of readiness, referred to as normal readiness operations.
DEFCON 4: Increased intelligence watch and strengthened security measures, step above normal readiness.
DEFCON 3: Increase in force readiness above that required for normal readiness, with the Air Force ready to mobilize within fifteen minutes (SAC on October 22, 1962).
DEFCON 2: One step short of nuclear war operations. US armed forces are ready to deploy and engage in less than six hours (SAC on October 26, 1962).
DEFCON 1: Nuclear war is imminent, with US armed forces at maximum readiness.[20]

Bath added:

> He [Grady] and Lt. Hancock (DMCCC) took their side arms out, cocked them, and laid them on the launch console. Next, they took their keys and unlocked both buttons. The commander told us our job was to get the missile into the air. He said it was what we were trained to do and we would do everything in our power to do just that. I can't remember how long we stayed at DEFCON 2, but we were glad when things started to calm down.[21]

W-38 warhead inside a re-entry vehicle being mated to the top of an Atlas F ICBM. *Strategic Air Command, Ashland, Nebraska*

Charles Condit, 578th SMS, BMAT, provides another look at the Cuban Missile Crisis as an Atlas F alert crew member:

> During the Cuban Missile Crisis I was a BMAT on launch crew R-54, assigned to the 578th SMS, Dyess AFB, Texas. Our crew consisted of Major Cox (MCCC), Lt. English (DMCCC), A1C Condit (BMAT), A2C Rowly (MFT), and A2C Jensin (EPPT). Tours of duty were twenty-four hours on and two days off. On Monday, October 22, 1962, the Primary Alerting System (PAS) went off and we received a decoded message that put us in DEFCON 3. We spent the rest of the tour checking and rechecking equipment and procedures. The following morning, we were relieved from duty by a sister team and, of course, there was plenty of discussion on what was going on with Russia and Cuba, what we were going to do or not do. Anyway, our next tour of duty was when the PAS went off again and the message put us in DEFCON 2 on October 24, 1962. We knew for sure this was going to be the real deal—scared, worried about our families, worried about the world situation. We sat on pins and needles for several days before the situation settled down and we returned to DEFCON 3, however, it was mid-November 1962 before we returned to normal alert status, DEFCON 4.[22]

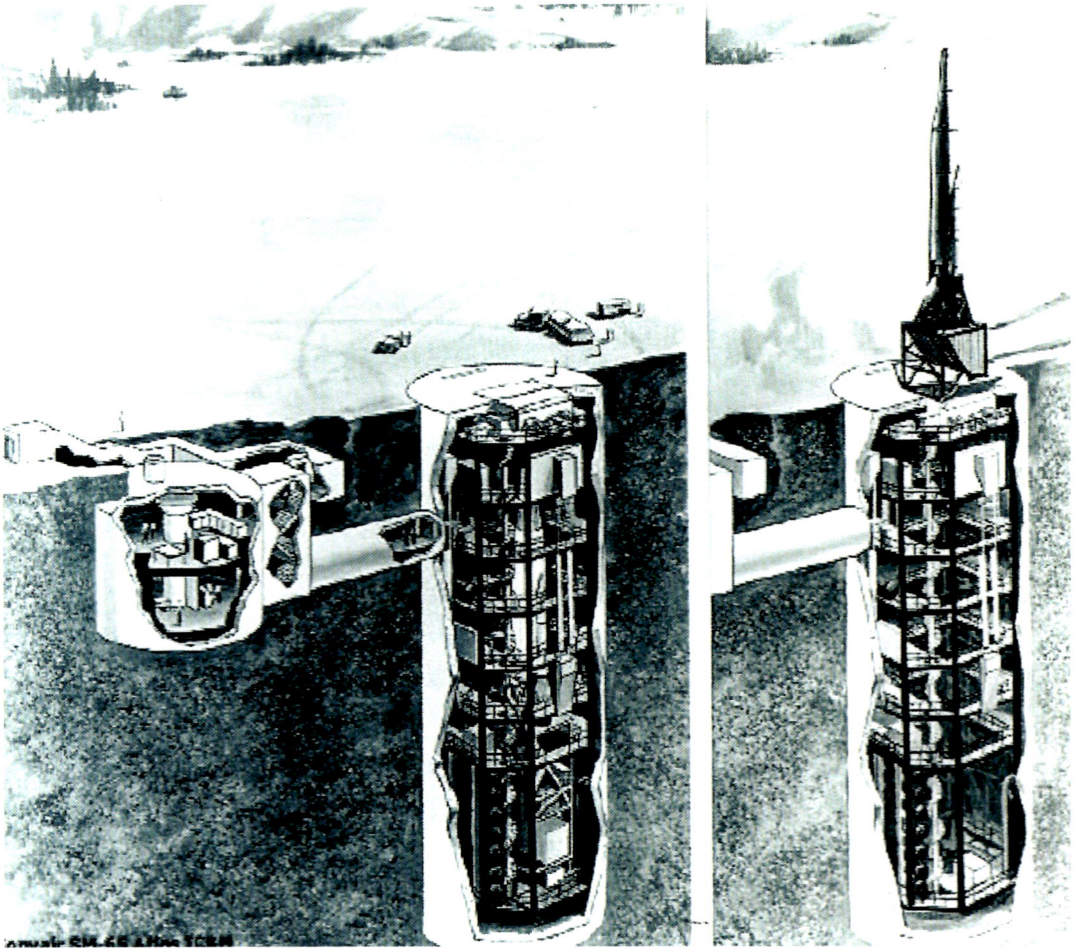

Atlas F launch sequence. *National Museum of the United States Air Force archives, Wright Patterson Air Force Base, Dayton, Ohio*

The nine-man Atlas F alert force crew (five in the LCC and four outside to maintain and guard the site) worked twenty-four hours on and three days off. During high alerts or increased DEFCONs the LCC would receive its launch orders from SAC Headquarters via the Dyess Command Post. The metal structure that supported the Atlas F was set on a platform and supported between shock struts, allowing the silo to vibrate and move side to side from the shock waves and overpressure of a nearby detonating thermonuclear warhead. The Atlas F silo was protected on the surface by two five foot thick, heavy seventy-ton blast doors set on top of a nine foot thick slab. The doors were so heavy they required special electric motors to open them to a vertical position. Once the missile was elevated to the surface, silo storage tanks provided the LOX to fill the fuel tanks, taking approximately four and one-half minutes to five minutes. The kerosene or RP-1 could be stored inside the missile fuel tanks for an extended period. The LOX replaced the inert nitrogen, keeping the fuel tanks from collapsing. After fueling the missile was ready for launch.[23]

On October 28, 1962, Soviet Union leadership agreed to remove its offensive missiles from Cuba. On November 20, they also announced that their light bombers (IL-28 Beagles) would be crated and shipped back to the Soviet Union. SAC started bringing down its bomber and missile alert posture, returning to normal SAC nuclear ready alert.[24]

The final Dyess AFB Atlas F launch site was completed in November 1962. Colonel William L. McDowell Jr., commander, 96th SAW, accepted the twelve Atlas F ICBM launch sites from Col. Hugh B. Manson, commander, Site Activation Task Force. Col. Ray M. Cole, commander, 578th SMS, assumed control of the missile sites. At this time, the number of civilian workers on the construction project dropped from 3,500 to a small technical advisory team assigned to provide guidance and training to squadron personnel.

> The first Atlas F arrived at Dyess AFB in a Douglas C-133B Cargomaster on December 15, 1961, and was stored until the Oplin launch site was ready for missile placement. The C-133B could carry the Atlas F ICBM on its transporter/erector. The loading and unloading process followed a precise procedure, given the close tolerances of the cargo doors and ramps. C-133Bs were vital to SAC's high-priority air movement of Atlas F missiles from the factory to Atlas bases.[25]

578th SMS command post at Dyess Air Force Base. *Bruce Townsley, Atlas F Museum, Clyde, Texas, to author, October 16, 2012*

The 578th SMS set a first in SAC. From May 28 through June 2, 1963, the missile squadron underwent the rigors of a SAC No-Notice Operational Readiness Inspection (ORI). This was the first Atlas F SMS to go through a SAC ORI.

The phaseout of Dyess AFB's Atlas F launch sites was made public by Secretary of Defense Robert McNamara in November 1964, to be completed by March 31, 1965. The first Atlas F was removed from alert on December 1, 1964. The transfer of Atlas F missiles began on January 1, 1956. The transporter/erector trailer was used to truck the missiles to the storage depot at Norton AFB, California. The missile was no longer considered a high priority air cargo and was trucked over roads from Dyess AFB to Norton AFB. The 578th SMS was inactivated on March 25, 1965. The silos and LCCs were demilitarized, with seventy-two launch sites at the six former Atlas F ICBM squadrons offered for sale on the civilian market.[26]

Unlike the Titan I ICBMs placed in storage at Norton AFB that were declared non-operational reusable missiles and destroyed, the Atlas missiles carried on as a satellite launch vehicle. It was used to launch John Glenn into orbit. The Atlas satellite launch vehicle variants were the Agena, Centaur, and Atlas V (modernized with a Russian RD-180 stage one oxygen/kerosene engine and aluminum Isogrid fuel tanks with a Centaur upper stage engine). The Atlas V is reliable and able to launch a heavy payload for commercial and Department of Defense classified payloads. The design has proven its worth, first as a nuclear deterrence ICBM and then in the exploration and exploitation of space.[27]

Atlas F slowly unloaded from an Air Force C-133B at Dyess AFB on December 15, 1961. *Bruce Townsley, Atlas F Museum, Clyde, Texas, to author, October 16, 2012*

4th STRATEGIC SUPPORT SQUADRON and the DOUGLAS C-124C GLOBEMASTER II

The Air Force expanded rapidly after becoming an independent service branch and needed a heavy strategic, long-range cargo/personnel transport. Douglas Aircraft Company took its C-74 Globemaster I transport, which flew cargo delivery missions during the Berlin Airlift in limited numbers, and built a new transport. Douglas Aircraft took the C-74 design and modified it with a deeper fuselage, a strengthened tricycle landing gear, and more powerful piston engines (later upgraded to the higher performance R-4360 engines on the C-124C). Douglas Aircraft designed the C-124 based on the Air Force's requirement for a heavy logistic hauler, not an adaptation of an existing passenger aircraft into a cargo transport. The C-124 was provided with all-weather radar (distinctive nose-mounted radome), wing tip fairings to accommodate combustion heaters to deice the wing, and tail plane leading edges for all-weather flying.

Douglas Aircraft engineers designed front fuselage clamshell doors with a built-in loading/unloading ramp for drive on/drive off cargo handling and an electronic hoist at the top of the cargo compartment at mid-ship with two overhead rail-mounted traveling cranes traversing the length of the cargo hold. A modification allowed the folding down of two metal deck sections secured to the upper cargo interior, creating an upper deck and allowing the aircraft to hold 200 troops/passengers or 123 stretchers, or forty-five ambulatory patients with fifteen attending medical personnel.[1]

Douglas C-124C at the Air Mobility Command Museum, Dover Air Force Base, Delaware. *Courtesy Air Mobility Command Museum*

Douglas C-124C forward view its clamshell doors open. The crew access ladder is visible in the middle of the area between the internal loading/unloading ramps, which move forward and then down onto the ground in front of the aircraft. The tricycle landing gear allowed the aircraft to load and unload through the forward nose section. *Courtesy Air Mobility Command Museum*

Side view of extended and secured web personnel seats. *Courtesy Air Mobility Command Museum*

SAC operated fifty-four C-124Cs from 1950 to 1962. The four strategic support squadrons' mission was to transport nuclear weapons between stateside air bases and forward deployed B-47E Reflex Action bases and provide airlift of SAC personnel and equipment during exercises and overseas deployments. The C-124Cs were highly visible at SAC bases and were assigned to four primary operating locations.

Strategic Air Command Strategic Support Squadrons (SSS)

1st SSS: Activated on July 10, 1946, as the 1st Air Transport Unit (ATU) at Roswell AAF, New Mexico. The squadron was transferred to Carswell AFB, Texas, on January 13, 1948, and redesignated the 1st Strategic Support Unit (SSU) on June 1, 1948. The squadron was then transferred to Biggs AFB, Texas, on December 13, 1948, and redesignated the 1st Strategic Support Squadron (SSS) on January 17, 1949. It was inactivated on January 15, 1959.

2nd SSS: Activated on January 14, 1949, at Biggs AFB, Texas. The squadron was transferred to Walker AFB, New Mexico, on April 18, 1950; to Castle AFB, California, on May 16, 1951; to Pinecastle AFB, Florida, on September 1, 1956; and was inactivated on June 15, 1961.

3rd SSS: Activated on November 16, 1950, at Hunter AFB, Georgia. The squadron was transferred to Barksdale AFB, Louisiana, on January 5, 1953, and inactivated on June 16, 1961.

4th SSS: Activated on February 18, 1953, at Rapid City AFB, South Dakota. The squadron was transferred to Dyess AFB, Texas, on June 15, 1957, and inactivated on March 15, 1961.[2]

C-124 assigned to the 4th Strategic Support Squadron (4th SSS), Ellsworth Air Force Base, South Dakota, on a supply run landing at Thule Air Base. *Lieutenant Merle M. Allen Jr., pilot, 4th SSS, 1954-1957, to Ellsworth Heritage Foundation, South Dakota Air and Space Museum to Author*

In August and September 1953, 4th SSS received seventeen Douglas C-124C Globemaster IIs flown to its base from the Douglas Aircraft, Long Beach, California, production facility.[3] The squadron's primary mission was to maintain a constant state of readiness so that SAC could provide air transportation, direct operational (nuclear readiness) support for the command, and perform operational and logistic support of all other strategic combat units. The squadron was assigned to the 15th Air Force and SAC since April 1, 1954. The 4th SSS moved to its permanent home at Dyess AFB, Texas, starting June 1, 1957. The squadron's presence at Ellsworth AFB was intended to be temporary; a permanent base of operations with sufficient facilities to better carry out its operational mission was needed. The movement of equipment to Abilene was begun on June 5, but it was not until June 17 that the first aircraft arrived at Dyess AFB, landing late in the evening of June 17: Capt. Ralph Anderson, aircraft commander; Capt. Thomas Slaven, copilot; Lt. Kenneth Gaaschus, navigator; Master Sgt. Euland Zecher, flight engineer; Staff Sgt. William Wofley, loadmaster; Airman 1st Class Dennis Albrecht, radio operator; and Airman 1st Class Benny Wilson, crew chief. From June 17 to July 1, 1953, there was a shuttle trip almost every day between Ellsworth AFB and Dyess AFB. Every load was planned in advance and loaded before the crew arrived at the aircraft to fly to Dyess AFB. On Monday, July 1, 1953, at 1300, the last of the C-124Cs assigned to the 4th SSS took off for the last time from Ellsworth AFB, South Dakota, for Dyess AFB, Texas, exactly four years to the day when the unit's first aircraft was flown to Ellsworth AFB. After taking off from Ellsworth AFB the crew made a low-level flight past Mount Rushmore National Memorial in their plane "The Shrine of Democracy," named for the four presidential faces below. A photograph of this fly-by is on display inside the real "Shrine of Democracy" visitor's center. On board the aircraft were Captain Louis Sales, aircraft commander; Lt. Leon Leaps, copilot; Capt. Allen Gay, navigator; Maj. Walker Reynolds, 4th SSS Operations Officer; Tech. Sgt. Nolan Brooks, flight engineer; Staff Sgt. Teddie Taylor, radio operator; Staff Sgt. William Cannon, loadmaster; and Airman 1st Class George Fuller, crew chief. During the move from Ellsworth AFB to Dyess AFB the squadron continued to perform periodic flight line and limited maintenance on assigned aircraft away from base and organizational maintenance on its powered ground equipment. During the transfer of operations the squadron flew 53,524 nautical miles, carrying 1,134,963 pounds of cargo and 870 passengers. Six C-124Cs were used during the airlift—three from Ellsworth and three from Dyess—shortening the effective mission time for each aircraft. Aircrews logged a total of 225 flight hours.[4]

John Watts, 4th SSS, indicated he was probably the youngest pilot assigned to the squadron. He was only twenty years old when he was assigned to Dyess AFB after completing flight school in a class of sixty pilots. The squadron appeared to have two groups of officers when it moved from Ellsworth AFB to Dyess AFB. One was a group who had been with the squadron from the start, moving from Biggs AFB to Ellsworth AFB. The second was a group who had been flying the Convair B-36 and moved from that unit over to the 4th SSS. The crew navigator on Watts' crew was a B-36 performance engineer who transferred to navigator training. Watts was a C-124C copilot and younger than the aircraft's commander and navigator.[5] Watts recalled a story that one of the loadmasters told that he was part of a SAC team that Gen. Lemay sent to the Douglas Aircraft Company's factory during the development of the C-124. The loadmaster and a Military Airlift Command (MAC) colonel discussed whether there should be one or two Auxiliary Power Units (APUs) on the C-124. The MAC colonel believed one APU was sufficient for MAC's use and two were not needed. The loadmaster called SAC Headquarters, General LeMay's office, and told General LeMay that because the C-124's primary mission was the transport of special weapons a second APU was essential. By the time the loadmaster returned to the MAC colonel, he found Gen. LeMay had already called and informed the colonel of the correct decision that there would be two APUs on the C-124. Gen. LeMay also informed Douglas Aircraft Company officers that this was his (SAC's) decision.

July 1, 1957, the last 4th SSS C-124 took off from Ellsworth Air Force Base for the flight to Dyess Air Force Base, Texas. The aircraft was named "Shrine of Democracy" and it made a low-level, photographic pass over Mount Rushmore before turning south. *Lieutenant Merle M. Allen Jr., pilot 4th SSS, 1954–1957, to Ellsworth Heritage Foundation, South Dakota Air and Space Museum to Author*

A C-124C from Dyess AFB was flown to the Lockheed Aircraft Company's top secret Skunk Works in Los Angeles to covertly load a U-2 spy plane on board and fly it to the desert (Groom Lake—today referred to as Area 51) for flight testing far away from prying eyes.[6]

In 1958, while operating at Dyess AFB, the 4th SSS participated in two history making operations. The first was Operation Power Flight, in which the squadron contributed to the successful around-the-world flight completed by the Castle AFB, California, 43rd SW Boeing B-52Bs. These SAC bombers were supported by KC-97G tanker aircraft (including those assigned to the 11th ARS, Dyess AFB) operating from Clark AB, Philippines. The squadron assisted moving equipment and personnel to the Philippines. Later in the year, the squadron was tasked to assist Project Ice Skate. The squadron allocated three C-124Cs to assist the supply of Ice Station T-3, near the North Pole. During this project, the three C-124Cs airlifted over 400 tons of cargo in nine days from the forward staging base at Thule Air Base, Greenland.[7]

The following lists the C-124Cs assigned to the squadron.

Douglas C-124C Globemasters Assigned to the 4th Strategic Support Squadron

SERIAL NUMBERS	DATE RECEIVED FROM DOUGLAS AIRCRAFT COMPANY
52-0973	August 15 to 26, 1953
52-0974	August 15 to 26, 1953
52-0975	August 15 to 26, 1953
52-0976	August 15 to 26, 1953
52-0977	August 15 to 26, 1953
52-0978	August 15 to 26, 1953
52-0979	August 15 to 26, 1953
52-0984	September 1953
52-0985	September 1953
52-0986	September 1953
52-0987	September 1953
52-0988	September 1953
52-0989	September 1953
52-1016	September 1953
52-1018	September 1953
52-1019	September 1953
52-1020	September 19538

Arctic operations showed the squadron was able to airlift 240,000 to 440,000 pounds of cargo in a single operation while performing flight line, periodic, and limited maintenance on assigned aircraft away from Dyess AFB, with personnel performing organizational maintenance on its ground powered equipment.[9]

From April 1 to 30, 1959, the 4th SSS had little trouble completing their thirty-seven missions allocated in 1959, the fifth anniversary of its assignment as a unit directly under the 15th Air Force and the Strategic Air Command. No aircraft were out of commission for parts during the month and the number out of commission for maintenance held steady at four—the average held since the beginning of the year. The number of missions increased by five over the March total and the flying time only increased 45:50 hours. Even with the small increase, April's flying time of 865,000 hours topped all previous totals and marked the highest month since the squadron was formed. With the increase in time came an increase in nautical miles flown from 114,592 to 149,198 and an increase in passengers from 1,571 to 1,856. The only decrease was the amount of cargo hauled from 1,766,402 to 1,677,106 pounds.

The missions accounting for these totals were flown under SAC Operation Order 37-59 (Operation SNUFFY SMITH) and as 15th Air Force VOCOs (Verbal Orders, Commanding Officer). The classified weapons airlift was flown in three separate segments and consisted of thirteen missions, one of which was not scheduled and was only utilized to deliver replacement parts for their aircraft in operation. The first five flights departed on the thirteenth and returned by the twenty-second. The next five left on the twentieth and were back at Dyess AFB on the twenty-fifth. The last three Operation SNUFFY SMITH flights conducted in April departed on the twenty-seventh from Dyess AFB, returning to on May 1. The 15th Air Force VOCO missions

C-124C at the *National Museum of the United States Air Force* Author

totaled twenty-four and included an overseas trip to the Pacific. Among the 15th Air Force VOCO flights in April were one in support of the 15th Air Force Inspector General's Team, one in support of the 15th Air Force Band, one in support of Civil Air Patrol Cadets (CAP), and one in support of Reserve Officer Training Corps (ROTC) cadets. There was also one mission—the last one of the month—supporting the 8th Air Force. By participating in these operations, the squadron proved itself capable of airlifting 240,000 to 444,000 pounds of cargo in a single operation, providing all-around support of various combat units, and performing flight line, periodic, and limited aircraft maintenance away from Dyess AFB, including the performance of organizational maintenance of its ground powered equipment.

The number of officer personnel in the squadron remained constant at seventy-nine during April: one lieutenant colonel, nine majors, thirty-six captains, thirty-two first lieutenants, and one warrant officer. Enlisted strength consisted of 288: two senior master sergeants, forty-two master sergeants, forty-five technical sergeants, sixty staff sergeants, forty-three airmen 1st class, sixty-three airmen 2nd class, twenty-eight airmen third class, and four airmen basic. All losses and gains for the month in squadron personnel strength were in the enlisted grades. There were four gains in four different Air Force Specialty Codes (AFSCs) as the squadron changed to meet SAC's different operational demands during the Cold War: one flight engineer technician, one aircraft loadmaster, one administrative helper, and one administrative clerk. The squadron had eleven losses in five AFSCs: four aircraft maintenance technicians, four personnel specialists, one apprentice personnel specialist, one apprentice reciprocating engine mechanic, and one organizational supply specialist.

The on the job training (OJT) program remained at 100 percent in April, with three airmen tested and passed and all sixteen eligible airmen engaged in the program. Eleven airmen were upgraded during the month. The Manning In Required Spaces (MIRS) was ninety-nine percent for all officers and 100 percent for officers on flying status: airmen crew members had 100 percent MIRS; non-crew member airmen, 92 percent; and MIRS for all airmen was ninety-two percent. The flight engineers, radio operators, and loadmasters were all 100 percent MIRS. The squadron MIRS, less flying personnel, was ninety-one percent and overall squadron MIRS was ninety-two percent.

During April, forty squadron aircraft were loaded and off-loaded at Dyess AFB by the Personal Equipment Section to service cross-country flight operations, with twenty-nine additional aircraft loaded and off-loaded for local training and test flights.[10]

In May 1959, the squadron provided a special weapons airlift when Maj. Welborn's crew loaded a Nike-Hercules surface to air missile in a C-124C. Dyess was in the process of constructing two Nike-Hercules SAM sites to protect SAC's B-47E medium nuclear bombers, KC-97G Stratofreighters, and the planned Atlas intercontinental ballistic missile. The crew flew the Nike-Hercules in a transporter to El Paso, Texas, for display during Armed Forces Day 1959. During the month the squadron flew a total of 888.35 hours. The squadron loaded and unloaded forty aircraft for cross country flights, with an additional twenty-two local flights. A look at the squadron's flight log indicates many SAC operational support flights and special classified flights to Kirkland AFB, New Mexico. These were flights to Albuquerque, New Mexico, where up to the time of the Cuban Missile Crisis the Atomic Energy Commission stored and controlled the US stockpile of atomic weapons. As SAC shifted to controlling its own atomic and then thermonuclear weapons, it started to build its own on-base nuclear weapons storage areas, including the one at Dyess AFB. There were classified flights to Kirkland AFB to change out tritium initiators (triggers) for nuclear weapons. SAC used its C-124Cs to move these nuclear materials to its expanding bomber bases. The logs only indicate the cargo was "classified," with no specifics. The squadron's strength remained fairly stable until the squadron was inactivated on March 15, 1961.[11]

During July, 4th SSS flying time diminished by 210 hours, but it was still very busy. The squadron was tasked with supporting SAC's Operations Order 37-59 with twenty-eight missions: ten VOCO missions, one overseas mission to the Atlantic, two to Alaska, and more classified SAC missions from Dyess to Kirkland and other SAC bomber bases. There were also thirty-eight local flying missions, giving the squadron a monthly total of 971 and one-third hours.[12]

Operational activities during August were not as great as the previous month. A decrease in flying time by 350 hours and lower figures for total cargo carried, passengers transported, and nautical miles flown reflected in the Consolidated Report substantiate the lighter workload for the squadron during the month. Twenty-seven operational missions were flown, of which fifteen were under SAC Operational Order 37-60. One, Operation MOON MULLINS, was an overseas mission in Europe. The remainder of the missions were VOCOs directed by the 15th Air Force. Of these VOCO missions, two were ferry flights taking and returning squadron aircraft after completing inspection and repair as necessary. General cargo airlifts accounted for the rest of the 15th Air Force VOCO sorties. All missions assigned were successfully completed and overall general support by the various bases was improved over previous months. The following is typical of the squadron support of SAC missions:

Captain Boyd and crew were detailed to fly to Davis-Monthan AFB on the fifth to pick up an engine at McChord AFB. The engine was not ready for shipment on the fifth and the crew was unable to proceed with the mission until the following day. Crew rest was taken at McChord AFB on the sixth while all spark plugs in engine number two were changed. The crew returned to Dyess AFB August 8, after stopping at Offutt AFB to pick up squadron personnel attending a conference there.[13]

The 4th SSS was inactivated on March 15, 1961. The squadron's personnel and aircraft were reassigned to various Military Air Transport Services (MATS) bases. After the 4th SSS was officially broken up, personnel from the squadron were assigned to three different units' Light Support Squadrons (LSS): the 7th, 19th, and 28th. In January 1966, MATS became the Military Airlift Command (MAC) and in the years that followed MAC began a transfer of C-124s to the Air Force Reserve (AFRES) and Air National Guard (ANG) units, with transfers complete in 1970. In September 1974, the ANG became the last military unit to fly and then retire the C-124C. The last recorded flight of a C-124 was on October 9, 1986, when the aircraft was flown nonstop from Selfridge Air National Guard Base in Michigan to McChord AFB, Tacoma, Washington. Today, nine C-124Cs have survived the scrape yard and are on display at eight US air museums in the United States; the other one is at the Seoul Military Academy Museum, Sacheaon Air Base, Seoul, Republic of South Korea.[14]

C-124C at Travis Air force Museum, Travis Air Force Base, California. *Author*

DEFENSE OF DYESS AIR FORCE BASE and the NIKE-HERCULES SURFACE-TO-AIR MISSILE

In the 1950s, US national intelligence agencies believed Russian Air Force Long-Range Aviation (LRA) bombers were a serious threat to the security of the United States. Supposedly, the Soviet Union was developing and producing a large force of four-engine, nuclear bomb carrying intercontinental bombers that would launch from Russian Arctic staging bases, flying over the North Pole to attack SAC bases and major US cities. The Tupolev Tu-20 Bear had a 159 foot wingspan and was 155 feet long, powered by four eight-blade twin sets of counter-rotating propellers powered by turboprop engines with an incredible unrefueled range of 13,400 miles. It is still flying today, as is its contemporary, the Boeing B-52H Stratofortress. The Myasishchev Mya-4 was a swept wing, four turbojet powered bomber with a 156 foot wingspan, 154 feet long and a range of 6,835 miles. For a time in the early 1950s, because the United States possessed no photo-reconnaissance satellites to collect intelligence on Soviet strategic systems, it was believed the Soviet Union was conducting a large bomber building program and this led to what the Pentagon referred to as a "bomber gap" with the Soviet Union. This resulted in SAC's development and production of over 2,000 B-47 Stratojet medium bombers, followed by the B-58 Hustler supersonic medium bomber and the B-52 Stratofortress heavy bomber. In reality, the Soviet Union had shifted from a large manned bomber force to ICBMs in substantial numbers, with large megaton warheads and eventually multiple independently targeted re-entry vehicles that would allow them to conduct a large attack on many US targets at the same time.

It was believed these two Russian LRA bombers would be launched in WWII type B-29 Superfortress massed bombing attacks against the United States over the North Pole at high altitude. The B-52 was initially designed as a high-altitude nuclear bomber carrying large megaton gravity free-fall bombs. The initial Nike-Ajax Surface to Air Missile (SAM) was designed as a weapon of last resort in a point defense role for air defense around important US military installations, which at that time were SAC bomber bases (including Dyess AFB, Texas). Later, this air defense coverage was expanded to include the first generation of US ICBM launch sites. It was not until the Atlas F that ICBMs were placed in hardened, vertical, underground silos. The Nike sites were placed in circles around major US urban areas to provide protection from Russian LRA bombers.[1]

On July 31, 1959, United States House of Representatives representative (congressman) Burleson, Texas, received a routine memorandum from the Pentagon, Department of the Army, prepared by the Army Chief of Legislative Liaison, stating:

> ...the Department of Defense and the United States Army announced today that in implementation of the Department of Defense Plan for Air Defense of the United States and in accordance with the Military Construction Act of 1959 as amended, the Department of Army is to construct nine Nike-Hercules facilities.

This included two near Dyess AFB to protect SAC's B-47Es, KC-97Gs, Atlas F ICBM sites, and the Special Weapons Storage Area (which at that time stored thermonuclear warheads and free-fall gravity weapons).[2]

Nike-Hercules site DY-50's administration area. *Carlisle Barracks, Pennsylvania, United States Institute for Military History, Photo Archives Division, United States Army War College*

The 5th Missile Battalion, 517th Artillery, US Army was activated at Dyess AFB, Texas, on March 15, 1960, to be equipped with the Nike-Hercules surface to air missile (SAM). Each missile cost approximately $3,000,000. The south site (DY-50) was on San Angelo Highway, fourteen miles south of Dyess AFB. Each Hercules battery was a complete military installation (Army post), with barracks, administrative buildings, dining halls, fire control equipment, and missile testing and launching facilities. These sites had above-ground launching facilities. The two Nike-Hercules sites protecting Dyess AFB were among the first above-ground SAM batteries constructed by the US Army Corps of Engineers.

Nike-Hercules site DY-10's administration area. *Carlisle Barracks, Pennsylvania, United States Institute for Military History, Photo Archives Division, United States Army War College*

The Barkeley Nike-Hercules Site (DY-10) was eighteen miles southwest of Abilene, Texas, on the San Angelo Highway. The first site was occupied on July 22, 1960, when Battery B of the 5th Missile Battalion moved from its temporary home to the site. Construction of the site continued until October 1960, but landscaping and communications were not completed until April 1961. The name Barkeley Nike Missile Site was selected to honor the WWII training facility. The battalion headquarters, motor pool, barracks, and mess hall were at Dyess AFB.

Nike-Hercules site DY-10's launch battery site. *Carlisle Barracks, Pennsylvania, United States Institute for Military History, Photo Archives Division, United States Army War College*

The Battalion Tactical Command Post was set up at the North American Air Defense Control Center at Sweetwater Air Force Station (AFS). The 3rd Surface to Air Missile Support Detachment provided supply and maintenance support for the battalion. More than fifty military technicians and Department of Army civilian employees worked in the large missile shop and office building near the Dyess AFB motor pool. Personnel for the 5th Missile Battalion came from 240 different US Army Air Defense Command (ADC) missile units around the United States to provide experienced missileers without decreasing the combat effectiveness of those units. This permitted training of new personnel in equal numbers versus an entire battery at the same time. A cadre of officers and enlisted men were especially trained on the Nike-Hercules at Fort Bliss, Texas, prior to reporting to Dyess AFB. During their training, personnel fired four missiles at radio controlled (drone) targets. The 5th Missile Battalion was responsible for defending Abilene, Texas, and surrounding military installations against aerial attack by manned Russian strategic Long-Range Aviation (LRA) bombers and air-supported missiles. The battalion was directly subordinate to the 2nd Region, US Army ADC, one of six regional command units dividing the United States for effective air defense purposes. The 2nd Region US Army ADC was headquartered in Oklahoma City, Oklahoma. It was directly subordinate to the nationwide US Army Headquarters at Colorado Springs, Colorado. Headquarters of the 2nd Region Army ADC also had command responsibility and administrative control for Army ADC organizations deployed at Dallas-Fort Worth and Austin, Texas; Shreveport, Louisiana; and Macon and Albany, Georgia. Each battalion had two or more Nike-Hercules missile battery sites. Each missile site was connected to a tactical command post that supplied early warning information and tactical control in the event of attack. The Tactical Command Post was in turn connected to NORAD communications. Operational control of the site near Abilene, Texas, was exercised by the NORAD Control Center at Duncanville AFS, Dallas, Texas.[3]

Nike-Ajax modification to a Nike-Hercules launch battery site. *Carlisle Barracks, Pennsylvania, United States Institute for Military History, Photo Archives Division, United States Army War College*

Western Electric—the Nike system's original prime contractor—modified and redeveloped the power and electrical systems to meet Air Force specifications for an upgraded Nike, resulting in the Nike-Hercules. It dramatically increased the flight performance of the existing Nike-Ajax. This allowed an improved missile system to be installed at former Nike-Ajax sites. Two new Nike-Hercules SAM sites were constructed in the Dyess Defense Area. The new system became operational in January 1958, and by June, initial Nike-Hercules missiles were deployed and operational at former Nike-Ajax sites protecting New York City, New York; Washington, DC; and Chicago, Illinois.

Conceptual model of a Nike-Hercules launch battery site at the Department of the US Army, Pentagon. *Carlisle Barracks, Pennsylvania, United States Institute for Military History, Photo Archives Division, United States Army War College*

The Nike-Hercules burnout speed was Mach 3.35 in early production models and increased to Mach 3.65 in following production models. Except for targets intercepted at extreme range, it was possible to intercept airborne targets up to 150,000 feet. The expected interception altitude for Russian LRA bombers was 40,000 to 45,000 feet. The missile's boost motor was a four-barrel cluster produced by Radford Arsenal and Borg Warner containing four Nike-Ajax solid fuel rockets. Thiokol Longhorn Division, Marshall, Texas, built the high-performance sustainer rocket engine with a solid charge positioned on the center of gravity. AiResearch produced the Advanced Auxiliary Power Unit, which among other operations powered the ailerons on the trailing edges of the four extremely swept delta wings. As with the Nike-Ajax, there were four small delta aerials to indicate the position of the guidance bay, and behind them was a large Type T-45 fragmentation warhead, but as a weapon of last resort in defense against an all-out nuclear attack by Russian LRA bombers, it could be armed with a variable nuclear warhead. It had a variable range: low (two kilotons), medium (twenty kilotons), and high (thirty to forty kilotons). It would take an actual nuclear attack on the United States by the Soviet Union for the president of the United States to authorize the arming and firing release orders and detonation of nuclear warheads over the United States (its major cities and military installations).

At the peak of Nike-Hercules deployment (1957 to 1960), Douglas Aircraft Company operated four ordnance missile production plants in North Carolina: Burlington, Charlotte, Greensboro, and Winston-Salem. Thiokol was unable to develop and produce a self-consuming booster as the technology was not available at this time. General Electric produced the fusing equipment and electronics for the W-31 thermonuclear warhead and most of an enhanced guidance system, including High-Power Acquisition Radar (HIPAR). This system, despite having a forty-three-foot aerial, could fit into three trailers—compared to twenty to twenty-one trailers for the original system—and this opened the way to a semi-mobile system tested in early 1960, when a Nike-Hercules at the Western Missile Test Range (WMTR) destroyed an inbound Corporal SSM. Later in the year, a Nike-Hercules shot down another Nike-Hercules at a combined (closing) speed of Mach 7 and an altitude of 100,000 feet. The Nike-Hercules was less effective at intercepting low-level penetrating aircraft attempting to sneak under US ADC radars designed to locate and identify hostile enemy aircraft over the North Pole, across Canada, and into the northern United States. This information was passed onto the Nike-Ajax and Nike-Hercules SAM sites as well as ADC fighter-interceptor squadrons around the United States. The US Army's peak deployment of 134 Nike-Hercules batteries occurred in 1963. The last Nike-Hercules came off alert and the site was deactivated in 1974.[4]

On November 19, 1959, the US Army conducted a groundbreaking ceremony at Dyess AFB for battalion headquarters, 5th Battalion, 517th Artillery, US Army ADC. The two Nike-Hercules sites' primary mission was to defend Dyess AFB's SAC bombers, tankers, Special Weapons Storage Area, and Atlas F ICBM launch sites. The two Nike-Hercules sites were under control of the "BIRDIE" system installed and operating at Sweetwater AFS.[5]

The Army Air Defense Command Post (AADCP) at Sweetwater AFS worked together with various Air Force units. Battery headquarters was at Dyess AFB. Battery DY-10 Fort Phantom Hill/Abilene, designated A Battery, 5th Battalion, 517th ADA Regiment, was active from October 1960 through June 1966. It contained twelve Nike-Hercules missile erector/launchers. Battery DY-50 Camp Barkeley/Abilene, designated B Battery, 5th Battalion, 517th ADA Regiment, was active for the same time period as A Battery and also contained twelve Nike-Hercules erector/launchers. These sites were built from the ground up as new missile installations. Even though they could be armed with the W-31 thermonuclear warhead, research in neither former SAC nor Air Force historical archives would confirm or deny the installation of active warheads on the Nike-Hercules, although these warheads were stored at the Dyess AFB Special Weapons Storage Area.[6]

Nike-Hercules missile launch site DY-10 was near Fort Phantom Hill at 32 degrees 34 minutes 49.48 seconds north latitude and 99 degrees 43 minutes 3.38 seconds west longitude. Site DY-50 was twelve miles southwest of Abilene, Texas, in the northeast corner of former Camp Barkeley at 32 degrees 16 minutes 16.47 seconds north latitude and 99 degrees 57 minutes 31.50 seconds west longitude.[7]

The Nike-Hercules site was divided into the Battery Control Area and the Launch Area. The Battery Control Area consisted of the following facilities:

SENTRY GUARD HOUSE: This was a small, square structure constructed of cinder block walls at the entrance to all areas of the Hercules site. The two areas were secured by two sets of security fencing with a fire break indicating the installation's boundaries.

ADMINISTRATIVE BUILDING: This housed the administrative support services for the missile base. The one-story, cinder block building contained a day room, offices for the battery commander and officers (site manning comprised 115 officers and enlisted personnel), a supply room, supply office, mail room, and a small arms storage room (armory).

BARRACKS: One for site launch personnel and one for battery control personnel. Each contained an officers' lounge, non-commissioned officers' lounge, several storage rooms, restroom, shower room, and a large common area/sleeping room. It was a slanted roof, one-story structure with cinder block walls in an L-shaped floor plan.

MESS HALL: This was the common eating area for the personnel stationed at the base. It included a well equipped kitchen, storage area, and boiler room for heat and hot water. It had cinder block walls and a slanted roof and was equipped with twenty vestibules.

PAINT AND OIL SHED: Looked similar to the sentry guard house; cinder block construction used to store flammable liquids.

POST EXCHANGE (SUPPLY STORE): A simple, gable-roofed rectangular building with sheet metal walls and roof only used for a few hours a day by personnel within the missile site.

WATER TREATMENT/SEWAGE FACILITIES: To maintain security an on-site water treatment and sewage pond was provided as a precaution against Russian agents in the United States conducting sabotage of civilian support facilities off-base in unsecured areas. The missile site had its own well providing secure water access, as well as state-of-the-art pump houses, sewage pumping equipment, holding tanks, and or/septic tanks. At this time there were no EPA rules regulating the odor from open sewage ponds/pools.

BASKETBALL COURT: When not on alert, Hercules personnel exercised and played basketball on the basketball court.

BATTERY CONTROL AREA: Referred to as the Integrated Fire Control (IFC) Area, it held the necessary radar, computer, and control equipment to detect and identify incoming (approaching high-altitude hostile aircraft) and launch and guide a missile to intercept the target. In general, the missile area was on higher terrain than the surrounding topography, but was still relatively level and well drained. The site was clear of visual obstructions such as trees, commercial radio towers, posts (power and telephone), electrical transmission lines, and smoke stacks. It needed a minimum crew of ten serving as the focal point for information and communications for the battery. There were cables everywhere in the Launch Control and Battery Control Areas.

BATTERY CONTROL TRAILER: The US Army designed the Nike-Hercules to be used as a mobile missile system like the Nike-Ajax missile system, suitable for setup with a mobile army, although not in the class of move and shoot area defensive SAMs. On US bases they were permanent installations. The equipment was still capable of mobile missile operations and dispersing from a permanent site in case of the threat of nuclear war to confuse Soviet targeting of bases, or to move missile defenses to protect a threatened area and/or installation. Consequently, key pieces of the Hercules radar system (launch and battery control equipment) were contained in mobile wheeled trailers connected by on-the-ground communications cable. A Hercules site was not neat, with cables running every direction. Other trailers were used to store spare parts and maintenance and antenna equipment. The battery control trailer was the center of the Hercules missile site. The Army equipped the trailers so they could provide the battery control officer with all the information required to direct battery operations. The trailer contained the battery control assembly, the acquisition radar cabinet, an event recorder, and a switchboard cabinet. The battery commander directed the acquisition of targets and firing of missiles from this trailer. The acquisition radar operator and computer operator were also stationed in the battery control trailer.

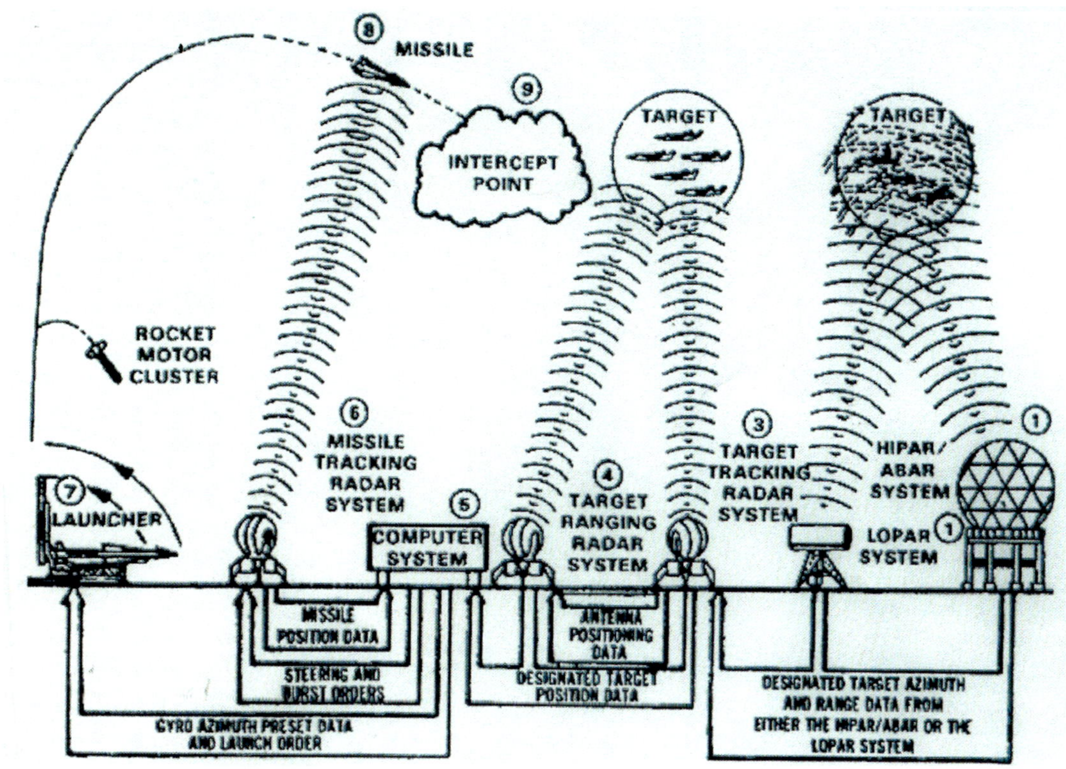

Drawing of a Nike-Hercules radar interception of a hostile, airborne enemy aircraft. *Carlisle Barracks, Pennsylvania, United States Institute for Military History, Photo Archives Division, United States Army War College*

RADAR CONTROL TRAILER: Housed the target radar console assembly, the missile tracking radar console, the radar power cabinet, and the radar range and receiver cabinet, as well as additional equipment associated with target and missile tracking radars. The target track radar console provided the control and displays for the target tracking radar. The missile track console provided the control and displays for the missile tracking radar. Generally, the battery control and radar control trailers were positioned back to back, allowing access to both trailers by assigned personnel.

LOW-POWER ACQUISITION RADAR (LOPAR): This search radar was composed of the acquisition antenna, receiver, and transmitter. The radar rotated constantly at a pre-determined speed. Through the acquisition radar scope, the battery commander or battery control officer received an image of possible airborne enemy (hostile) aircraft approaching within range of the battery. The battery commander determined whether the target was friend or foe. Hercules radars were positioned on top of ground level concrete pads. If any obstructions were in the area the site's radars were mounted on top of steel towers with sufficient elevation to provide line of sight, unobstructed radar transmission, and reception. The acquisition radar was positioned between the targeting and missile tracking radars.

HIGH-POWER ACQUISITION RADAR (HIPAR): This radar was capable of locating incoming targets at high altitudes. Since a ballistic missile or high-speed aircraft may not be detected until it entered the antenna beam, high-altitude coverage provided adequate reaction time to allow for interception at a safe distance. This was critical if the launched Hercules was armed with a thermonuclear warhead. The HIPAR was set on a 50-foot high support tripod steel platform covered with a radome protecting the main, Omni, and auxiliary antennas.

HIPAR EQUIPMENT BUILDING: Adjacent to the HIPAR system, it housed electronic equipment to operate and maintain the HIPAR radar.

TARGET TRACKING RADAR: It tracked the hostile aircraft's range, direction, and elevation, transmitting the information electronically to the site's main computer system. The radar consisted of tracking antenna, receiver, and a transmitter.

MISSILE TRACKING RADAR: Similar in appearance and operation to the target tracking radar. The missile tracking radar followed the missile throughout its outward, powered flight, continuously transmitting information to the site's primary computer system. The computer then transmitted steering commands to the missile through the missile tracking radar, directing the missile toward its predicted interception point with the approaching hostile target. Continuous electronic commands were transmitted to the missile to correct for evasive maneuvers by the approaching hostile target. When the approaching target and launched missile converged the missile was detonated and the missile tracking radar automatically transferred to the next missile designated to fire at another approaching hostile target.

GENERATOR BUILDING: Housed diesel generators for electrical power to operate the site if commercial power was disrupted. Transformers were mounted outside the building for receipt and disruption of commercial power for the missile site. Commercial power—with electrical converters to change sixty cycle power to 400 cycle power—was used where available. Power source switching control was also provided at this point.

RADAR COLLIMATION MAST ASSEMBLY: Composed of a radar mast that had two track radar frequency band generators; the radar collimation mast—which was usually sixty feet high; the target head assembly; and cross arms for correcting bore sight. The mast assembly was used for collimating or adjusting line of sight and adjusting the missile tracking and target tracking radars. The mast assembly was approximately 600 feet from the missile-tracking and target tracking radars, forming a triangle.[8]

The Missile Launch Area was manned by twenty-one personnel, including the launch control officer and section chief who operated launch control. Of these twenty-one personnel, six missile crew members manned each of the three launching sections. The launch area consisted of the following:

LAUNCH CONTROL TRAILER: Contained the equipment to function as the control center between the battery control trailer and the launching sections. Similar in appearance to the battery control and radar trailers, the launch control trailer contained the launching control panel, launching control switchboard, and test responder. Included with the launching control panel were the controls, displays, and communications to supervise and monitor the launching sections and to act as a relay station between the launching sections and the battery control area.[9]

MISSILE TEST AND ASSEMBLY BUILDING: Missiles arrived disassembled and unarmed under peacetime interstate commerce commission restrictions preventing the transportation by military convoys of launch capable missiles from a central assembly facility on a military support base serving multiple missile sites. In the building and its adjacent hardstand, site personnel uncrated, assembled, and tested the missiles. Assembly consisted of the installation of the missile control fins, main fins, ailerons, and fairings. The missile's hydraulic and propulsion systems were checked. The site crew visually inspected the various components and lines of both systems for correct assembly and serviceable condition. Personnel ran leak tests on the missile's lines and components. Following system tests, the crew performed a complete missile test. In preparation for this test, crewmen connected the missile to an external hydraulic power source and to the radio frequency and electrical test sets. The missile was then operated from these external sources. The missile was made to perform as it would in flight and its performance parameters were carefully observed. After this test the crew connected the missile to a compressed air source and both the hydraulic air tank and propulsion air tank were pressurized. The crew installed a charged battery in the missile guidance section and conducted a pressure test to assure it was properly sealed. The missile test and assembly building had two large garage doors at either end, through which the missiles rolled in and out. In addition to the main test and assembly room, the building included a stockroom and a boiler room. A concrete walkway for missile movement connected the missile test and assembly building with the acid fueling station.

ACID FUELING STATION: Here crewmen fueled and joined the missile to the booster with a crank-operated lift approximately twelve feet high. Crewmen hoisted the fuel onto this platform, allowing the fuel to flow into the missile gravitationally. Likewise, the acid server had an assembly that automatically inverted the barrel as it was raised. Crewmen wore rubber suits during the fueling process as protection against the caustic acid.

ACID STORAGE SHED: Near each fueling station was a metal storage shed. Also nearby were shower facilities in the event of contact with dangerous chemicals and fuels.

WARHEAD BUILDING: For safety in the case of an explosion, the missile warhead operations were also performed at the acid fueling station, which was encircled by an earthen berm eight to ten feet high. The warhead mating process involved installing two arming devices and the warhead and connecting these components with detonating cord. The crew attached the warheads in the warheading building near the fueling station.[10]

If authorized, the W-31 boosted fission nuclear warhead would be mated to the Hercules missile. This provided a smaller, lighter, less fissile material for variable yield detonation at a lower per unit production cost. Cost was an important consideration, given the number of Nike-Hercules missiles deployed to operational sites. Again, although never officially confirmed, the Air Force planned for the dispersal of W-31 warheads at nuclear weapons storage areas supporting the Nike-Hercules sites. Given the Cold War ideology of the time period, US military war planners believed it was possible to fight and win a thermonuclear war like a large-scale conventional arms conflict. The W-31 was designed to be operational under enemy nuclear detonations near a missile site. Nuclear detonations produce electromagnetic pulses (EMPs) bursts that can knock out electronics and render them inoperable. These detonations produce intense radar interference that can damage the plutonium pits in US warheads. The W-31 warhead was 39 to 39.5 inches long and 28 to 30 inches in diameter and weighed 900 to 945 pounds. It entered the US nuclear warhead inventory in 1959 and remained operational until 1989—long after the Nike-Hercules was deactivated—and was then used as an Army atomic demolition munition. Its primary yield setting when mated to the Nike-Hercules was about twenty kilotons.[11]

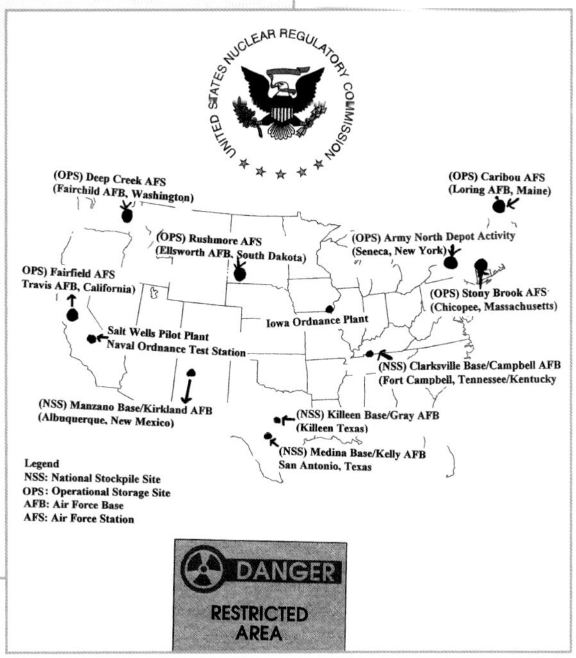

Atomic Energy stockpiles map. *Author*

THE 96th BOMBARDMENT WING and the BOEING B-52 STRATOFORTRESS

The 96th BW, 337th BS, replaced its three squadrons of B-47Es with one operational Stratofortress squadron on December 23, 1963. SAC's wing authorization for bomber bases was fifteen aircraft (B-52s or B-58s). Between 1963 and 1967 wing aircraft numbers fluctuated between thirteen to seventeen B-52s. The wing received B-52Cs from the 99th BW for aircrew transitional training from B-47Es to B-52Es, continuing until 1971 for aircrew training.[1]

The author was assigned to the 93rd BW from July 1976 to June 1978 as wing intelligence officer, target materials officer, SIOP officer, and an instructor with B-52s. He gathered historical information on the 93rd BW and SAC Stratofortress operations at this time. Most of this information is no longer available for research, being either misplaced or destroyed. The 93rd BW (medium) received its B-47s in May 1954, but its involvement with B-47s ended on June 29, 1955, when it transitioned to the B-52B. Castle AFB trained SAC's B-52 bomber crews, including those who were assigned to the 96th BW where they received training for assuming nuclear alert duties.[2]

The 96th BW's first operational Stratofortress was the B-52E.[3] The US Strategic Command historian was able to locate a Dyess AFB aircraft authorization sheet during SAC's presence in their files that had not been transferred to historical storage at the Air Force Historical Research Agency, Maxwell AFB, Alabama. Unfortunately, many of these former SAC bomb wing records cannot be located. The following is a reconstruction of the B-52Es assigned to the 96th BW at Dyess AFB:

56-0637	57-0015	57-0095	57-0115	57-0123
56-0646	57-0016	57-0100	57-0118	57-0126
	57-0024	57-0108	57-0120	57-0134[4]
	57-0025	57-0109	57-0121	

B-52Es at Dyess AFB stood nuclear alert as part of SAC's SIOP thermonuclear deterrence response against possible Soviet nuclear attack. Standard nuclear alert posture at Dyess comprised five B-52Es supported by four KC-135As. SAC had standardized its bomber wing to consist of three squadrons, each with fifteen B-47s, but SAC cut the number of B-52s per wing to fifteen. SAC had to use intelligence estimates of the number of deployed Russian ICBMS because of a lack of operational overhead satellite photo-reconnaissance.

SAC's alert procedures called for the first B-52 to take off within seven minutes of receipt of confirmed positive control launch from SAC headquarters, with the entire alert package airborne and cleared of the alert base to a safe distance within fifteen minutes. SAC's alert force was trained to reach a safe area away from their bases and clear of a Soviet ICBM thermonuclear detonation.[5]

The B-52Es on thermonuclear SAC alert (1963 to 1967) had various arming options. Even though the Cuban Missile Crisis had passed, SAC retained a large bomber force to maintain nuclear deterrence. SAC commander Gen. LeMay did not wholeheartedly support the introduction of ICBMs into SAC's thermonuclear inventory, but the trend toward ICBMs and SLBMs could not be stopped. SAC war planners rapidly pushed ahead with the development and deployment of ICBMS. The B-52E could be armed with four B-57s—a lightweight, multi-purpose thermonuclear bomb. The B-52E could also be armed with the B-28, SAC's primary free-fall gravity thermonuclear bomb from 1958 to 1991.

The B-52E could carry two (four) clip thermonuclear bombs, however, the standard SAC thermonuclear alert bomb load was one clip in the forward bomb bay on a MHH-14 Assembly/ Launcher for optimum aircraft airborne balance. The aircraft could be loaded with one B-53 thermonuclear bomb to attack and destroy super-hardened, underground targets such as command and control bunkers, ICBM launch command centers, or large area targets like Moscow. Two variants were produced between August 1962 and June 1965, classified as either clean or dirty. The Y2 clean fissile material consisted of High Explosive Uranium (HEU) with no plutonium fissile material. Unfortunately, its weight required three parachutes if deployed (released) at low altitude to slow its descent to detonation altitude, giving the aircraft enough time to reach a safe distance. The B-52E could carry the B-61. It had the distinction of being the oldest thermonuclear bomb in the US nuclear weapons stockpile.

The B-52E could carry two North American-Rockwell AGM-28A Hound Dog Air to Surface Missiles (ASMs) on pylons under the wing, between the fuselage and inboard engines. The B-52's onboard navigation systems and the missile's onboard computer worked together, allowing the missile to be constantly updated on its current airborne position in relation to its programmed or designated target. The missile had a high to low launch to target profile. The original SAC mission profile launched the Hound Dog at 45,000 feet, with the missile climbing to 56,000 feet, diving to as low as 200 feet at the Initial Point (IP) for the low-level, high-speed run into the target. The missile had a maximum launch range of 600 miles. The missile's engine was used during the B-52's takeoff and to supplement available aircraft thrust when airborne, and was refueled from the B-52 prior to launch.

In 1969, the 337th BS began converting to the B-52D, which it flew from 1969 to 1982. As of December 1969, it operated six B-52Cs for training, along with eight B-52Es and sixteen B-52Ds to complete SAC mission requirements. The B-52Es were slowly withdrawn from the 96th BW. The B-52 proved its conventional combat support in Southeast Asia, including during Linebacker II.[6]

The 96th BW operated the B-52D from 1969 to 1981. The unit was redesignated the 96th BW (Heavy) on March 31, 1972. During several months of 1970, and for a lengthy period in 1972 and 1973, all wing aircraft, crews, and most support personnel were loaned to other SAC organizations based in the Far East or Southeast Asia for combat operations.[7]

A B-52E being refueled by a Boeing KC-135A Stratotanker. *National Museum of the United States Air Force*

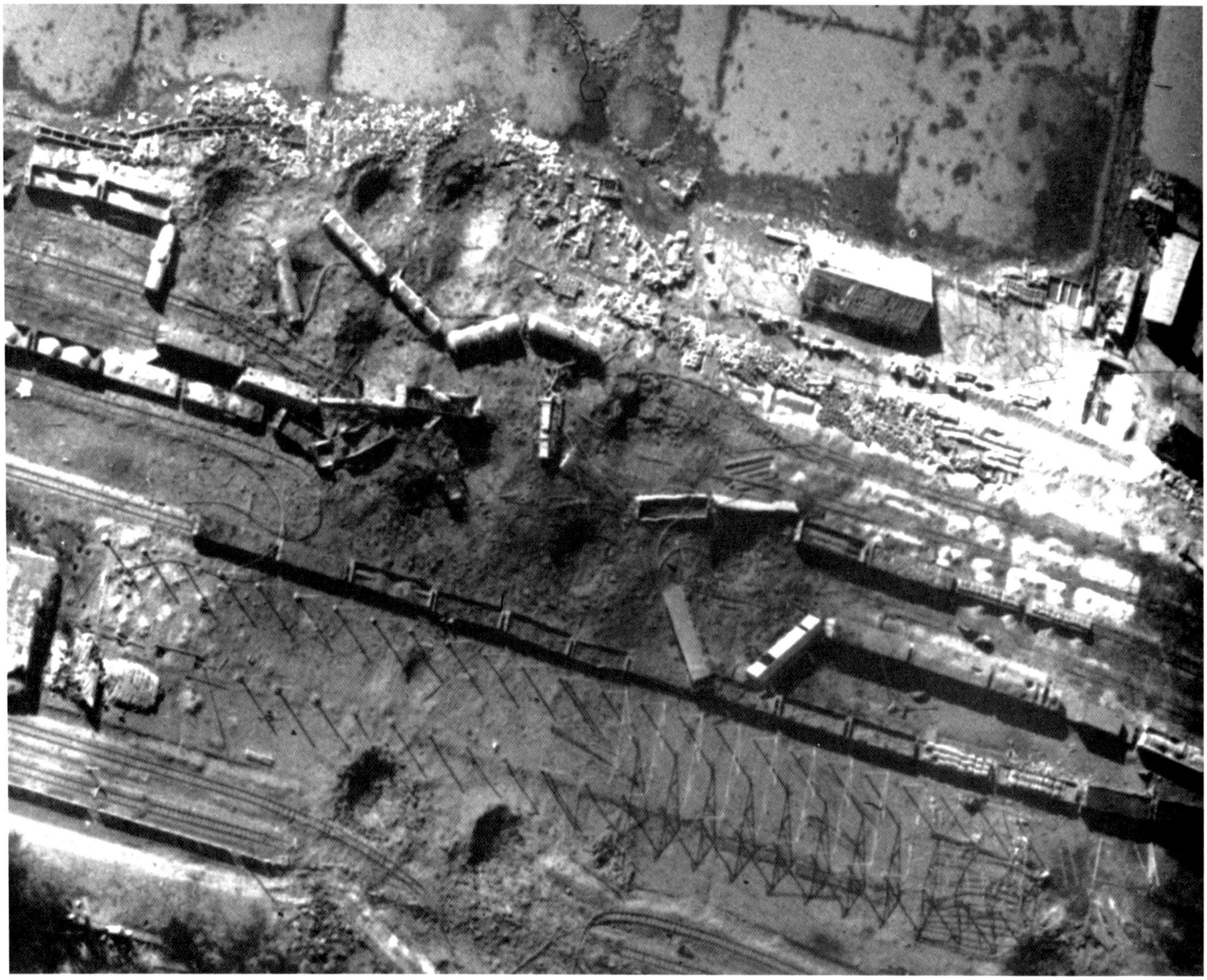

A B-52 bomb strike during Linebacker II. The photograph was taken by an unarmed, high-speed, low-level F-101 Voodoo aerial reconnaissance aircraft and shows massive destruction at the Giap Nhi Railroad Yard near Hanoi. *Headquarters Eighth Air Force, Andersen Air Force Base, Guam, headquarters historian*

After the end of the Vietnam War, the 96th BW's B-52Ds returned to Dyess AFB, resuming SAC's primary nuclear deterrence mission. The wing retained its B-52Ds until 1982, when it began transitioning to the B-52H, the final production variant of the Stratofortress. Except those selected for static display at aviation museums or at military installations, the delivery of the last operational B-52D to the Aerospace Maintenance and Regeneration Center at Davis-Monthan AFB, Arizona, marked the end of the first generation of the Stratofortress. B-52Es were retired in 1970, followed by B-52Fs in 1978. SAC retained a force of 169 B-52Gs and ninety-six B-52Hs.[8]

The final production version of the Stratofortress (B-52H) first flew on March 6, 1961, with series production ending in June 1962 and only 102 produced. Boeing engineers significantly upgraded the B-52H, including changes introduced on the B-52G:

1. The "wet wing" eliminated previous fuel bladders, creating a sealed wing fuel storage area and adding approximately 10,000 gallons of internal fuel storage.
2. The tail height was lowered eight feet, giving the aircraft a distinctive appearance.
3. Gunner's position moved from the pressurized, separated tail compartment into the forward crew compartment and was provided with radar and closed circuit television to remotely operate and fire the rear tail armament.
4. Ailerons were eliminated, with lateral control provided by wing spoilers.
5. The large external wing auxiliary fuel tanks were replaced by smaller, 700-gallon tanks.
6. A wide variety of internal changes were made, including new hydraulic and fuel management controls and enhanced crew comfort for extended flights.
7. Pratt & Whitney TF-33 fanjet engines replaced the previous J-57s.
8. The four .50-caliber machine gun tail turret was replaced with a six-barrel 20-mm M61 Gatling gun.
9. Advanced electronics were incorporated to allow very precise, low-level terrain following penetration into heavily defended areas, along with extremely accurate target acquisition.
10. Dual chin forward turrets housing low-light television and infrared sensors to allow precise navigation and bombardier directed bombing under any light conditions and in all weather.
11. Weapons upgrades:
    a. Hound Dog ASM replaced by the AGM-69 Short Range Attack Missile (SRAM).
    b. AGM-84: Harpoon anti-shipping missile.
    c. AGM-142: Have Nap conventional standoff cruise missile.
    d. AGM-86B: conventional warhead armed ALCM.
    e. AGM-129A: Advanced Cruise Missile (ACM).
    f. CBU-87/89/97: family of conventional cluster munitions.
    g. CBU-103/104/105: Wind Corrected Munitions Dispensers (WCMD).
    h. CBU-31/31: Joint Direct Attack Munitions (JDAMs).
    i. AGM-154: Joint Standoff Weapon (JSOW).
    j. AGM-158: Joint Air to Surface Stand-off Missile.
12. Improvements to offensive and defensive avionics
13. Weight reduction as old systems and electronics were removed, decreasing strain on the airframe and increasing range and munitions upload capabilities.[9]

AGM-69/A Short Range Attack Missile (SRAM) at the National Museum of Nuclear Science and Technology, Albuquerque, New Mexico. *Author*

To equip the 96th BW with B-52Hs, the 319th BW gave up its H model Stratofortresses. While on SAC nuclear alert at Dyess AFB, the B-52Hs were armed with AGM-69/A SRAMs. The standard SAC SRAM alert package consisted of the following weapon configuration:

1. One Common Strategic Rotary Launcher (CSRL) with eight SRAMs.
2. Two under wing pylons:

Each with six SRAMs mounted on a MAU-12 ejection rack (or) Four B-61 thermonuclear bombs in the bomb bay replacing eight SRAMs.[10]

The 96th BW only operated the B-52H until June 1985, when the wing transitioned to the B-1B Lancer. As of 2013, only two Air Combat Command bomb wings operate the B-52H: the 2nd BW at Barksdale AFB, Louisiana, and the 5th BW at Minot AFB, North Dakota.[11]

A B-52D landing at U-Tapao Royal Thai Air Base, Thailand, while a KC-135A holds short of the runway prior to beginning its takeoff. The B-52D wears the Southeast Asia muted jungle camouflage color paint scheme. *Headquarters Eighth Air Force, Andersen Air Force Base, Guam, headquarters historian*

The B-58 became SAC's primary Cold War, free-fall gravity Thermonuclear bomb. On display in the National Museum of Nuclear Science and Technology, Albuquerque, New Mexico. *Author*

An Ellsworth 28th Bomb Wing B-1B Lancer nose to nose with a Minot 5th Bomb Wing B-52H. Dyess Air Force Base went through the process of exchanging its B-52Hs for B-1B Lancers. *Author*

A B-52H nose on view. The two chin-mounted turrets house the AVQ-22 low light level television referred to as EVS. The side fuselage mounted blister cockpit (one to either side) holds the Forward Looking Infrared (FLIR) system. At the top of the nose (centered) is an ECM antenna. *Author*

917th AIR REFUELING SQUADRON and the BOEING KC-135A STRATOTANKER

Dyess AFB was home to the 11th Air Refueling Squadron, operating the piston-powered Boeing KC-97G Stratofreighter from August 1, 1955, to June 1, 1960. It was not able to meet SAC's increased refueling requirements of its new turbojet bombers, the B-52 and B-58. On September 19, 1985, the 917th Air Refueling Squadron was consolidated with the 617th BS. It was activated on May 1, 1959, at Biggs AFB, Texas, equipped with the Boeing KC-135A Stratotanker. Its SAC mission was to provide air refueling for the 95th BW's B-52s. It was reassigned to the 96th Strategic Aerospace Wing (SAW) and later the 96th BW at Dyess AFB, Texas, on January 15, 1965.[1]

The Air Force announced its intention of purchasing an undisclosed number of tanker transports developed from the prototype Model 367-80 jet transport in August 1954. The first of these aircraft came out of the final assembly and production building at Boeing Airplane Company, Renton, Washington, on July 18, 1956, and was named "The City of Renton." The tanker made its initial flight on August 31, 1956. SAC and the Air Force received its first KC-135As at Castle AFB, California, on June 28, 1957. Boeing built 732 KC-135As, of which 582 had a short tail fin; the remaining production aircraft had a tall tail that improved takeoff stability. Eventually, the entire fleet was retrofitted with a tall tail fin.

In external appearance, the KC-135A is similar to the Boeing 707 commercial passenger jet, but with increased structural strength. It is a swept wing, long range, high altitude, high speed turbojet transport. The KC-135A can carry either 83,000 pounds of cargo or airlift up to eighty passengers/troops or 285,000 pounds of JP-4 fuel. The amount of onboard fuel that is off loaded during refueling missions can vary due to the distance the tanker has to fly to the nearest air base. During a thermonuclear war, the tanker could off load its entire fuel capacity to meet US SIOP/EWO mission requirement and let the bombers complete their nuclear attack mission.

During air refueling operations, Boeing's flying boom—attached to the tanker's lower fuselage—allowed fuel transfer as high as 6,500 pounds per minute. The primary mission of the KC-135A is the refueling of US strategic, long-range bombers. It also provides air refueling support to Air Force, Navy, and Marine Corps aircraft, as well as aircraft of allied and coalition nations in support of the global war on terrorism. The transition from the Cold War to the global war on terrorism continues the demand for aerial refueling.

Normally during in-flight refueling the boom operator is in constant radio contact with the receiver aircraft, but if stealth is required he directs the receiver aircraft to the flying boom using colored lights on the bottom of the tanker. The hookup is made by final direction to the receiver aircraft using these lights. The KC-97G pioneered this system of in-flight refueling. The fuel cells in the tanker are made of nylon fabric less than one-sixteenth of an inch thick that only weigh eighty pounds but have a fuel capacity of 14,000 pounds.

A Boeing flying boom underneath a KC-135A, on display at the South Dakota Air and Space Museum, outside the main gate to Ellsworth Air Force Base, South Dakota. *Author*

One KC-135A Stratotanker (aircraft number 56-3939) arrived at Dyess AFB on May 26, 1981, assigned to the 917th ARS. It was the third Dyess KC-135A sent to Incirlick, Turkey, in support of Operation Desert Shield combat sorties. After SAC was inactivated this tanker transferred to ACC, with its final operational sortie flown on June 8, 1992.[2]

The 917th ARS was operational from January 15, 1965, to September 1, 1991. The squadron's KC-135As stood SAC nuclear alert at Dyess AFB in support of B-52Es, B-52Ds, B-52Hs, and B-1Bs, consisting of four KC-135As and five B-52Hs (prior to the transition to B-1Bs). At Dyess, the tankers were positioned at the end of the parking apron, inside a secure, guarded area and ready to launch under nuclear launch orders. Under SAC's fifteen minute ground alert posture, the first B-52 took off within seven minutes under Minimum Interval Take Off (MITO) and the alert tankers were the last aircraft to take off, following the bombers.

Boom operator's window behind the flying boom on the KC-135A. Aircraft on display at the South Dakota Air and Space Museum, outside the main gate to Ellsworth Air Force Base, South Dakota. *Author*

In 1964 and 1965, growing US military involvement in Southeast Asia placed heavy demands on SAC's KC-135A air refueling operations. Transferring fuel from tankers required two different techniques, depending on the type of receiver aircraft. All bombers and some fighters—particularly those employed late in the war (1970–1972)—were equipped with receptacles for the flying boom. To make a hookup, the pilot of the receiver aircraft simply positioned the aircraft behind and slightly below the rear of the tanker. The boom operator directed the forty-six-foot flying boom into the receiver's refueling receptacle, beginning the transfer of fuel. Several fighters used in the early years of the Vietnam War, such as the North American F-100 Super Sabre, were equipped with a probe refueling transfer that required the tanker to use a drogue refueling system. In this instance, the KC-135A trailed a drogue device at the end of a flexible hose that could be quickly installed on the end of the flying boom. It was extended and maintained in a stable flight configuration, allowing the fighter pilot to fly the aircraft's probe into the drogue and begin transferring fuel.[3]

During nine years of operations in SEA, KC-135As completed 813,000 aerial refuelings of combat aircraft. During several months in late 1970 and deployments in 1972 and 1973, the 917th ARS, 96th BW, and 917th ARS sent bombers and tankers, crews, and the majority of the wing's support personnel to SEA. They were temporarily assigned to SAC SEA combat operations.[4]

In-flight refueling depended on precise timing and navigation. Bombers, fighters, and reconnaissance aircraft were carefully scheduled to meet tankers at given times and locations. When meeting B-52 bombers on long-distance combat bombing missions (B-52s flying from Andersen AFB, Guam, on ARC Light strikes in South Vietnam and massive air refueling operations during Linebacker II) three or four KC-135As flew together. The lead tanker was responsible for navigation and refueling timing. The other tankers followed one mile in trail and slightly higher, separating during refueling operations to create a safe zone around each tanker and receiver.

Refueling fighters and reconnaissance aircraft near combat zones was dangerous and complicated. Several meeting areas called "anchors" over Thailand, Laos, South Vietnam, and the Gulf of Tonkin were set up so fighters could select the nearest airborne gas station on the way into and out of target areas. Sometimes fifty or more aircraft met and fueled planes that otherwise would not have made it home. Many pilots owed the success of their missions and many owed their lives to being refueled by tankers after receiving heavy battle damage. Tankers also refueled helicopters. The Air Force tested the concept of in-flight helicopter refueling in 1965 and began normal refueling missions in the middle of 1967. Air Force HC-130P tankers helped search and rescue operations by HH-3 Jolly Green helicopters, extending their range into enemy controlled areas to pluck up downed airmen.

The Air Force based KC-135As in Japan, the Philippines, Thailand, and Guam. During the Vietnam War, Air Force tankers flew 200,000 sorties, completing more than 800,000 aerial refuelings. From 1964 to 1973, tankers pumped approximately 1.4 billion gallons of fuel into receiver aircraft. At the height of tanker deployment in late 1972, 195 KC-135As—thirty percent of SAC's tanker force—were in Southeast Asia. U-Tapao Royal Thai Air Base, Thailand, was the largest Air Force tanker base in SEA with forty-six aircraft assigned flown by eighty-eight crews flying sixty sorties each day to keep pace with aerial refueling operations. By mid-August 1973, with the final US combat air strike in Cambodia, SAC tankers had logged a total of 911,364 flying hours is SEA. Air Force tanker operations continued in 1975 during support of air evacuations near Phnom Penh, Cambodia, and Saigon, South Vietnam, as US involvement in SEA ended.[5]

The KC-135A on display at the South Dakota Air and Space Museum outside the main gate to Ellsworth Air Force Base, South Dakota. *Author*

Starting in 1980, the 917th ARS deployed KC-135As to Europe, Alaska, and the Pacific to support SAC Tanker Force operations/requirements. The 96th BW transitioned to the B-1B Lancer on June 29, 1985, and became the first wing to operate SAC's new strategic bomber. The squadron's tankers provided refueling support to units involved in the invasion of Panama in December 1989. The squadron ferried personnel and equipment to Guam for further movement to Southwest Asia in August 1990. Single KC-135As provided refueling support throughout Southwest Asia from August 1990 to March 1991.[6]

Starting in 1981, work began re-engining the KC-135A fleet with more powerful and fuel efficient turbofan engines, replacing the loud and smokey J57-P-59W turbojets. This was followed by upgrading to the CFM International CFM56—military designation F108—high by-pass ratio turbofan engine, offering greater fuel efficiency, noise reduction, and operational flexibility. A great modification to the tanker was the installation of the Quick Start Auxiliary Power Unit (QSAPU), characterized by intake and exhaust ports on the port side of the rear fuselage. The QSAPU allows the tanker to be used or based at unsupported airfields. The KC-135R was a great improvement over the KC-135A. It can offload fifty percent more fuel, is twenty-five percent more operationally fuel efficient, costs twenty-five percent less to operate, and is ninety-six percent quieter than the older KC-135A.[7]

Dyess AFB was the site of a fatal KC-135A (aircraft number 63-7990) crash on January 31, 1989, at 12:10 p.m. The official Air Force account via Dyess AFB public affairs news release summarizes what happened. The tanker was assigned to K.I. Sawyer AFB, Marquette, Michigan, where the flight originated. The KC-135A from K.I. Sawyer stopped at Dyess AFB prior to flying to Hickam AFB, Hawaii, on a training mission, and had a maximum capacity fuel load necessary for the tanker's flight plan and aerial refueling (155,000 pounds of fuel) of F-16 fighters flying from the US West Coast to Hickam AFB.[8] The tanker never really got off the ground. The tanker's engines were heard backfiring and missing by those on base. The aircraft veered left of center of the runway, crashing. The Air Force Accident Investigation Report indicated the KC-135A had trouble shortly before initiating rotation to clear the runway toward the end of the tanker's take-off roll, at the point where the two pilots had no alternative, since the aircraft was too far down the runway to safely ground abort. The two pilots attempted a take-off and circle back for an emergency landing. The wreckage fiercely burned for more than an hour at the south end of the runway near Highway 277, six miles southwest of Abilene. The Stratotanker's wreckage was at a forty-five degree angle with one burned wing tip slanted upward. A Dyess fire and rescue team rushed to the crash site, with firefighters extinguishing the fires caused by aviation fuel from the tanker's ruptured tanks. The rescue team set up portable generator-powered flood lights and searched throughout the night, recovering all nineteen bodies of those on the flight (seventeen from K.I. Sawyer AFB and two from Dyess AFB), including the seven tanker crew and passengers.[9] SAC headquarters provided a news release on the fatal crash at Dyess AFB. Any aircraft accident is bad, but the many fatalities made this a particularly terrible one.

Many older KC-135As have been retired. For the last years of operation the KC-135As at Dyess were assigned to the 7th BW, beginning on October 1, 1993. Eventually, these tankers were retired from active operations at Dyess and flew to Davis-Monthan AFB and the 309th Aerospace Maintenance and Regeneration Group (AMARC), under the Air Force

Material Command (AFMC).[10] Aircraft of the 917th ARS were reassigned to the 43rd Operations Group (OG) at Malmstrom AFB. It was inactivated in 1994 after Malmstrom's flight line was closed and the 43rd Air Base Wing (ABW) became an Air Mobility Command (AMC) wing at Pope AFB.[11] The KC-135R continues to carry on and will eventually be replaced by the new tanker approved by the Air Force and under production by the Boeing Aircraft Company designated the KC-46A. Currently, the Air Force retains and continues to operate 360 KC-135Rs, fifty-four KC-135Ts, and fifty-nine McDonnell Douglas DC-10 Extender aerial tankers.

A KC-135R on display during Ellsworth Air Force Base's "Dakota Thunder" open house in 2000. *Author*

THE 64th TROOP CARRIER WING/317TH AIRLIFT GROUP and the LOCKHEED C-130 HERCULES

On February 8, 1961, Dyess AFB became home to Tactical Air Command's (TAC) 64th Troop Carrier Wing (TCW), medium. At the same time, the 64th Consolidated Maintenance Squadron (CMS) was activated. The wing's mission was to provide command and staff supervision to tactical units engaged in air transportation of airborne forces, their equipment and supplies, long-range movement of personnel, equipment, supplies, and air evacuation within theater of operations.

By May 1, the 17th Troop Carrier Squadron was operational and helping the construction of the Distant Early Warning (DEW) radar stations in Greenland. These DEW line radar stations were designed and built to provide tactical warning of Russian Air Force Long Range Aviation (LRA) bombers penetrating North American airspace over the North Pole. The wing used a specially modified C-130D with skis below the wheels for landings and takeoffs on snow or ice to move heavy equipment and supplies to the DEW line construction sites. The squadron was the only C-130D equipped Hercules unit in the Air Force, flying twelve C-130Ds.[1]

C-130A. Washington, DC. *Department of the Air Force Historical Photo Archives*

Two C-130s damaged on the Dyess Air Force Base aircraft parking ramp on July 14, 1962. *Dyess Air Force Base, 317th Airlift Group, Brian Smith, 317th Air Group historian to author, January 2012*

On June 1, 1961, the 64th began using Tye Army Airfield's surviving runway—now adjacent to the base's main runway—to train crews in dropping supplies and equipment. The 17th Squadron procured miniature parachutes to simulate all phases of an actual airborne operation. The 64th added the 18th TCS on January 18, 1962. On July 14, a tornado hit Dyess AFB, causing over $500,000 in damage. Just after 6:15 p.m. the tornado followed a path directly down the Dyess AFB flight line. It did not touch down as it passed over the 96th BW's B-47Es but did in the middle of the 64th's C-130As. Nine of the wing's aircraft sustained varying degrees of damage with none destroyed. The tornado picked up one of the C-130As, slamming it back onto the parking apron. At the time two officers were conducting a preflight check. Four personnel suffered disabling injuries, while thirty-eight people required some form of on site first aid. Fortunately, no one was killed.

On September 15, Headquarters Air Force assigned a highly classified project to the 64th TCW code named Project Skyhook. This was similar to an Army project that allowed in-flight ground retrieval of personnel or cargo. The technique was developed from satellite recovery after re-entry through the earth's upper atmosphere. The person to be picked up inflated a plastic balloon that lifted a line into the air. A C-130 with special equipment attached to its nose caught the line, cut the balloon loose, and lifted the person or object, which was then retrieved through the open cargo ramp. The 64th's primary role was testing the equipment used during the evaluation of the system. Personnel developed operational techniques and procedures for the specialized equipment and an aircrew training curriculum designed to qualify aircrews from all services that would use Skyhook aircraft. The results of this testing were incorporated in Special Operations Command's (SOC) MC-130 Combat Talon aircraft.

On October 22, the 64th TCW received its first call for assistance during the Cuban Missile Crisis, requesting not only aircraft but officers and airmen. In less than twelve hours the wing processed 235 people for deployment. Most personnel and equipment were sent to designated areas in Florida. The wing's mission logs indicate aircrews flew 107 missions traversing the United States. Some missions were flown from Dyess AFB to distant locations, such as McChord AFB,

Washington, near Seattle, and the Coast Guard station in Niagara Falls, New York, terminating at Key West, Florida, and other bases throughout that state. By mid-December, most of the wing's personnel had returned to Dyess AFB.

For almost nine and one-half years, the 516th Tactical Airlift Wing (TAW) called Dyess AFB, Texas, home; it was activated in place of the 64th TCW on January 1, 1963. The 17th and 18th Troop Carrier Squadrons (TCS) remained active and were assigned to the 516th the same day. During 1963, the wing expanded rapidly, adding three tactical airlift squadrons (345th, 346th, and 347th) and transferring the 18th Squadron to Stewart AFB, Tennessee, keeping personnel in a constant state of change. From January 1 to December 31, the wing's assigned personnel increased from 1,110 to 1,939. On March 23, the first C-130E Hercules arrived at Dyess AFB. By June 30, the wing's complement of C-130s consisted of:

19 C-130Es
13 C-130As
8 C-130As (equipped with skis for snow and ice landings and takeoffs)
3 C-130Ds (with skis removed)

The removal of the skis from some of the wing's aircraft allowed the 17th to participate in non-ski operations while flying the DEW line resupply missions from Sondestrom AB, Greenland. The last C-130A departed in July and the final C-130E arrived on October 2.[2]

In addition to the 17th Squadron's commitment to DEW line support operations, the 516th picked up another rotational commitment to Panama. On September 18, seven aircrews and six aircraft rotated to Howard AFB, Panama, making up the assault airlift force for Operation GREENLEAF. While at Howard AFB, the crews were under operational control of USAF Southern Command. Perhaps one of the most unusual missions undertaken by any of the airlift units that flew from Dyess AFB occurred while two of the 516th's aircraft were deployed to India and Iran. At that time Iran was under the control of the Shah of Iran. During the deployment to India and Iran the wing's aircraft participated in Operation SHIKSHA in November 1963. The operation was a successful application of joint tactics and air doctrine with British RAF and Indian Air Force personnel.

The year 1964 was marked with many large-scale deployments of personnel and aircraft. In late March, the wing ended its rotational commitment in Panama and deployed to France. On May 18, the first of sixteen aircraft rotations began to Eureux-Fau AB, France, sixty-five miles east of Paris. The rotation committed almost an entire squadron for ninety days. Other deployments followed. Exercise POLAR SIEGE was held in an area along the Alaskan and Fort Richardson Highways in the interior of Alaska. It was the first Arctic deployment for F-105s assigned to George AFB, California, requiring airlift support. The 516th provided twenty-seven C-130Es and two C-130Ds, along with personnel to man en route support teams, a combat airlift support unit, and tactical support elements. Exercise DELAWAR was conducted on March 24, with the wing sending fifty combat ready crews and twenty-eight C-130Es to the Middle East. Exercise INDIAN RIVER required deployment of fifteen C-130Es and crews to test and evaluate operational procedures at the Tactical Air Warfare Center (TAWC), Eglin AFB, Florida. On June 15, 1964, the 17th TCS was transferred to Elmendorf AFB, Alaska. All of the wing's C-130Ds and some of its most experienced personnel were transferred along with the Greenland Support Mission. In 1995, the Arctic Airlift Support Mission continued with squadron support, this time by the re-designated 517th Airlift Squadron (AS).

Early in 1965, a deployment to Okinawa increased the wing's operational tempo. Aircrews flew the first group of US Marines to Da Nang, South Vietnam, and later transported airborne troops to Bien Hoa AB. Additional crews were sent to retrieve those deployed in December 1964 and by March 1965, aircrews were deployed in lesser numbers but more frequently. The 346th TCS deployed three crews on March 2, two on April 6, three on April 13, and three on April 20. From January to June, the wing deployed forty-eight crews for a total of 180 days. By November, with the wing maintaining sixteen aircraft and eighteen aircrews and maintenance personnel at

Naha AB, the necessity for deployment support of Operation ONE BUCK concluded. On November 28—a prelude of the realities of war—two of the wing's C-130Es landed at Dyess AFB sporting SEA camouflage.

On August 1, 1966, the wing's C-130Es deployed from Dyess AFB to France, followed by a deployment to England. In September, the US Army Corps of Engineers built a temporary assault landing strip at the Marrion Drop Zone—the former WWII Army airfield—for use as a tri-service test of aluminum matting aircraft landing strip. The Department of Defense requested the testing of aluminum matting to determine the most suitable type/design for joint service use around the world. The first matting was laid on October 18 and the runway was completed on November 15. The testing period (December 1966 through April 1967) saw many different aircraft test the aluminum matting: F-4 Phantoms, C-141 Starlifters, US Army OV-1 Mohawks and CH-47 Chinooks, and C-130Es. The AM-2 aluminum matting continues to be used today in the construction of forward airstrips or main operating bases where operations are critical and cannot wait for the construction of asphalt or concrete runways. On May 1, 1967, the designation of troop carrier units with TAC changed: wing and flying squadrons were under the control of the 516th Tactical Airlift Wing (TAW), 346th Tactical Airlift Squadron (TAS), and 347th TAS.

In January 1968, a crisis of immense national importance occurred when North Korea's military forces seized the USS *Pueblo* (electronic surveillance and collection ship) operating in international waters in the Sea of Japan. As a result, TAC ordered the deployment of the 347th TAS to Clark AB, Philippines, on January 27. The wing sent twelve aircraft with twenty-four aircrews to fly F-106 parts and personnel from Myrtle Beach, South Carolina, to Phu Cat AB, South Vietnam, before arriving at Clark AB, Philippines. These aircrews worked around the clock during the execution portion of the deployment. Wing crews flew personnel, equipment, and cargo to South Vietnam and Japanese air bases. The majority of the wing's missions flown by deployed crews were in combat conditions to Cam Ranh Bay, South Vietnam, with additional missions flown to South Korea from Japan. On average eighty-nine wing maintenance personnel manned a detachment at Cam Ranh Bay and were assigned there for the entire deployment. All aircrews flew Vietnam Shuttle missions and spent several days at a time there.

C-130s assigned to the 347th and 348th TAS received new unit markings in 1969. TAC began marking their aircraft with the TAC emblem, a unit code in large white block letters, and a tail number. The new unit codes for the 516th's squadrons were DB for the 348th TAS, DZ for the 347th TAS, and TD for the 18th Tactical Airlift Training Squadron. Eventually the wing's emblem was added to the nose of each aircraft, with some aircraft sporting unit emblems.

With Pacific deployment requirements no longer levied against the 516th, Abilene Airlifters began a routine that would continue for twenty-three years: deployments to Europe. On January 23, 1970, the 347th TAS deployed fourteen aircraft to Rheine-Main AB, Germany, as Delta squadron. This was a change from the usual rotation to Mildenhall, England. From February 15 to March 2, the 347th and 348th TAS participated in Exercise ARCTIC EXPRESS, supporting NATO operations in Norway along the northwest frontier with the Soviet Union and developing war plan countermeasures to the Russian Northern Fleet based at Murmansk. The 347th TAS provided inter-theater airlift from Continental Europe to Norway while the 348th TAS deployed sixteen aircraft and twenty aircrews and support personnel from Dyess AFB to RAF Mildenhall AB, England. The 348th TAS completed its portion of the exercise and returned to Dyess AFB on March 2.

The wing continued deploying to Europe after 1970. The wing supported major exercises and contingencies with names like CORONET CAPE, GARDEN PLOT, ALOUD LIMA, and others. The wing continued training operations with the C-130 and C-7 throughout the year.

Headquarters USAF approved the inactivation of the 516th TAW. On January 11, 1972, the 463rd TAW—a unit inactivated at Clark AB, Philippines, in December 1971—was to replace the 516th on June 1. During the first three months of the year, the 18th TAS continued a phase-down of training operations for SEA-bound pilots. The e mphasis in training was directed to include Air Force Reserve pilots. Pilot training classes shifted from Dyess AFB to Maxwell AFB, Alabama.[3]

The 463rd TAW started initial operations on June 1, 1972. On August 25, the last C-7A departed Dyess AFB. On February 23, 1973, the 773rd squadron deployed to Ching Chuan Kang AB, Taiwan. Their primary mission was to reposition troops in SEA as the drawdown of US forces in the theater of operations continued after the conclusion of the Paris Peace Talks in December 1972. One of the most gratifying missions Dyess airlifters were ever involved in occurred during the squadron's extended deployment. In March, the squadron participated in Operation HOMECOMING, the release of American Prisoners of War (POWs) from North Vietnamese prisons. The squadron flew the released American POWs from prison camps and scattered facilities throughout North Vietnam to eventual airlift by Air Force C-141s home to the United States. The squadron also transferred North Vietnamese POWs from detention centers in Saigon to Hanoi. On May 6, the 772nd deployed to Ching Chuan Kang to replace the 773rd, whose members returned to Dyess AFB on a C-141 on May 12. On July 6, another C-130 squadron was activated at Dyess AFB. The 774th TAS was activated with sixteen aircraft and personnel from the former 47th TAS, previously assigned to Forbes AFB, Kansas. When Arab countries bordering Israel attacked that nation on October 6, 1972 (Yom Kippur War), the wing was tasked to deliver emergency supplies. The 774th, on its first rotation to Europe, was the lead unit for the wing. It delivered United Nations peacekeeping forces to Cairo, Egypt, after a cease fire was agreed to by Arab nations and Israel.

On December 1, 1974, the 463rd and its units were transferred from TAC to Military Airlift Command (MAC). The US secretary of defense directed the consolidation of the worldwide airlift mission, resources, and responsibilities under the command and control of a single airlift manager.

In January 1975, the 772nd deployed to Mildenhall, England, returning home on March 16. The squadron returned in time to witness the first Lockheed C-130H Hercules delivered to Dyess AFB on March 31. On December 6, 1956, the 463rd became the first Air Force Airlifter unit equipped with the C-130A. The C-130H was equipped with upgraded (more powerful) engines, a new air conditioning system, and longer range.[4]

During 1976, the wing participated in many different exercises and Army test support missions. The most notable achievement was the many hours flown during earthquake relief missions, sending members of the wing globe-trotting to areas on opposite sides of the earth.

In 1977, life among Abilene Airlifters settled into a distinct pattern. Each of the three flying squadrons took their turn in European rotation, flew training and support missions for the Army, and completed the phase-in of the C-130H. The wing was assigned sixteen C-130Hs to each squadron, with fifty-three assigned total. Because the swapping of C-130Es to C-130Hs took longer than anticipated and there were more C-130Hs arriving than C-130Es departing, the wing quickly ran out of aircraft ramp parking spaces. On January 10, a new aircraft parking plan was started, increasing ramp space from forty-eight to fifty-two Hercules. At this time, the wing's C-130s required more ramp space than the larger B-52s and KC-135s assigned to the 96th BW.

On August 3, 1978, Albany, Texas, was hit hard by flooding caused by Hurricane Amelia. Members of the wing deployed to the area as part of a large emergency relief team from Dyess AFB to provide immediate assistance to victims and survivors of the flood-ravaged town. Personnel from the 1st MAPS continued the effort the following week by offloading over 13,000 pounds of relief supplies staged at Dyess AFB for land transport to Albany. The supplies were flown in from Albany, New York, in 109th Tactical Airlift Group C-130s.

On January 26, 1979, the 463rd TAW won the Air Force Outstanding Unit Award for exceptionally meritorious service for the period May 1, 1977, through July 15, 1978. The award was given to the wing and its personnel for "consistently displaying the highest degree of professionalism while participating in world-wide airlift missions, joint service exercises, and humanitarian operations." This was the fourth such award for the 463rd and only the second awarded to a Dyess AFB Airlifter unit.

In January 1980, the wing earned an excellent rating during an Operational Readiness Inspection. The 773rd Squadron deployed sixteen aircraft and maintenance support personnel for rotation to England in February.

On May 7, 1981, the wing flew all-out for a national training exercise for a second time. During this training mission, thirty-six of the wing's aircraft took to the air in ten minutes. From end to end, the line of C-130s awaiting take off took up nearly all the Dyess AFB taxiway.

On March 19, 1982, Abilene Airlifters took off from Dyess AFB, flying to California in a twenty-ship formation. The aircrews and support personnel took part in the large-scale Exercise GALLANT EAGLE 82 that was held at the desert training area at Fort Irwin, California.

From October 24 to November 2, 1983, members of the 463rd were involved in Operation URGENT FURY, the US invasion of Grenada. The invasion was ordered by President Ronald Reagan to rescue American students and prevent the spread of communist Cuba's military influence in the area. The wing supplied nine C-130Hs during the operation. The first C-130H from the 43rd landed in Grenada on October 25, about six hours after initial US troops landed on the island. 1st Lt. James D. Davidson, 772nd Squadron, landed at Point Salinas, Grenada, delivering ammunition to support AC-130 Specter gunships during the invasion for support of ground troops against Cuban troop concentrations. On October 26, three additional wing aircraft flew fuel bladders and additional fuel to Grenada. Their initial attempts to land at the airport were aborted by hostile ground fire and fuel limitations from the previous day.

From August 3 to September 1984, the 463rd supported Exercise GALLANT EAGLE 84, a joint chiefs of staff field training exercise held at several locations in the western United States.

On September 19 to 20, 1985, massive earthquakes rocked Mexico City, Mexico. The wing deployed several members of its Airlift Control Element (ACE) and 1st Mobile Aerial Port Squadron (MAPS) to support thousands of injured and homeless disaster victims. Overall, the teams provided ground support for over 217 tons of supplies and equipment flown in during September 23 to October 1. Wing members received the Humanitarian Service Medal for their efforts.

In February 4, 1986, the Air Force announced that the 774th TAS would inactivate as part of several proposed structural changes designed to ease budgetary constraints. The 744th was chosen to inactivate based on Military Airlift Command's need to station C-130Hs with the 17th TAS at Elmendorf AFB, Alaska. On June 19, the first three of eleven aircraft transferred to the 17th TAS. The 744th inactivated on June 27, after its last rotation to England from April 5 to June 13. The number of C-130Hs assigned to the wing dropped from forty-six to thirty-five. Wing members came to the assistance of the people of Sweetwater, Texas, forty-five miles west of Abilene, on June 26, after a tornado ripped through the city. The largest exercise of its kind held by the US Army, Exercise MARKET SQUARE featured the construction of a heavy, division-size force through the use of an expanding Army and Air Force planning sequence. The 772nd squadron provided twelve C-130Hs responsible for multiple airborne assault drops and realistic emergency and planned resupply operations. The highlight of the exercise occurred on October 18–19, when all twelve wing aircraft flew a total of six waves of twelve-ship formations from Charleston, South Carolina, to Salerno, Netherlands, to the Luzon Drop Zones at Fort Bragg, North Carolina. The wing's C-130Hs flew 229 missions during a sixty-hour period, airlifted 1,481 passengers and 3,203,121 pounds of cargo, and air dropped 3,384 paratroops.

In 1987, the number of exercises the wing flew continued to increase. Deployments of small numbers of aircraft, aircrews, and support personnel were more frequent as large-scale exercises were scheduled, and the wing flew all over the world supporting many different exercises.

In February 1988, the 463rd combined its local Operational Readiness Inspection (ORI) with that of the 96th BW. From February 16–20, both wings tested joint operations with the C-130H and B-1B, and their capabilities in meeting contingency and Emergency War Orders (EWO). Both units deployed all available aircraft and support teams, and relocated critical work centers. The wings also exercised battle staffs and crisis action teams.

From January 2 to February 12, 1989, the wing deployed sixteen C-130Hs and twenty-eight combat ready aircrews, along with 180 maintenance and support personnel to participate in Exercise BRIM FROST 89. It was held throughout the state of Alaska, with the majority of the wing's aircraft and personnel deployed to Elmendorf AFB, near Anchorage. Initial estimates said the exercise would call for over 400 employment missions and up to 130 airdrops, but wing personnel were disappointed when the weather did not cooperate. Extremely cold weather during the exercise hampered airlift operations, from maintenance to troops not arriving at the aircraft for transportation. The weather was so severe that the Federal Aviation Administration (FAA) suspended all instrument flight rule approaches during the final days of the exercise due to a barometric pressure of over thirty-one inches of mercury registered during a stationary cold front that settled over Alaska. Most US manufactured aircraft instruments register only 30.08 inches of mercury; consequently, aircrews could not rely on the accuracy of their altimeters while flying under instrument conditions in the mountains and trackless Alaskan terrain. Ironically, clear skies created by high pressure systems created conditions that were classified as "almost too perfect to fly in." In preparation for an upcoming ORI, from February 13–17, 1989, the wing deployed 300 personnel and fifteen aircraft to the Abilene Regional Airport during a five-day exercise called Operation CROSSTOWN. The exercise was the first time a unit from Dyess AFB used Abilene Regional Airport and its facilities as a simulated remote operating base. Plagued by rain and overcast skies, the wing managed to launch twenty-eight missions from the simulated remote operating location.

On June 14, 1990, the 463rd received its final wing commander prior to its inactivation. The wing was reassigned to Headquarters, 15th Air Force, which moved from March AFB to Travis AFB, California. This marked the second time the 463rd came under the command of the 15th Air Force: the first was during WWII combat operations. In August, Headquarters ACC announced that Dyess AFB's 96th Wing would inactivate and be replaced by the 7th Wing from Carswell AFB at Fort Worth, Texas.

From February 9–16, 1990, the 463rd conducted Operation CROSSTOWN II at Abilene Regional Airport. Ironically, the lessons learned during this exercise in mobility, deployment, and employment paid off handsomely later in the year. On June 2, the 773rd squadron deployed to RAF Mildenhall on rotation. When military forces of Saddam Hussein invaded Kuwait in August, the 463rd responded. On August 14, the 773rd was released from its rotational duties in Europe and was ordered to return to Dyess AFB as quickly as possible. Within twenty-four hours thirteen of the squadron's fifteen aircraft had returned from RAF Mildenhall. The two remaining aircraft were still flying support missions in Europe, but returned to Dyess AFB within forty-eight hours of the notification to terminate European operations. The first deployment of wing personnel came on August 29, when thirty-five personnel from the 1st Mobile Aerial Port Squadron deployed to Sharjah Air Base, United Arab Emirates, in support of Operation DESERT SHIELD. The 772nd squadron was scheduled for a normal rotation to Europe beginning on December 4, but the increased need for Persian Gulf operations caused the squadron to deploy earlier, on October 19. As the end of the squadron's rotation neared, Headquarters MAC extended their deployment until December 27. However, the squadron's redeployment was halted in mid-flow and six of the squadron's aircraft were retained in England to augment another C-130 squadron taking command of Bravo Squadron. They would not return to Dyess AFB until March 1991.

On December 27, the 773rd Squadron deployed eight aircraft, crews, and maintenance and support personnel to Alkharj Air Base, Saudi Arabia. These aircraft and personnel became the 1670th TAW (Professional) during Operations DESERT SHIELD and DESERT STORM. During August to December, the 463rd Airlift Control Squadron was busy assisting US forces deploying to the Persian Gulf. Overall, the squadron deployed three Army divisions, a critical air defense artillery brigade, and elements of other units. In all, they coordinated the movement of over 45,600 passengers and 15,059 tons of equipment on 577 aircraft of various types. The squadron's controlled airlift operations maintained an average ninety-one percent on time launch rate.

The year 1991 began in the middle of air operations for Operation DESERT SHIELD. After completing their assigned tasks in the United States, the 363rd Airlift Control Squadron deployed to Southwest Asia, where they eventually processed over 59,000 passengers and 7,800,000 tons of cargo. The 773rd's deployment lasted until March, when the majority of personnel returned to Dyess AFB. While deployed, the squadron flew 2,810 Operation DESERT SHIELD and Operation DESERT STORM missions, racking up 4,285 flying hours while moving 17,422 passengers and 8,764 tons of cargo. In addition to flying supplies, munitions, and personnel throughout the Southwest Asia Theater of Operations, the 773rd also airlifted elements of the XVIII Airborne Corps in preparation for the famous "end run" flanking maneuver, during which US forces drove deep into Iraq, cutting off Iraqi forces from their lines of communication during the ground operations phase of Operation DESERT STORM. Squadron crews were some of the first airlifters into liberated Kuwait City, Kuwait, returning the US ambassador and embassy staff to their former residence. The squadron evacuated almost 8,000 Iraqi POWs to safety in Saudi Arabia.

Many welcome scenes played out during March, April, and May 1991, as more than half of the 463rd's personnel began returning from the desert. However, supporting the forces remaining in the Southwest Asia area after the allied coalition victory over Iraq became a priority mission for the wing. From June 26 to September 6, 1991, the 772nd deployed to King Abdul Aziz Air Base, Dhahran, Saudi Arabia, for Military Airlift Command's first "desert rotation." Their operations consisted of daily scheduled resupply missions across Saudi Arabia, into Kuwait, and to most other countries in the Persian Gulf area. They primarily flew in replacement troops and supplies needed to sustain the scattered units in 120 to 130 degree summer heat. They also flew routine and emergency medical evacuation missions when required. During the rotation the squadron flew 1,284 sorties in 308 missions. Although the war in Southwest Asia required an additional rotational commitment, the rotation to RAF Mildenhall still had to be accomplished. From October 4 to December 10, 1991, the 773rd took its turn. They finished a very big year, flying 1,142 sorties that required 2,739 hours and airlifting 3,799 tons of cargo and 7,492 passengers. In May 1992, the wing deployed the 772nd to King Abdul Aziz Air Base, Dhahran, Saudi Arabia, in support of Operations SOUTHERN WATCH and DESERT STORM. Operation SOUTHERN WATCH was the enforcement of the United Nations sanctions and the United States imposed "no fly zone" over southern Iraq. The desert rotation had changed dramatically in scope; now a ninety-day rotation, the wing's two flying squadrons split the time deployed in half, with a swap out at the deployment's midpoint.[5]

The creation of the ACC on June 1, 1992, resulted in part from dramatic changes in international politics. The collapse of the former Soviet Union and the end of the Cold War led senior US department of defense war planners to conclude that the structure of America's military was not suited to the new world situation. The likelihood of a large-scale thermonuclear war seemed far more remote, but US military forces would be increasingly called upon to participate in small-scale regional contingencies and humanitarian operations. The Air Force began to reconsider the long-standing distinction between two major commands: Strategic Air Command (SAC) and Tactical Air Command (TAC). The term "strategic" had become almost exclusively linked to the concept of nuclear deterrence. The focus of "tactical" operations, on the other hand, was on cooperative missions, with the Air Force in tandem with ground and naval forces. The distinction did not lend itself to a limited conflict. During the fighting in Southeast Asia, "strategic" B-52 bombers performed "tactical" missions, including close air support, while "tactical" fighter aircraft carried out "strategic" bombing deep in enemy territory. The conduct of Operation DESERT STORM in early 1991 further blurred the distinction between the two terms. Consequently, as senior Air Force officers and department of the Air Force civilian employees sought to re-examine roles and missions, the redundancy of this former division came under examination. Senior Air Force planners then reviewed numerous options available before settling on the official conclusion of merging most SAC and all TAC resources and a reorganization of the Military Airlift Command (MAC). This restructuring of forces consolidated airlift and most refueling assets under a single umbrella, the new Air Mobility Command (AMC). This command represented the "global reach" facet of the Air Force's mission, while the new ACC provided the Air Force's "global power."

The birth of the ACC on June 1, 1992, took place amidst numerous changes within the Air Force and the Department of Defense. A brief ceremony held at Langley AFB marked the inactivation of TAC and the activation of Air Combat Command, with its new headquarters at Scott AFB, Illinois. Following the inactivation of SAC at Offutt AFB, the US Strategic Command replaced it, which was created to manage the combined strategic nuclear forces belonging to the Air Force and Navy. The ACC became responsible for providing combat ready forces for deterrence and air combat operations. It assumed control of all fighter resources based within the continental United States: B-1B bombers, reconnaissance platforms, battle management resources, and ICBMs. The ACC had some tankers and C-130s in composite, reconnaissance, and other combat wings. Since its activation, the ACC has found itself in an almost constant state of operational flying. Air Force Global Strike Command took control of ICBMS and B-2 and B-52 bombers. The ACC controlled nearly all the tankers and a large training mission, and has gained combat rescue and theater airlift missions. At the same time, sweeping changes in US military policy have imposed not only force structure reductions on the ACC, but a requirement for much greater flexibility than ever before. The ACC's forces remain "on call" to perform a variety of missions, including support to international peacekeeping operations, to humanitarian needs at home and abroad, and protection of America's interests around the world.

On September 26, 1992, the wing deployed to King Abdul Aziz Air Base, Dhahran, Saudi Arabia, to support Operation SOUTHERN WATCH. The significance of this second deployment in 1992 was that the wing was also sent to Mombasa, Kenya, to support Operation PROVIDE RELIEF and later Operation RESTORE HOPE. In August, Operation PROVIDE RELIEF started as a humanitarian mission undertaken by President George Bush to deliver food to the starving citizens of Somalia. On December 2, over 270 wing personnel and eight C-130Hs began the long journey to Mombasa.

The year of greatest change for the Abilene Airlifters was 1993. The wing was still deployed to Kenya with Operations PROVIDE HOPE and PROVIDE RELIEF. Almost all of the wing's personnel returned from Kenya by April and began preparations for their final desert rotation. From May to September, both of the wing's flying squadrons deployed to King Abdul Aziz Air Base, Dhahran, Saudi Arabia, swapping out in mid-rotation. They flew a combined 405 sorties in 626 flying hours. The squadron airlifted 1,485 tons of cargo and 3,470 passengers. On July 1, 1993, ICBM forces were transferred to the Air Force Space Command Headquarters, Colorado Springs, Colorado. C-130s came under ACC control in the United States and KC-135s went to the AMC, with a few exceptions.[6]

On October 1, the 7th Wing moved from Carswell AFB during ceremonies held at Dyess AFB's parade ground. The 463rd Wing (C-130H) and 96th BW (B-1B) were inactivated. The marriage of the C-130H Hercules and B-1B Lancer into a single integrated unit was a monumental task. The difference in missions was not the most difficult problem, because the two wings' personnel often exercised together and understood each other's roles. However, personnel formally assigned to the 96th BW were not familiar with all the mobility requirements associated with a C-130 unit. Whereas Dyess AFB B-1Bs often deployed one or two aircraft and some maintenance personnel to exercises, now the entire base was subject to the possibility of deployment to conduct C-130 operations.

From November 1–5, 1993, the 7th conducted simultaneous ORIs on C-130 and B-1B systems. The C-130 inspection, called PURPLE PENNY, tested the wing's ability to respond to a contingency of tasking sixteen C-130Hs with aircrews and support personnel. Although the exercise was not rated, it was significant in that it was the first opportunity for the wing battle staff to work a C-130 exercise.

On June 24, 1994, sixty-four Abilene Airlifters and five C-130s from the 39th and 40th Squadrons deployed to Incirlick AB, Turkey, for thirty days. Because the runway at Incirlick was being repaired a single C-130 could operate from the seventy-five-foot wide taxiway used to fly in supplies and equipment. On September 16, the 7th Wing deployed twenty C-130s with crews and support personnel to MacDill AFB, Florida, in preparation for Operation UPHOLD DEMOCRACY. After two days the 7th's aircraft formed with aircraft from Pope AFB, North Carolina, and Little Rock, Arkansas, for the aerial invasion of Haiti. An hour after the air armada departed MacDill AFB for Port-au-Prince, Haiti, all the aircraft were recalled. On September 22, the first 7th Wing C-130s landed at Cap-Haitian, Haiti, with elements of the US Army's 10th Mountain Brigade. The unit was charged with peacekeeping and nation building efforts undertaken by President Bill Clinton. Most of the wing's C-130s redeployed to Dyess AFB, but a contingent of eight aircraft began operations at Roosevelt Roads Naval Station, Puerto Rico, until late October.

The thirty-fifth year of C-130 operations at Dyess AFB began with a week-long exercise starting January 20, 1995. The exercise combined both C-130 and B-1B personnel and assets with e mphasis on deployment. Exercise participants set up a bare base at the Marrion Drop Zone to conduct operations. This was the first deployment exercise of its kind for the 7th Wing. In June, six aircraft, crews, and support personnel from the 40th Squadron deployed to King Abdul Aziz Air Base, Dhahran, Saudi Arabia, beginning a 120-day desert rotation for the 7th Wing. On July 4, sixty-four additional Dyess AFB personnel and two aircraft deployed to Southwest Asia. Abilene Airlifters set up operations and maintenance offices in an abandoned liquid oxygen plant to support two additional C-130s needed in the theater. When the 39th Squadron deployed to relieve the 40th on August 4, they took eight aircraft and 113 personnel needed to man both now firmly established C 130 operating locations. All of the airlifters redeployed to Dyess AFB in October. As 1995 came to an end, members of the 7th Airlift Control Squadron were notified to make preparations for deployment to Bosnia, in former Yugoslavia. The possible deployment, code named JOINT ENDEAVOR, was part of President Clinton's deployment of US forces to the country to separate warring Bosnian Serbs from Croats and Muslims after a peace agreement between them was signed in Paris, France.[7]

The 317th Airlift Group emblem. *Dyess Air Force Base, 317th Airlift Group, Brian Smith, 317th Air Group historian to author, January 2012*

On April 1, 1997, the 317th Airlift Group (AG) returned to Texas, stationed at Dyess AFB. In April 2010, the group started a thirty-month transition from its thirty-three C-130Hs to twenty-eight C-130J-30 Super Hercules.[8]

The 317th Airlift Group consists of the following Squadrons:

317th Aircraft Maintenance Squadron: The squadron performs flight line maintenance on C-130J-30s and global reach missions under the auspices of the 317th AG, 18th Air Force, and AMC. Personnel spanning nine Air Force specialties provide all aspects of flight line maintenance and are responsible for the condition of their aircraft. Together they support the mission "From the Ground Up."

317th Operations Support Squadron: Responsible for C-130J-30 combat effectiveness. The squadron directs flight operations, aircrew and aircraft scheduling, combat tactics, aircrew training, cargo delivery, deployment planning and execution, simulator training, mobility training, mobility processing, maintenance analysis, and aircrew flight equipment functions. The squadron coordinates with the host wing for airfield maintenance, weather support, and air traffic control.

Group photo of the 317th Airlift Group. *Dyess Air Force Base, 317th Airlift Group, Brian Smith, 317th Air Group historian to author, January 2012*

317th Maintenance Operations Squadron: Provides operations support for all airlift group maintenance squadrons. The squadron provides management oversight of all fleet health issues, formulates plans, establishes procedures for and provides training to group maintenance personnel, and directs logistic support for all group assigned aircraft and engines through engine management, plans, and scheduling. The squadron also manages the maintenance operations center, analysis, and quality assurance for the group.

317th Maintenance Squadron: Performs on-and-off equipment maintenance on C-130J-30s and components supporting the group's global reach airlift mission. Back shop maintenance includes fuel cell, propulsion, isochronal (equal interval) inspection, aero repair of key flight control surfaces and landing gear components, and propeller valve housing repair. The squadron partners with the host wing to provide crashed, damaged, and disabled aircraft recovery responsibilities world-wide.

39th Airlift Squadron, "Trail Blazers": Maintains quality aircrew and aircraft to mobilize, deploy, and provide intra-theater airlift world-wide for Department of Defense customers. The men and women of the squadron support theater commander requirements with combat delivery capability through tactical air land and airdrop operations, as well as humanitarian efforts and aeromedical evacuations. The squadron provides approximately forty-five combat ready aircrew and maintenance for assigned aircraft.

40th Airlift Squadron, "Screaming Eagles": Maintains quality aircrew and aircraft to mobilize, deploy, and provide intra-theater airlift world-wide for Department of Defense customers. The men and women of the squadron support theater commander requirements with combat delivery capability through tactical air land and airdrop operations, as well as humanitarian efforts and aeromedical evacuation. The squadron maintains thirty-two aircrews.[9]

On April 16, 2010, the 317th AG's first C-130J-30, nicknamed the "Pride of Abilene," landed at Dyess AFB. With twenty-eight authorized C-130J-30s, the 317th will be the largest single operator of the latest Hercules variant. Before the aircraft landed the group needed facility upgrades. The hangar was updated with a new fire suppression system in the ceiling, new officers, and a controlled tool crib on the floor, and new tow lines were painted on the ramp. To park two C-130J-30s inside the hangar, the aircraft had to be offset by ten feet, placing the aircraft's tails next to one another. A new 70,000 square foot, double-bay fuel cell maintenance hangar was completed in 2009.[10]

May 16–23, 2010, the 317th AG was one of three C-130 units representing each component of the Air Force that made history at the Gulfport, Mississippi, Readiness Training Center, AMC. The AMC Inspector General (IG) administered the inspection of the 123rd Airlift Wing (Kentucky Air National Guard), 317th AG (Dyess AFB, Texas), and 70th Aerial Port Squadron (Homestead Air Force Base, Florida, reserve members and equipment). As with a traditional ORI, this one tested the ability of each unit to mobilize airmen and equipment, fly to a remote site, operate in a hostile environment, defend against enemy attacks, and redeploy back home, all while AMC inspectors evaluated every phase of the operation. Unlike traditional ORIs, the three units were tasked with supporting civil authority's unconventional foe in the United States. This was a successful, first test of Homeland Defense Operational Readiness Inspection, after the threat to the United States changed after September 11, 2001.[11]

Cargo being loaded and secured inside a C-130J-30 at Dyess Air Force Base. *Dyess Air Force Base, 317th Airlift Group, Brian Smith, 317th Air Group historian to author, January 2012*

After the US Navy Seal team's penetration of Pakistani territory to attack Osama bin Laden's secret compound, Pakistan still called on the US for assistance. Even with drone attacks on terrorists in Pakistan the Air Force still maintained a humanitarian mission in that country. The 40th Airlift Squadron was part of the 386th Air Expeditionary Wing (AEW) at Bagram Airfield, Afghanistan. On August 30, 2010, airmen from the wing flew relief supplies into Pakistan. This was necessary because record-setting monsoons hit Pakistan, killing over 1,600 and leaving over 2,000,000 homeless. The wing delivered hundreds of thousands of pounds of food, water, and medical supplies. Loadmasters were key in delivering these supplies, with the majority airlifted to remote villages by pinpoint parachute extraction during low-level offloads. The 386th AEW is the primary tactical airlift hub for re-supply missions supporting coalition forces operating in the Southwest Asia area and providing combat support to land component forces throughout the Persian Gulf region.[12]

On February 22, 2012, the 317th AG successfully completed its first continental US Joint Precision Airdrop System (JPADS) airdrops on routine training lines by dropping two bundles totaling 2,400 pounds at Fort Hood, Texas.

Two loaded cargo pallets sliding along the floor rails inside a C-130J-30 and out its open cargo door. The initial pilot parachute is deployed, pulling out the main parachute. *Dyess Air Force Base, 317th Airlift Group, Brian Smith, 317th Air Group historian to author, January 2012*

JPADS is an airdrop system using GPS controlled parachutes and an advanced computer to steer loads to the designated point of impact in a drop zone, similar to JDAMs precision weapon strikes. While JPADS has been issued on Southwest Asia Theater of Operation missions since 2006, the majority of aircrews do not have the opportunity to fine tune their skills during training missions prior to executing this air drop method during combat support missions. These GPS guided airdrops offer many benefits, including an increase in the number of available drop zones, as well as an increase in cargo precision delivery. This system increases the survivability of the drop aircraft and its aircrew by being able to complete standoff deliveries. Traditional airdrops by Air Force airlifters, C-130s, and C-17s fly missions at altitudes of 400 to 1,000 feet. With JPADS, these aircraft have the potential to guide air-dropped bundles from as high as 25,000 feet, out of the range of hostile small arms gunfire.[13]

On April 24, 2012, the 317th AG successfully completed a precision airdrop capability demonstration for a distinguished panel of visitors at Fort Hood, Texas, during the US Transportation Command Component Commander's Conference. A C-130J-30 released a JPADS bundle packaged by the National Guard 29th Quartermaster Company over Fort Hood's Antelope Drop Zone. AMC units were tasked to start JPADS training in the continental United States at higher altitudes to replicate combat air drops in Afghanistan. Due to the amount of air space needed to conduct high-altitude JPADS training, only a few selected locations can facilitate this airdrop method, making the 317th AG the premier unit conducting this training. In May, the 317th AG was the first unit to drop JPADS above 10,000 feet on a routine mission. Most precision airdrops performed in the combat area in Afghanistan are high altitude, meaning aircrews must wear supplemental oxygen masks and helmets, as well as deal with the physiological effects of flying in the unpressurized C-130 cargo compartment.

From April 25 to 30, the 317th Air Group underwent a Headquarter Air Mobility Command/Inspector General Consolidated Unit Inspection (CUI). This over-arching inspection included a maintenance Logistics Compliance Assessment Program (LCAP) inspection, an Aircrew Standardization and Evaluation Visit (ASEV) inspection, and a compliance Inspection (CI). The 317th Airlift Group performed well, earning a CI "Excellent," an ASEV "Excellent," and an LCAP "Outstanding.[14]

On July 2, 2012, a group of sixteen C-130J-30 Super Hercules filed onto the runway at Dyess AFB as part of a training exercise. This was the largest massed C-130J-30 formation by AMC. The simulated mission was an airdrop above two different drop zones: the first drop was to reinforce current ground troops and the other was to place heavy equipment to set up a headquarters.[15]

For thirty-seven years, Dyess AFB C-130s and its airmen have built a legacy in the Air Force. That legacy came to an end on September 27, 2012, as the last C-130Hs (tail numbers 1667 and 2063) departed for Little Rock, Arkansas. With the departure of the C-130Hs, 317th AG aircraft will no longer carry navigators and flight engineers; these positions are no longer part of the C-130J-30 crew complement.[16]

On September 18, 2012, a 317th AG C-130J-30 and aircrew were already assigned to deploy to Afghanistan on a tail swap mission. This allows an aircraft already in theater that needs to return to Dyess AFB for maintenance to be replaced by another aircraft from Dyess AFB. This gave the 317th AG an opportunity to conduct their mission and help the people in Afghanistan as well by participating in the Denton Program, transporting school supplies to students and teachers. Under the Denton Program, the secretary of defense may transport to any country, without charge, supplies that have been furnished by a non-governmental source and are intended for humanitarian assistance. Such supplies may be transported only

C-130J-30s on Dyess Air Force Base's runway. *Dyess Air Force Base, 317th Airlift Group, Brian Smith, 317th Air Group historian to author, January 2012*

on a space available basis. The aircrew stopped at Charleston AFB, South Carolina, to pick up school supplies from Denton Program officers before continuing on to Kandahar Airfield, Afghanistan, where the supplies were dispersed.[17]

On November 7, visiting 18th Air Force commander Lieutenant Gen. McDew presented the 317th Air Group with its third Air Force Meritorious Unit Award, covering the period July 21 to June 2010. The award citation read in part:

> The 317th AG qualified for this award by contributing to Air Mobility Command's (AMC) global airlift mission and the direct support of overseas contingency operations. During the period of the award, the 317 AG flew 9,359 sorties that delivered over 137,000 personnel and 28,000 tons of cargo in support of Operations ENDURING FREEDOM (OEF) and Combined Task Force Horn of Africa. These efforts were instrumental to the closure of combat operations in Iraq [at that time] while sustaining the surge in Afghanistan.

The year 2013 began with twenty-five assigned C-130Js, with the final three delivered in March, April, and July. Air Mobility Command commander Gen. Silva delivered the twenty-eighth and final new C-130J on July 25, 2013. The transition from C-130Hs to C-130Js began in April 2010, when Gen. Schwartz—then Air Force chief of staff (and C-130 pilot)—delivered the first C-130J. The transition took forty-one months. The protracted transition allowed the 317th Air Group to continue to support its OEF commitment.

A C-130J-30 (top) and C-130H (below). *Dyess Air Force Base, 317th Airlift Group, Brian Smith, 317th Air Group historian to author, January 2012*

The eight 40th Airlift Squadron C-130Js on the first ever six month long OEF deployment returned to Dyess AFB in March 2013. The last aircraft to return was tail number 10-5701—with Maj. Sean Callahan as aircraft commander—landing at Dyess AFB on March 20, 2013. With all 317th Air Group C-130Js home from OEF, this marked the end of 3,378 days of continuous deployment for 317th Air Group aircraft and personnel that began on December 20, 2003.

From March to September 2013, the 41st Airlift Squadron from the 19th Airlift Wing, Little Rock AFB, covered C-130J duties in Afghanistan. The 317th Air Group returned to Afghanistan in September 2013, with the 39th Airlift Squadron arriving in theater for their September 2013 to March 2014 deployment of eight C-130Js.

In addition to the main OEF deployment, the 39th Airlift Squadron was also tasked to send two aircraft to Ramstein Air Base, Germany, to augment the 317th Airlift Squadron's C-130Js, supporting their Africa Command alert mission. The two aircraft arrived in Germany in August 2013. In addition to sitting AFRICOM alert duty, the C-130Js flew occasional European Union Command missions and moved their alert locations to Spain, Crete, and Djibouti as requirements dictated. This AFRICOM/EUCOM commitment continued through June 2014.

C-130J-30 aircrew in Southwest Asia. *Dyess Air Force Base, 317th Airlift Group, Brian Smith, 317th Air Group historian to author, January 2012*

The 40th Airlift Squadron's eleven deployed aircraft in Germany, Africa, and Afghanistan will continue through September 2014, when all are scheduled to be replaced by a Little Rock Air Force Base squadron.

When six 39th Airlift Squadron C-130Js returned from six months in Afghanistan, three of them returned the normal route through Europe and the North Atlantic, while the other three returned to Dyess Air Force Base via the Indian and Pacific Oceans. All six returned to Dyess Air Force Base at the same time, on March 18, 2014.

On April 22—four years after the first C-130J arrived at Dyess Air Force Base—the 317th Air Group's one and only C-130J flight simulator celebrated its ribbon cutting ceremony, with Congressmen Conaway and Neugebauer cutting the ribbon.

On May 4, 317th Air Group crews deployed to OEF took part in the relief mission to northeast Afghanistan following the massive landslide in Badakhshan that killed over 2,000 villagers. A 40th airlift Squadron C-130J delivered 28,000 pounds of food, water, tents, and blankets.[18]

A C-130J-30 on the taxiway at Dyess Air Force Base. *Dyess Air Force Base, 317th Airlift Group, Brian Smith, 317th Air Group historian to author, January 2012*

The six airmen assigned to the 455th Air Expedition Wing at Bagram Airfield, Afghanistan, who died on 2 October when their C-130J Super Hercules (317th Airlift Group) crashed were identified by the Department of Defense on 3 October: Capt. Jordan Pierson, Capt. Jonathan Golden, Staff Sgt. Ryan Hammond, Senior Airman Quinn Johnson-Harris (deployed from the 317th Airlift Group), Senior Airman Nathan Sartain, and Airman 1st Class Kcey Ruiz (deployed from the 66th Security Forces Squadron, Hanscom AFB, Massachusetts). The wing held a mourning fallen ceremony to honor the airmen who made the ultimate sacrifice while doing their duty on the combat frontier, thus allowing their fellow wingmen to pay their respects and mourn their loss. After a brief prayer from a wing chaplain, the squadron commanders of the fallen were given the opportunity to address the gathered service members and offer their thoughts.

Lt. Col. Mitchell Spillers, 774th Expeditionary Airlift Squadron commander, offered condolences and a message to support those grieving, while reminding all to stay focused on the mission at hand to honor the sacrifices of the lost airmen:

We've taken a blow, but I'm proud of the way we've come together...that must continue. We're a tactical airlift unit that provides a lifeline to our forces that no else can. Our mission will continue and we must carry on. This was one of my best crews; they had a positive impact on everyone around them. They served honorably and will forever be remembered as true tactical airlifters. Our thoughts and prayers are with their families and we will do everything in our power to comfort them during this time of loss.

Major Met Berisha, 455th Expeditionary Security Forces Squadron commander:

The fallen airmen loved what they did and they did their duty without regard for their own safety to deliver airpower capabilities here [Afghanistan]. Airmen must stay strong and continue their mission. We must mount up and get back to our posts, get back to our patrols, and get back in those aircraft and continue to do what we do best...project combat airpower for our nation. We all know deep in our hearts, Defenders, that's exactly what Sartain and Ruiz would have wanted.

I knew without a doubt, that when our nation sent an aircraft into harm's way into an unsecured and dangerous Afghan airfield the aircrew were defended by the finest security forces airmen our Air Force could deliver. Simply put, Ruiz and Sartain loved securing and projecting combat airpower for our nation. Their families not only raised fine American patriots, but they raised heroes that I had the humble honor and phenomenal privilege to serve alongside with here.

Chief Master Sgt. Matt Gregg, 455th AEW Command chief:

Airmen across the wing grieve for the lost airmen; let everyone pull together and continue the mission to honor their sacrifice. Today, we paused to remember those who made the ultimate sacrifice as part of the Vulture Nation. We can only hope that the anguish of the families of these fallen heroes is tempered by the knowledge that their loved ones died doing what they loved for the nation they loved...they did not die in vain. It is our duty to finish the work of these fallen comrades.

CHAPTER 11

DYESS AIR FORCE BASE SPECIAL WEAPONS STORAGE AREA: NUCLEAR and CONVENTIONAL WEAPONS STORAGE

Initially, control of America's atomic bombs after their use against Hiroshima and Nagasaki, Japan, was a complicated and disorganized process as stated under SAC's mission to deploy these atomic bombs (prior to the development of thermonuclear or hydrogen bombs).[1] The author (at the time an Air Force 2nd Lt., 1970) was an intelligence officer assigned to SAC, 544th Aerial Reconnaissance Technical Wing, and a member of the Offutt Air Force Base Junior Officers' Council, 1971–1973. He was presented with a framed, signed copy (signed by SAC Commander-in-Chief Gen. Bruce K. Holloway) of SAC's original mission:

> The Strategic Air Command will be prepared to conduct long-range offensive operations in any part of the world either independently or in cooperation with land and naval forces; to provide combat units capable of intense and sustained combat operations employing the latest and most advanced weapons; to train units and personnel for the maintenance of the Strategic Forces in all parts of the world; to perform such special missions as the Commanding General, Army Air Force may direct.

This was written in 1946, prior to the creation of an independent Air Force on September 18, 1947.[2]

W.A. Garner, Sandia Corporation, prepared a summary of construction projects at Special Weapons Storage Areas, including the one at Dyess AFB (1955). This was the first reference found as to when weapons storage construction started on a nuclear weapons storage area at Dyess AFB. Construction of Special Weapons Storage Areas was a highly classified subject, making it difficult to locate remaining historical documents on the construction of the Dyess AFB Special Weapons Storage Area. There was no information available at Dyess AFB due to records transfer after the inactivation of SAC and the loss of the wing historian. A search of the Air Force Historical Research Agency added no direct or specific records. Looking at a summary of Sandia Corporation's "Project Responsibilities" (for nuclear weapons storage sites) does provide interesting information:

1. Maintenance and repair.
2. Upgrades of existing facilities for thermonuclear weapons.
3. Construction of new facilities for thermonuclear weapons.
4. Construction of igloo storage vaults for increased thermonuclear weapons storage capacity.
5. Construction of new storage sites.

According to this summary, the total dollar value (FY 1955) scheduled, under construction, and completed was a total in excess of twenty-two million dollars.[3]

Sandia Corporation was assigned the responsibility of nuclear assemblies, fissile materials, and initiators for thermonuclear bomb assemblies to arm SAC's bombers (including those assigned to Dyess AFB: the B-47E, B-52E, B-52D, B-52H, and B-1B). In 1949, SAC was moving to create a formidable thermonuclear striking force consisting of:

Three heavy bomb groups, each with eighteen aircraft

One heavy bomb group with Convair B-36s and two heavy bomb groups in the process of becoming operational with the B-36

Eleven medium bomb groups:

1. Boeing B-29 Superfortress
  A. Eight bomb groups
  B. Three with forty-five aircraft assigned
  C. Five with thirty aircraft assigned
2. Boeing B-29s and B-50s
  A. Three bomb groups, each with forty-five aircraft assigned

Most of the critical nuclear assembly operations were conducted away from SAC bases at Los Alamos, New Mexico. This created a bottleneck, because in 1949, SAC nuclear trained munitions personnel could only assemble an average of two operational atomic bombs per day, which was far below what SAC required to conduct its nuclear deterrence mission.[4] This memorandum of the assigned responsibilities of Sandia Corporation formalized procedures, in which Sandia Corporation nuclear weapons trained personnel would meet incoming nuclear material shipments with an AEC custodian to render technical assistance and advice. Sandia Corporation went further, assisting SAC personnel in their assumption of nuclear weapons responsibilities. Sandia Corporation advised SAC Headquarters that changes would affect its operations after Quality Assurance (QA) Inspection Agencies were established. The evolution from a limited stock of nuclear bombs to a sufficient stockpile allowed SAC to rapidly arm its bombers and meet nuclear alert/deterrence mission requirements. Sandia Corporation personnel would be withdrawn from the "plants" (unclassified reference to SAC Special Weapons Storage Areas), leaving military personnel responsible for maintenance activities. Sandi personnel would perform QA inspections in their own areas, referred to as "S" structures.[5]

The "S" structure's common name was the "surveillance building," where QA inspections were conducted, along with wagon (weapons preloaded into munitions trailers stored inside the earth-covered munitions storage igloos) testing of the stockpile at that time. Personnel performed hands-on assembly work of stockpile weapons to validate the quality and accuracy of maintenance operations inside the Special Weapons Storage Areas, as well as to verify the functionality of limited-life components. (Tritium initiators had a relatively short operational life cycle and needed to be frequently replaced or swapped out from one shipped in from AEC to the one on the operational bomb/warhead, with the removed unit(s) shipped back to AEC for refurbishment.) The surveillance building also contained electrical and mechanical bays and a calibration room. There was no shielding or earth mounding around the building.[6]

There is a small earth-covered igloo munitions storage bunker with a vault door inside the Dyess Special Weapons Storage Area, which is currently a conventional munitions storage area for B-1B operations. The "S" building is across from this small bunker and was initially used to store Tritium initiators. All of this was necessary because to carry out its primary Cold War mission to maintain the capability of launching a sustained airborne attack in a nuclear environment, SAC needed its bomb and ICBM warheads fully protected. Fighter-Interceptor Squadron (FIS) aircraft's (North American F-86D Sabre Dogs armed with unguided rockets and Lockheed F-89J Scorpions armed with Genie AAMs tipped with thermonuclear warheads) primary airborne interception targets were incoming Russian Air Force long-range, heavy strategic bombers. SAC installations were priority defense objectives, followed by AEC/AFSWP facilities: AEC research facilities and testing and nuclear weapons storage areas, as well as component fabrication and assembly facilities. AEC requested this enhanced protection immediately after its creation in the middle of 1947, on the eve of the creation of an independent Air Force. Air Defense Command (ADC) was undergoing a dramatic expansion to meet its growing responsibilities. Stockpiling of atomic bombs began slowly, with only thirteen produced and

Tritium earth-covered igloo bunker at former Rushmore Air Force Station, Ellsworth AFB, which is similar to the one at Dyess Air Force Base. The one at Dyess Air Force Base is covered with a thicker layer of compacted earth due to its proximity to above ground buildings. Power poles with top-mounted lights visible in the background have a metal lighting arrestor spike on top to prevent electric charges from detonating explosives stored in the magazines. *Author*

stored in 1947. The pipeline from the production facilities had just begun after the slowdown of production after the end of WWII, with limited output thereafter. It was only later, during the Cold War, that mass production of nuclear bombs started.[7]

This was highlighted when President Harry Truman and former Prime Minister Winston Churchill boarded a train in Washington, DC, for a trip west to Fulton, Missouri, where Churchill made his famous Cold War speech at Westminster College. Part of his speech hit home, as the United States was rebuilding its military forces. The March 3, 1946, speech included the following:

> From Stettin in the Baltic to Trieste in the Adriatic, an iron curtain has descended across the continent. From what I have seen of our Russian friends and allies during the war, I am convinced there is nothing they admire so much as strength and there is nothing for which they have less respect than for military weakness.[8]

SAC continued to expand its stockpile of nuclear bombs, which by 1948 had grown to fifty-six and 298 by 1950. The increase was needed, heightened by concerns raised during the Korean War (1950 to 1953), when US nuclear weapons stockpiles reached 832. One of the drawbacks for SAC was their timely assembly. By the end of 1955, the United States had a stockpile of 2,280 nuclear weapons (bombs and warheads). The standard SAC Special Weapons

Storage Area—referred to as "Q" areas—typically consisted of forty buildings, inclusive of the igloo storage area that comprised about forty percent of the buildings and was distinctively sited within the larger segregated environment. Construction began on these Special Weapons Storage Areas in 1950 to 1951, with Dyess AFB construction occurring from 1953 to 1955 (estimated, with no official Air Force confirmation). These areas were distinctive inside SAC bases, with seven foot high steel chain link fences topped with razor strands of barbed wire surrounded by security patrols and maintenance roads. There were signs secured to the chain link fencing, "The use of deadly force is authorized." This meant Air Force Security Police would shoot first and ask questions second. SAC took security of its nuclear bombs and aircraft seriously, with nothing but 100 percent security at all times. Gen. LeMay, as SAC commander from October 19, 1948 to June 30, 1957, burned this into his SAC base commanders and all personnel.

The Special Weapons Storage Areas evolved in three phases:

Initial Phase: "Q" areas, augmented by their administrative components, focused on the full hardening of command and control buildings and the articulation of their multiple communications, adding a Special Weapons crew building and replacing personnel alert quarters at the assembly plant. Key additions were the nuclear booster storage buildings—the A-25—and security bunkers or guard towers—the "S" buildings. "Q" areas indicative of the emergency Cold War era are those tied to the assembly, checkout, and storage of the first atomic and thermonuclear (TN) bombs. Atomic bombs functioned as fission devices, using strictly fissile material. The early thermonuclear bombs were actually fission weapons boosted through a fission-fusion-fission chain reaction. A fission bomb initiated a TN device that in turn enhanced the original fission process. In the mature TN weapon or "super bomb," TN fuel was greatly increased and although set off by a fission device, was truly a TN weapon many times more powerful than the first atomic bombs.

Phase Two (middle of 1950): "Q" areas added a plant that was also earthen embanked and similar in exterior. Usually the two plants (atomic and TN) were described as Plants I and II, or "A" and "B," with the bombs completed in stages at each. The "A" structure stored nuclear capable fissile material, also called detonators or pits. The "A-2" structure did not become part of the "Q" area until the shift toward TN bombs in 1954. The roles of the "A" and "A-2" structures paralleled one another, both housing the critical fissile material that, when assembled with the bomb, created the atomic and early TN (boosted fission) bombs. These structures were windowless, with faux fenestration (false window placement) camouflage to fool foreign intelligence collection efforts. They were constructed with ten-foot thick, reinforced concrete walls and seventeen-foot thick roofs. The "C" structure assured the current usefulness of the stored bomb components and was formally designated a nuclear capsule surveillance structure. These four building types served as the character-defining elements of the "Q" areas.[9]

Black & Veatch Architecture Firm of Kansas City, Missouri, designed the Air Force "Q" areas. Design Group Number 115 was responsible for the Special Weapons Storage Areas at SAC bases. The firm developed a unique expertise in radioactive and electromagnetic environments, clean rooms, weapons (atomic and thermonuclear) research facilities, laboratories, nuclear and chemical waste treatment, blast resistant design, blast containment design, and igloo storage magazines. SAC standardized its Special Weapons Storage Area designs. Eventually, the US Army Corps of Engineers supervised the construction and completion of twenty "Q" areas by June 1957. This was a large and expensive construction project. SAC required more atomic weapons as its B-47E bomber force grew, along with the larger B-36 and the follow-on B-52 Stratofortress and B-58s.[10]

Phase III (1956): The "A-2" structure had only one above-ground story and was more elongated. In 1956, the exposed fissile detonators became obsolete with the development of a true TN

Aerial view of the Dyess Air Force Base Special Weapons Storage Area, in the sparse northeast corner of the base. *United States Geological Survey (USGS)*

bomb that did not require on-site assembly. This speeded up SAC's arming of its bomber force and reduced personnel requirements to assemble the bombs. The assembly plants, "A" and "A-2" structures, and "C" structures were no longer needed for their original, highly critical mission. At operational storage sites, one or two generations (different construction types) of alert personnel quarters were present, with a command post enlarged to direct SAC's larger assigned mission in the late 1950s. The igloo storage design used to store atomic and thermonuclear bombs and warheads changed to the storage of conventional munitions at many former SAC bases. Some bases retained a mix of thermonuclear weapons and conventional munitions storage. Again, there is no official confirmation from Air Force sources on the existence of these Special Weapons Storage Areas for the storage of atomic or thermonuclear weapons. There are two distinct rows of seven earth-covered storage igloo magazines inside Dyess AFB's Special Weapons that were initially used to store atomic and thermonuclear bombs and warheads and are currently storing conventional munitions.

"Q" areas stored SAC bombs and warheads, along with ADC Genie AAM warheads. On some SAC bases there were also FIS aircraft (the F-89J, which was assigned to Ellsworth AFB under ADC) armed with thermonuclear warhead air to air missiles. SAC "Q" areas were critical during the early years of the Cold War, but were essentially an active infrastructure during the 1950s and early 1960s, following the same progression as the Navy's Polaris, Poseidon, and Trident.[11]

SAC finally gained independent control of its thermonuclear weapons toward the end of 1962, after transfer deficiencies from nuclear storage areas to SAC bomber bases during the Cuban Missile Crisis and after AMC nuclear storage areas were absorbed by SAC bases. Special storage and transfer facilities like those at Gray AFB and Killeen National Stockpile Site Base were determined no longer necessary to support SAC's bomber forces.[12]

After SAC B-47Es deployed to England under REFLEX ACTION—including Dyess AFB's 341st BW—nuclear weapon storage igloos were built and became highly visible objects of the Cold War around SAC bases in the US and SAC bombers and tankers at RAF Air Bases. There are still Cold War bunkers in the English countryside. Many were built during WWII for storing large amounts of conventional bombs dropped on Nazi occupied areas and Germany that were upgraded for the storage of atomic and early thermonuclear bombs. The early munitions storage bunkers were also built by the RAF for its first generation of atomic weapons based on the Manhattan Project's design in a partnership between British and American scientists. SAC added upgraded earth-covered igloos for its B-47E bombers operating from RAF air bases, including deployments by Dyess AFB B-47Es. Many of these relics from the Cold War remain relatively intact, and unlike official Air Force confirmation of the locations of active atomic and thermonuclear weapons storage sites, a large number of the former British and US Special Weapons Storage Areas are marked on English road maps. The next generation of storage igloos was built to US/SAC standards, but are now considered obsolete for the storage of modern, miniature, precision thermonuclear weapons. Most are being used to store conventional munitions, such as precision guided air to ground munitions; those no longer considered viable or too far from bases were demolished. This is an expensive process, given the thickness of the concrete and type of construction.[13]

It has been difficult to locate information on buildings inside the Dyess AFB Special Weapons Storage Area. The following is a best attempt to look at nuclear and conventional munitions storage activities inside this facility. This separate area, as is common with these sites (such as Ellsworth AFB and Rushmore AFS), stored atomic and thermonuclear bombs and warheads before becoming a conventional munitions storage area after the B-1B stood down from nuclear alert after President George Bush ordered the US Strategic Command to stand down from nuclear alert on September 27, 1991. It was not until 1996 that thermonuclear weapons were removed from Dyess AFB for active reserve stockpile storage at Kirkland AFB, New Mexico.[14]

After 1991, Dyess AFB's Special Weapons Storage Area began storing a complete spectrum of conventional munitions, dumb bombs, and precision weapons. The most visible section of the storage area is the two rows of seven, earth-covered munitions storage igloos. These earth-covered magazines are preferred for storing munitions because they provide excellent protection from outside exposure. Earth-covered magazines provide temperature stability and are particularly desirable for the storage of propellants and pyrotechnics and are the best and safest storage type.[15]

The fourteen igloo magazines are one-story and rectangular, externally measuring twenty-eight feet wide and forty-four feet long, with an interior height of eight feet. The interior space provides 1,008 square feet of usable floor storage. The structures are constructed out of reinforced concrete with steel rebar, poured and compacted foundations, with one-foot thick steel rebar reinforced concrete floor slabs and walls. The flat roofs were constructed with twelve-inch-thick concrete with steel rebar reinforced bar joists for added strength, covered on the exterior with three-ply, built-up tar and gravel roofing material to create a waterproof moisture barrier. The front walls are exposed concrete with a heavy steel vault door and a concrete loading/unloading vehicle area. The side and rear walls are covered with compacted earth. Each igloo has twelve-inch thick, angled wing walls extending eleven feet to either side of the magazine's front, giving the igloo storage bunker a larger exterior appearance. The exterior concrete exposure is fifty feet wide. These wing walls serve as a retaining system for the surrounding compacted earth. The steel reinforced vault doors are set within the concrete face of the exposed walls and provide the single access point into the magazines. The magazines are equipped with recessed light

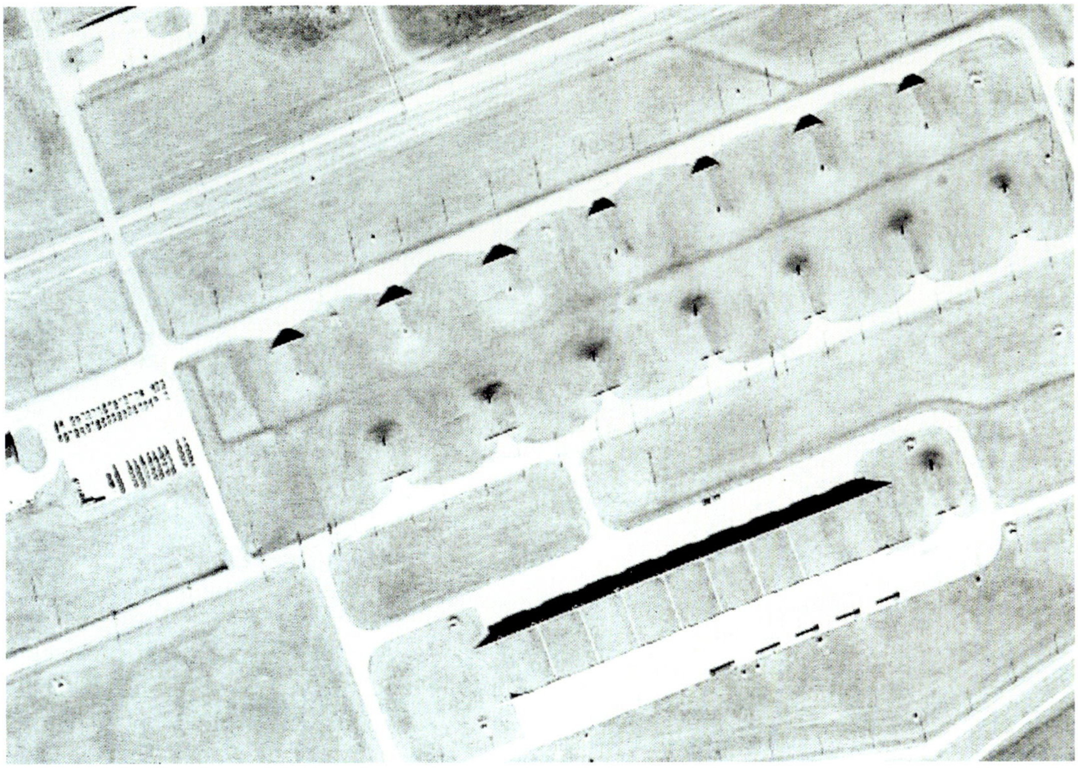

Aerial view of the twin rows (seven each) of earth-covered munitions storage igloos. *USGS*

Front view of a single-bay, earth-covered munitions storage igloo. This igloo is inside former Rushmore Air Force Station, Ellsworth Air Force Base, South Dakota. Its twin is at Dyess Air Force Base. *USGS*

fixtures over the doors, exterior mounted portable fire extinguishers, explosion-proof switches that are grounded to prevent static electricity buildup as an ignition source, amber warning lights that automatically turn on when the vault door is opened, and signs warning non-authorized entry is prohibited and use of deadly force is authorized. The area has wooden power poles spaced evenly throughout with flood lights attached on top to illuminate the storage area, removing shadows. Each pole also has a lightning rod with a copper cable running down the pole into a below-ground connector/diffuser. If the area is hit by a lightning strike, the powerful charge is directed away from the munitions storage bunkers and dissipates safely into the ground. The interior of each igloo's floor surface is coated with non-sparking, non-conductive floor finish. Bunker separation provides additional fraternization protection in case of an accidental detonation.

In the event of an accidental explosion, the blast would not trigger a nuclear detonation or conventional munitions; the compacted earth provides additional blast protection to lessen the disaster of any explosion within the igloo. Compacted earth adjacent to the front exposed vault wall and steel door is covered with asphalt, preventing soil slippage. This is rough, non-rolled asphalt that is covered with small gravel and then thick soil after pouring. This asphalt allows water to flow away from the igloo into depressions that direct the water out of the igloo area.[16]

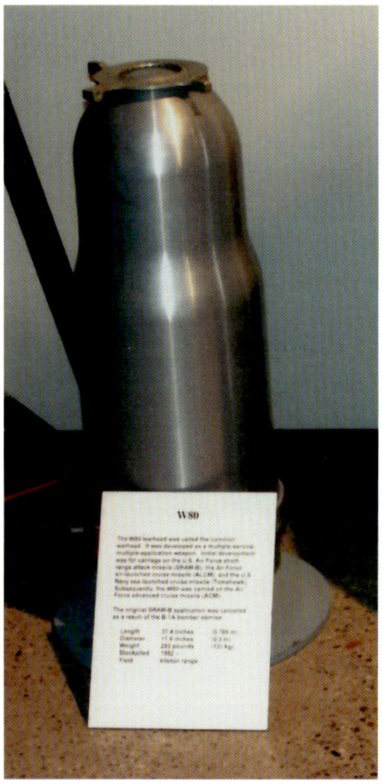

W-80-1 Fission fuel thermonuclear warhead at the National Museum of Nuclear Science and Technology, Albuquerque, New Mexico. *Author*

When nuclear weapons were stored in the Special Weapons Storage Area, a steel guard tower was manned twenty-four hours a day in all weather conditions to prevent unauthorized entrance and attempted access into the secured storage igloos. The top steel slated floor deck is accessed by exterior steel steps. The steel tower was built to a standard design; for example, its twin is in the former Rushmore AFS at Ellsworth AFB. The author had access to this tower. The guard tower has an enclosed room with windows on all sides and an exterior deck offering an unobstructed, 360 degree view of the storage area below. It was equipped with communications equipment to contact on and off-site security forces and contact the command center in the weapons area to coordinate access into and out of the separate storage igloos, high-powered telescopes, and powerful searchlights. The guard tower is forty feet tall, and is usually set on the highest point of elevation within the igloo storage area. The guards—a minimum of two per four-hour shift—were armed with pistols and shotguns—originally carbine rifles before replacement with M-16 fully automatic assault rifles. Security in these areas was absolute.[17]

As of 2013, the United States maintains a substantial thermonuclear warhead inventory (active operational, active stockpile, and pending dismantlement). In FY 2013, the federal budget indicates a spending level of 7.6 billion dollars for thermonuclear weapon activities in the Department of Energy's National Security Administration to maintain, secure, and modernize the US nuclear stockpile.[18] Under the New Start Treaty, US nuclear forces are permitted to deploy 1,722 strategic nuclear warheads on 806 operational deployed ICBMs, SLBMs, and strategic bombers. The non-deployed warhead count is 2,800, with another 500 warheads designated as tactical nuclear weapons. An undisclosed number of retired warheads are awaiting dismantlement, but there is no timetable available.[19]

Security of the movement of nuclear weapons into and out of the Dyess Special Weapons Storage Area before these bombs and warheads were removed in 1996 was strict and by checklist, under two-officer policy, heavily guarded, and with detonators or arming circuits moved separately. All weapons were under "safe" condition and disarmed, and unable to be detonated under any circumstances. The danger was that someone would attempt to acquire the radioactive material for the purpose of building a "dirty" bomb. Due to secrecy and deniability, it is difficult to verify the number of nuclear bombs and warheads stored, as these were removed for storage elsewhere. The following is an estimate based on scattered, unclassified nuclear watchdog sources on these weapons:

The steel guard tower in the area of the earth-covered munitions storage igloos. *Author*

Atlas F ICBM (June 1961 to June 1965)
13 W-38 thermonuclear warheads
Boeing B-47E Stratojets (November 1953 to March 1963)
170 various types of thermonuclear bombs
Nike-Hercules Surface to Air Missiles (two operational sites) (1960–1966)
24 W-31 thermonuclear warheads
Boeing B-52E, B-52D, and B-52H Stratofortress (1963–1985)
170 various types of thermonuclear bombs and warheads (the B-52 could be armed with the Hound Dog AGM)
North American (formerly Rockwell International, North American Aircraft) B-1B Lancer (1985–1991)
170 various types of thermonuclear bombs and warheads for precision guided AGMs

Best estimate is that Dyess AFB Special Weapons Storage area held between 170 to 204 thermonuclear weapons, depending on the weapons systems operational at the time. This was only one SAC base, but one can determine that the number of thermonuclear weapons stored at other SAC bases would probably come close to these numbers.[20] Absolute two-officer policy Positive Control procedures states "The strict policy which dictates the release of nuclear weapons with primary intentions to prevent, under any circumstances, either the accidental or unauthorized detonation of thermonuclear weapons."[21] The two-officer policy is the core of Positive Control,

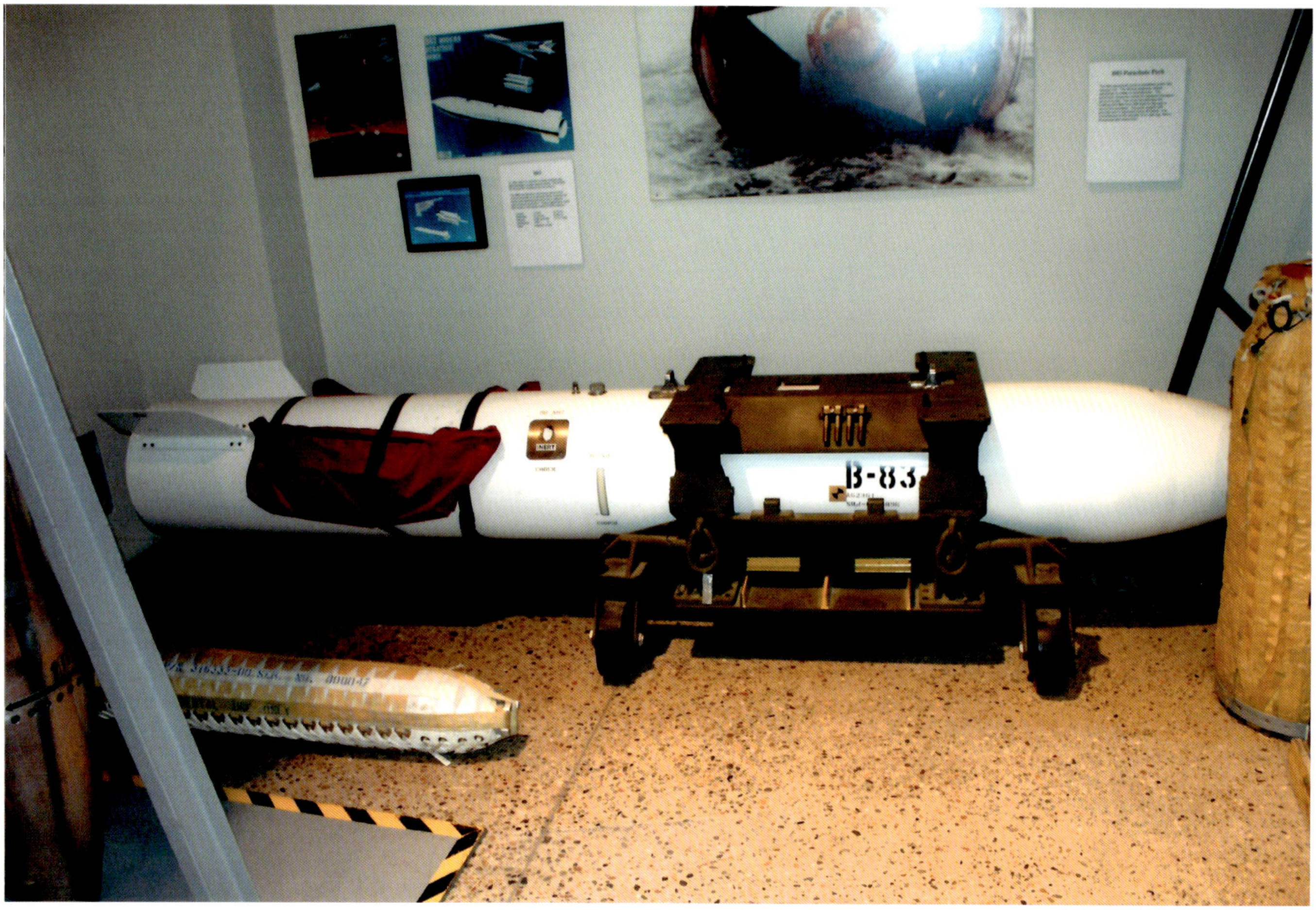

A B-83 thermonuclear bomb at the National Museum of Nuclear Science and Technology, Albuquerque, New Mexico. *Author*

which required the cooperation of two authorized individuals to launch a nuclear weapon (two bomber crew members, two missile launch officers, two missile launch officers at a Nike-Hercules SAM site, or two Positive Control/SIOP officers in a SAC Wing Intelligence Division). As strict is the training and operational procedures directing two SIOP officers who control the arming and disarming of loaded thermonuclear weapons, alert certification of weapons systems, the training of assigned personnel, and the movement and storage of thermonuclear weapons into and out of the weapons storage areas in corporation with munitions squadron personnel. Everything was done according to separate checklists verified by each officer and was intended to eliminate memory procedures. Everything was done by the checklist, with no variations allowed. SAC did not tolerate any mistakes with the storage, movement, handling, and loading and unloading of nuclear weapons.[22]

On August 7, 2007, regardless of multiple layers of controls and checklists, thermonuclear warheads were loaded into a Minot AFB B-52H assigned to the 5th BW. The mission profile specified inert Air Launched Cruise Missiles to be loaded into a B-52H to be transported from Minot AFB to the 2nd BW at Barksdale AFB, Louisiana. These ALCMs were designated to be removed from active Air Force and Air Force Global Strike Command inventory. Against operational nuclear security procedures, each ALCM was armed with an active W-80-1 thermonuclear warhead. After the B-52H landed at Barksdale AFB, the ALCMS were unloaded by 2nd BW Munitions Squadron personnel, transported to a missile storage area, and secured, remaining undiscovered for thirty-six hours. The Minot munitions personnel involved in this incident were decertified. A complete investigation of this mishap was conducted by the Department of Defense inspector general. Fortunately, the custody of these armed ALCMs was not compromised.[23]

After 1991, the B-1B's mission with the 7th BW transitioned from nuclear to conventional munitions delivery. The US Air Force *Munitions Facilities Standards Guide* indicates that munitions storage and handling facilities should be sited within an installation's explosive clear zone. The Dyess AFB Munitions Storage Area (MSA), at the northeast section of the base, is sufficiently isolated to prevent destruction of major base facilities and aircraft.[24]

B-1Bs at Dyess and Ellsworth AFBs have completed their transition from thermonuclear to conventional munitions delivery. A reference was found to an Air Combat Command conducted Nuclear Staff Assistance Visits (NSAV) to Dyess AFB in February 1994, August 1994, and September 1995. The 7th BW received a USAF Nuclear Safety Plaque in 1995 for "outstanding achievements" and "contribution" to nuclear security. The 7th Security Police Squadron received an "excellent" and "outstanding" rating during inspections. From February 20 to March 3, 1996, the 7th BW went through a Nuclear Operational Readiness Inspection (NORI); ACC conducted the last NSAV in October 1996. The remaining nuclear weapons stored at Dyess AFB were transported to Kirkland AFB, New Mexico, for storage in the Kirkland Underground Munitions Storage Complex as part of the US Thermonuclear Reserve Stockpile.[25]

Air Force Conventional Munitions

Air Force enlisted munitions systems technology personnel are important to the operation of modern conventional munitions. Their career tasks cover a wide range of munitions responsibilities, especially with the heavy conventional B-1B missions in Southwest Asia and now with the bombing targets in Iraq and Syria as of October 2014):

1. Receive, identify, inspect, store, re-condition, ship, and issue conventional and unguided non-nuclear munitions.
2. Handle, store, and transport weapons and locate munitions.
3. Transport munitions using forklifts, trucks, trailers, and special purpose vehicles.
4. Maintain and operate personal computers and the Special Conventional Ammunition System.
5. Proficiency in personnel management, warehousing, electrical systems maintenance, and operation and inventory management.

These enlisted personnel operate different types of equipment inside the munitions area:

Forty foot weapons trailer inside Ellsworth Air Force Base's weapons storage area. *Author*

1. Hand pallet jacks
2. Forty-foot tractor trailer combinations for movement of large volumes of munitions
3. All terrain 10,000 pound capacity forklifts
4. Heavy duty 50,000 pound forklifts
5. Light trucks and small tractor pullers

To perform these tasks, Air Force Specialty Codes (AFC) designate responsibilities:

1. (461x0) Munitions Maintenance
2. (462x0) Weapons Maintenance (referred to as Loaders)
3. (463x0) Nuclear weapons
4. (464x0) Explosive Ordnance Disposal[26]

Small weapons wagon inside Ellsworth Air Force Base's weapons storage area. *Author*

Equipment Maintenance: Perform maintenance and inspections of munitions handling equipment: MHU-141, MHU-110, LALS, UALS, and MHU-226 trailers.

Precision Guided Munitions: Responsible for testing and maintenance of all conventional air to air munitions used on aircraft and all air to ground missiles.

Line Delivery: Line delivery drivers are dispatched by Munitions Control and are responsible for the safe and expedient handling and delivery of munitions from the bomb dump or other storage locations to aircraft. Line delivery drivers are responsible for the accounting of their equipment and munitions movement via daily reconciliation reports for all movements.

Conventional Maintenance: Responsible for the construction, maintenance, and testing of all conventional air to ground munitions used on aircraft, ranging from chaff, to flares, to cannon ammunition and unguided bombs.

An MJ-40 Aerial Stores Lift Truck referred to as a "Jammer." It lifted single weapons into the B-1B stores bay and attached the bomb to an already installed launcher module. On display at Ellsworth Air Force Base, South Dakota, Dakota Thunder Open House 2011. *Author*

MHU-196 Munitions Heavy Lift Trailer at Ellsworth Air Force Base, South Dakota, Dakota Thunder Open House 2011. *Author*

Munitions Control: Direct and track work crews, coordinate requirements, act as a liaison for outside agencies, develop war plans, provide oversight for safety and security, and ensure the daily reconciliation of all munitions and related equipment against established inventories.

Storage and Handling: Responsible for storing and breaking out munitions required by Conventional Maintenance and Munitions Inspection, and is also responsible for the maintenance of munitions. Storage facilities are usually referred to as "igloos," "magazines," or "revetments." These personnel transport munitions over public right of ways (state highways and interstates) to transfer munitions between different storage or shipping and receiving depots/locations. Storage personnel operate the majority of the heavy equipment found in the bomb dump, including the eighteen-wheel flat-bed tractor trailer combinations, heavy-rated forklifts, and cranes. This is necessary under Air Force requirements (AFH 32-1084 facility requirements) to operate munitions storage facilities used to store munitions explosives material, inert components, and equipment.

Munitions Inspection: Inspects all munition items at various times for safety and compliance with technical instruction manuals and procedures.

Munitions Accountability: Under 645x0A supply career field, they are responsible for the accountability and logistics for the entire munitions stockpile.[27]

Adjacent to and south of the fourteen earth-covered igloos is what the US Army Corps of Engineers refers to as a "Box Type" earth-covered munitions storage bunker. The complex on Dyess AFB consists of a structure of nine side-by-side bunkers each seventy-five feet wide, one hundred feet long (deep), and ten feet high. The walls and roof are constructed of reinforced poured concrete or prefabricated (factory pre-cast) concrete panels joined together at the construction site. The choice of on-site concrete pouring or delivery of pre-fabricated concrete panels depends on the availability of construction materials. The bunkers are earth-covered, with each storage bay equipped with overhead supported steel double doors that roll to either side to provide open access to the storage compartment. There is a large, 100-foot wide concrete pad on either side of the bunkers running the entire length of the bunker. At the end of the bunker complex at Dyess AFB is a separated earth-covered bunker. Currently, according to standard Air Force munitions procedures, it is used to store electronics for precision guided munitions. The shift from nuclear to conventional munitions storage operations maximizes using existing facilities, thereby reducing new construction costs. The author was unable to determine the date of construction for this facility, although it was probably sometime after 1991.[28]

Earth-covered box type munitions storage bunkers currently used to store 2,000-pound bombs for adaptation to precision weapons using a JDAM kit. *USGS*

Ground view of a box type munitions storage bunker showing the two steel doors that slide to either side. The bunker is in Ellsworth Air Force Base's weapons storage area. *Author*

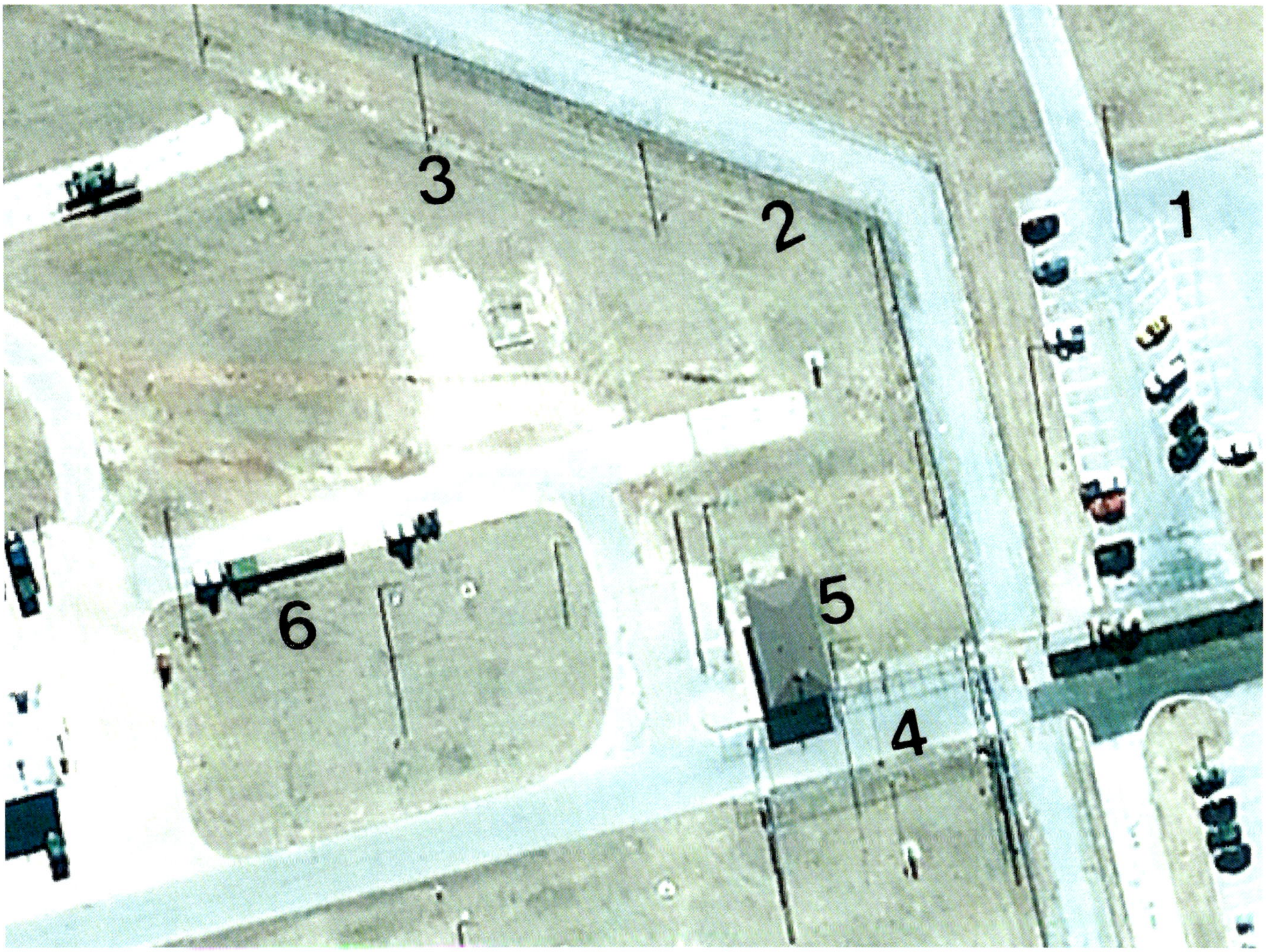

Entrance to Dyess Air Force Base's Special Weapons Storage Area: 1. POV parking lot outside the storage area; 2. Seven-foot high security fencing topped by razor wire; 3. Light pole with a lightning rod mounted on top; 4. Double sliding steel chain link access/egress gate; 5. Security building; and 6. Forty-foot munitions flatbed trailer and tractor. *USGS*

An aerial view of the weapons area reveals it as sparse and bare. Fire prevention in this area is the responsibility of all personnel who work in or enter into the storage area. It is their responsibility to keep the area in a condition that will prevent fires from starting and to prevent fires from entering into the munitions storage area from outside or surrounding areas. Firefighting facilities are of immediate importance to personnel within the weapons storage area. Fighting fires in their beginning stages can prevent a major fire or mass detonation of ammunition stored within. At the same time, on-site personnel must not be exposed to the hazards of an imminent explosion. Firefighting equipment will vary depending on the type of facility, the ammunition stored, and the availability of personnel.[29]

There is more to the Dyess AFB munitions storage area than fourteen earth-covered igloos. The munitions area is secured by a seven foot high chain link fence topped by coiled razor wire, along with a security patrol. It is well lit to prevent any potential intruder from hiding in shadows. The entrance is at a single access/egress double security gate with a corresponding security entrance building. Private vehicles are parked outside the secured area. Only government vehicles screened by security forces are allowed to operate inside the munitions area.

The former "S" structure has been converted to quality assurance inspections and testing of precision guided munitions. The building was originally designed to provide munitions personnel adequate space for quality assurance activities and to keep work spaces separated from other weapons maintenance activities. A nearby group of three buildings predominates the main entrance gate. The T-shaped building was originally used as a barracks and mess hall. It now serves as a mess hall and conventional munitions administration building, housing the munitions control office. There are two general purpose warehouses nearby.

To the southeast is an earth-covered bunker. When thermonuclear weapons were stored in the storage area it secured the tritium boosters used on the early TN bombs. The bunker had a safety feature at the top—similar to other storage igloos within the site—an exhaust vent that allowed any buildup of tritium gas to ventilate.

Tritium gas has a radioactive half-life of approximately twelve to thirty-three years, depending on its concentration due to the type of weapon to be boosted. Interestingly, in 1957, Sandia National Laboratory technicians determined the venting of tritium gas in small amounts produced little contamination downwind of the released gas. After 1957, tritium gas was no longer used in thermonuclear weapons. Possible side effects still remain uncertain for those who worked around this type of igloo.

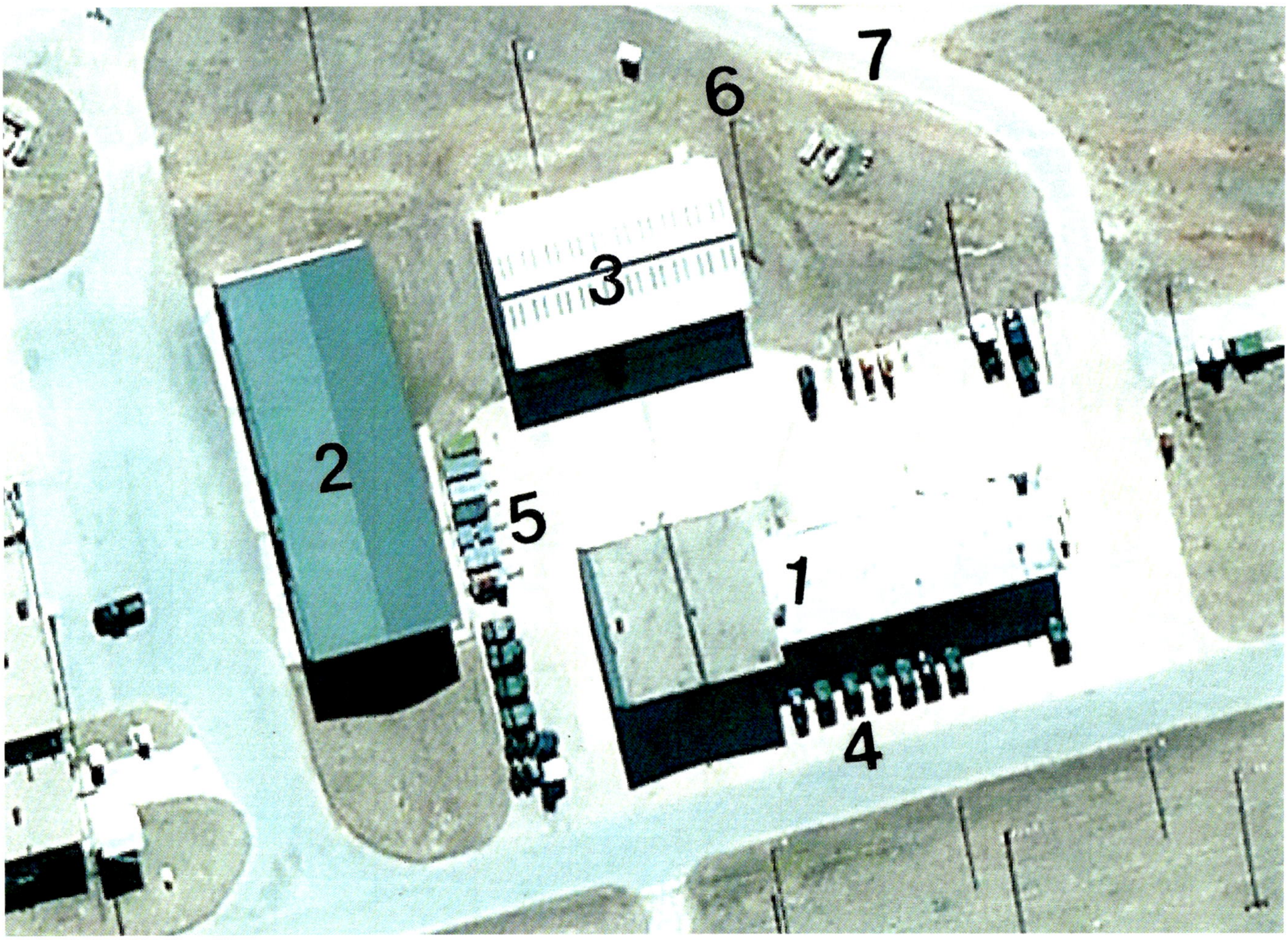

Dyess Air Force Base's Special Weapons Storage Area administration and general storage: 1. T-shaped building containing mess hall, munitions administration, and munitions control; 2. warehouse; 3. warehouse; 4. standard Air Force pickup trucks used for transportation in the weapons area and to pull various weapons trailers; 5. small weapons trailers; 6. light pole; and 7. general service road. *USGS*

1. Cold War, earth-covered tritium storage igloo. 2. Above ground explosive storage magazine. 3. "A" structure. 4. General explosive storage. 5. Light pole as part of area lighting.

To its left is an above-ground munitions magazine. It is considered a general storage magazine built out of steel and concrete framing, with hollow title walls usually filled with sand. It had a concrete floor covered with a sparkproof coating. They were designated to store fixed and separate loading projectiles, as well as small arms and rifle ammunition—classified as low-level explosives. Across from this building is a former windowless, above ground "A" structure forty-two feet wide and fifty-three feet long, with ten-foot thick walls. Its interior dimensions are twenty-one feet wide, thirty-three feet long, and nine feet high. A smaller building was originally used to store small nuclear capsules: seventy per room, with a total of three rooms. Access doors were fitted with dual combination locks.

The 7th BW Munitions Squadron is now responsible for the storage, maintenance, and delivery of quality conventional munitions and maintains munitions release systems, assuring mission readiness for B-1B and C-130J operations to meet the secretary of defense's taskings.[30]

Currently, the 7th Munitions Squadron supports B-1B conventional operations as directed by ACC while conducting the US "global war on terror." The B-1B can carry a wide variety of conventional weapons that are now maintained in the Dyess AFB Special Weapons Storage Area.[31]

The 7th Munitions Squadron services the B-1B's conventional weapons capabilities. The squadron earned the 2006 Air Force Explosive Award for its work in building more than 1,500

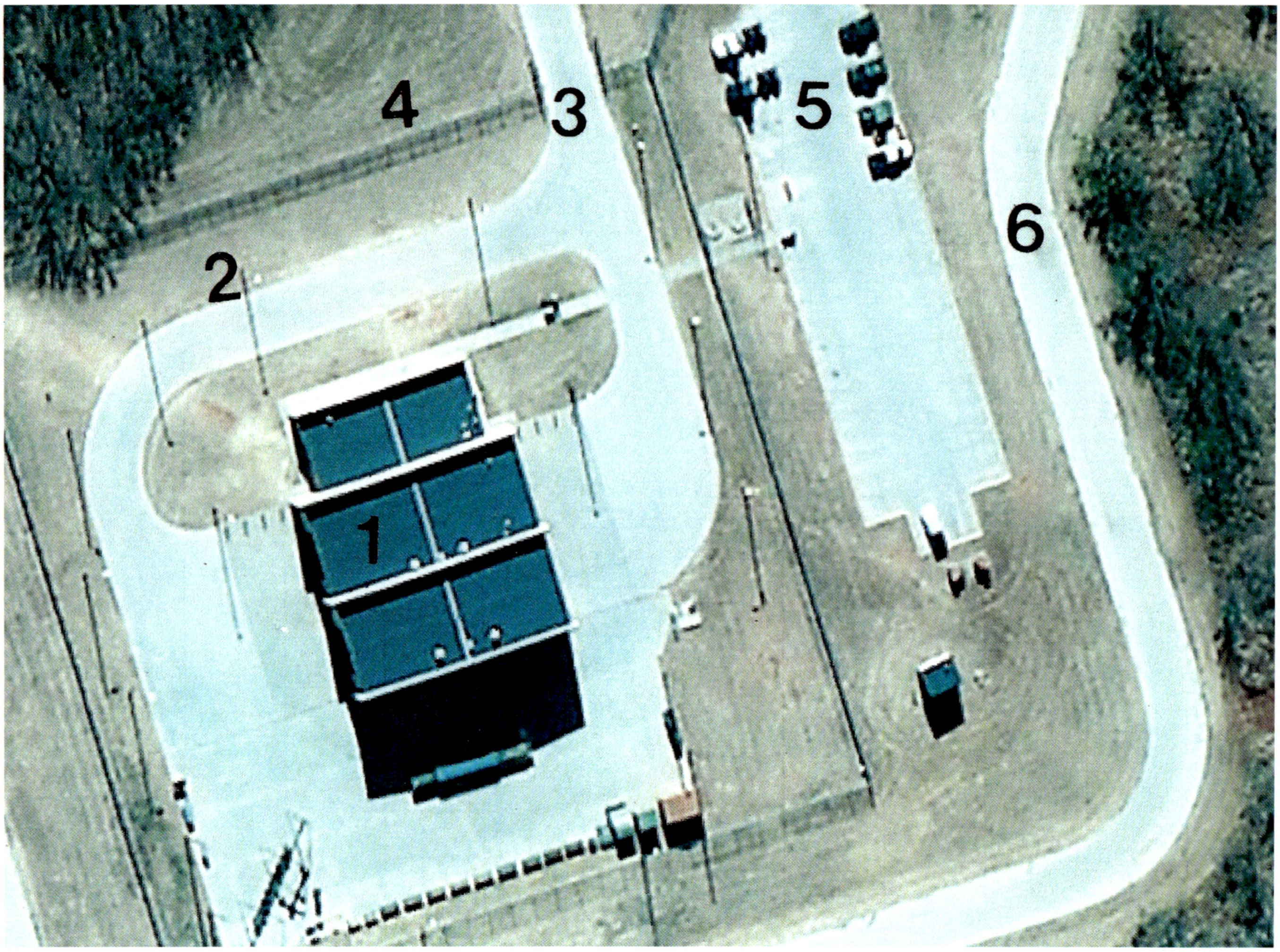

1. Former Atlas F missile assembly building equipped with heavy overhead traveling crane. 2. Security area lighting. 3. Entrance to area, which was closed when the facility held an Atlas F ICBM. 4. Security fencing. 5. Air Force trucks. 6. Service road.

munitions and 23,000 countermeasures with no safety incidents at Dyess AFB, or at an undisclosed location in Southwest Asia as part of the US global war on terror. In Southwest Asia, B-1Bs provide constant, on-call support for US, coalition, and Afghan Army forces. Normal procedures for the munitions airmen working with the weapons include regular safety briefings by crew chiefs and careful attention to Air Force Technical Orders and Instructions that specifically outline how to handle the bombs. Beginning the first day they attend technical school, their education continues every day in their operational squadron, as these airmen are constantly trained on safety operations. Airmen work armament breakout of munitions from storage, assemble the weapons, load weapons onto munitions trailers, and transport weapons to the flight line, where load crew airmen load the weapons into the B-1B's bomb bay, allowing the aircraft to take off with its designated bomb load. More than seventy 7th Munitions Squadron personnel—out of a designated strength of 248—deployed in the summer of 2006 to Southwest Asia, completing more than 1,200 munitions drops.[32]

The 7th BW deployed personnel to the 379th Expeditionary Maintenance Squadron Munitions Flight (EMSMF) at an undisclosed location in Southwest Asia. The fight for US troops on the ground in Afghanistan presents an operational challenge. The continued fighting faced by US ground troops remains a dangerous operation. When a ground team engages an enemy on the ground, regardless of terrain or weather conditions, and it needs immediate aerial support, they can call upon their airborne counterparts. The B-1Bs lay down precision delivery of conventional munitions. But how are these munitions assembled and how do they make their way into the aircraft? If they are dropped by a B-1B Lancer, they were most likely assembled by airmen assigned to the 379th EMSMF.

The munitions flight's primary responsibilities are to assemble and inspect bombs for the B-1Bs, such as the JDAM Guided Bomb Unit-31, which has a launch weight of more than 2,000 pounds, and the GBU-38 with a launch weight in excess of 500 pounds. They also assemble chaff and flares for the C-17 Globemaster II and the C-130 Hercules. The difference between working in a munitions flight at Dyess or Ellsworth AFB or in a deployed environment is significant from a mental stress standpoint. At deployed locations in Southwest Asia, munitions personnel handle live (armed) explosives and build bombs that are designated for use against specific targets. This differs from being at a home base (Dyess AFB or Ellsworth AFB for B-1Bs), where munitions personnel mainly assemble training weapons that contain no explosive fillers, usually referred to as "dummy" bombs. When dealing with multi-million dollar aircraft and facilities, this is the only acceptable training option to keep munitions airmen trained and operationally certified. Once munitions are assembled they are stored in a staging area until the airborne mission requires them. All munitions are inspected starting with assembly at the build site and throughout the entire process to ensure there is no corrosion, damage, or defects. Some precision munitions are inspected more than thirty times, and these checks/inspections do not stop until the munitions are loaded

7th Munitions Squadron airman working on a weapons trailer with three JDAM training bombs already loaded. Notice the box type munitions bunker, bunker doors, concrete facing, concrete apron, lighting, and lighting suppression poles. Heavy Air Force trucks are in the background. *Dyess Air Force Base, 7th Bomb Wing Public Affairs*

B-1B conventional bomb load. *Dyess Air Force Base, 7th Bomb Wing Public Affairs*

into the B-1B. Due to multiple inspections and munitions airmen's hard work, the Munitions Flight has achieved a detonation success rate of 98.2 percent.[33]

In the state of the union address to the nation on February 12, 2013, President Obama stated US combat ground forces were to be reduced by 34,000 in 2013, with the remaining by 2014, leaving a support force of 12,000 in Afghanistan. B-1Bs and the 28th and 7th BWs will continue to support US ground forces, requiring Munitions Flight personnel to continue to be deployed to Southwest Asia. This will continue the story of the Dyess AFB munitions storage area and its tradition of excellence and importance to the defense of the United States.

A B-1B's open bomb-bay, which can hold conventional munitions combinations in support of the US war on global terrorism. This 28th BW B-1B is at Ellsworth Air Force Base, South Dakota, Open House, 2011. *Author*

CHAPTER 12

THE 7TH BOMBARDMENT WING and the ROCKWELL-INTERNATIONAL B-1B LANCER

The 96th BW traded in its B-52H Stratofortresses for B-1B Lancers in June 1985. The first Rockwell International, North American Aircraft operational B-1B flew in October 1984. The first operational B-1B was delivered to SAC's Dyess AFB, 96th BW, on October 1, 1986.[1]

B-1B on Dyess Air Force Base's flight line. *Dyess Air Force Base, 7th Bomb Wing Public Affairs*

Dyess B-1Bs were part of SAC's nuclear deterrence SIOP package (War Plans Division) from 1985 to 1991, under the command's nuclear strike mission profile against the Soviet Union. Alert B-1Bs would sit "cocked" and alert, awaiting an Emergency War Order (EWO) and then launching to clear the base, making a rendezvous with alert-launched tankers under their portion of the SIOP mission profile and breaking away from the tankers, then penetrating to attack targets inside the Soviet Union. The B-1B's standard SIOP thermonuclear weapons load was able to be delivered over a variety of attack mission profiles:

B-1Bs on Dyess Air Force Base's flight line. *Dyess Air Force Base, 7th Bomb Wing Public Affairs*

High to low attack profile: considered to be the standard B-1B attack package.
8 B-61 thermonuclear bombs carried in the intermediate stores bay.
8 SRAMS carried in the aft stores bay.
1 Auxiliary fuel tank carried in the forward stores bay.
High-Altitude attack profile
16 ALCMs[2]

A walk around of a B-1B. The B-1B was flown from the Rockwell-International production facility at Palmdale, California, on January 13, 1986, to Dyess Air Force Base, Texas, and assigned to the 96th Bomb Wing. The aircraft was named "TEXAS RAIDERS." Its nose art is the same as that of a Confederate Air Force Boeing B-17 Flying Fortress restored to flying status. The aircraft was painted entirely in gunship gray. The B-1B was removed from operational service at Dyess Air Force Base and was flown to Ellsworth Air Force Base, South Dakota (28th Bomb Wing), on February 1, 2005. 28th BW maintenance personnel removed electronics, hydraulics, engines, brakes, tires (replaced by non-operational worthy tires), along with any wiring, crew compartment electronics, and aircraft systems, leaving the aircraft a hollow shell. It was towed through the base to the South Dakota Air and Space Museum for static display in front of the museum's entrance on a raised area. The aircraft reflects B-1Bs operating at Ellsworth Air Force Base. *Author*

The B-1B's radome opens to the left, providing maintenance access to the Westinghouse AN/APQ-164 Offensive Radar system. The oval antenna provides the B-1B's aircrew with low-altitude, terrain-following, and precision guided navigation. *Author*

On the lower side of the B-1B are the rear set of double doors for air conditioning hose, along with the forward round access external connection points. The three date probes are visible on either side of the fuselage in front of the forward crew compartment. The two composite material Structural Mode Control System (SMCS) vanes are mounted on both sides of the aircraft nose at a thirty degree downward angle to reduce aircraft oscillations caused by turbulence in low-level flight. *Author*

Covering of the crew access hatch that holds a retracting crew ladder deployed aft of the forward nose gear when open. *Author*

The B-1B's nose landing gear can be steered seventy-five degrees left or right of center for directional control during ground operations. The system is hydraulically operated and electronically controlled, with steering commands sent through the pilots' rudder pedals. Nose wheel steering is automatically disengaged when the landing gear retracts. The landing gear track is fourteen feet six inches wide with a wheel base of fifty-seven feet six inches. *Author*

The B-1B's left side, fixed dual air inlets for the two left side engines. *Author*

The left side, four-wheel main landing gear was strengthened on the 100 production aircraft to accommodate operational combat weights. The gear retracts inboard and aft into the fuselage. Multiple disk brakes are fitted to each wheel, including an anti-skid system for braking on wet runways. *Author*

Canvas-covered, inflatable rubber bladders seal the gap when the B-1B's wings are in full aft swept position. It replaced a less aerodynamic fairing on the four prototype B-1As. The engine exhaust nozzle actuator fairings were removed in the early 1990s to reduce maintenance and weight. The exhaust nozzle controls the expansion ratio of engine exhaust gases during flight operations. *Author*

General Electric (GE) F101-GE-102 30,780 pound thrust B-1B with afterburner for increased thrust. The engine is on its dolly used for maintenance access and removal and installation on the B-1B. *Author*

The B-1B's vertical fin tip fairing containing an ECMS antenna and rendezvous radar beacons. A white tail light and anti-collision strobe light are mounted below the fairing's rear area. Static discharge wicks are attached to the rudder trailing edge to dissipate static electric charges. *Author*

The front bomb bay doors (left) and middle and aft bomb bay doors (right). The forward weapons bay is divided by a bulkhead that can be moved or removed as required, allowing either two fifteen-foot long bays, one twenty-two-foot and one eight foot, or one thirty-one-foot long weapons bay. *Author*

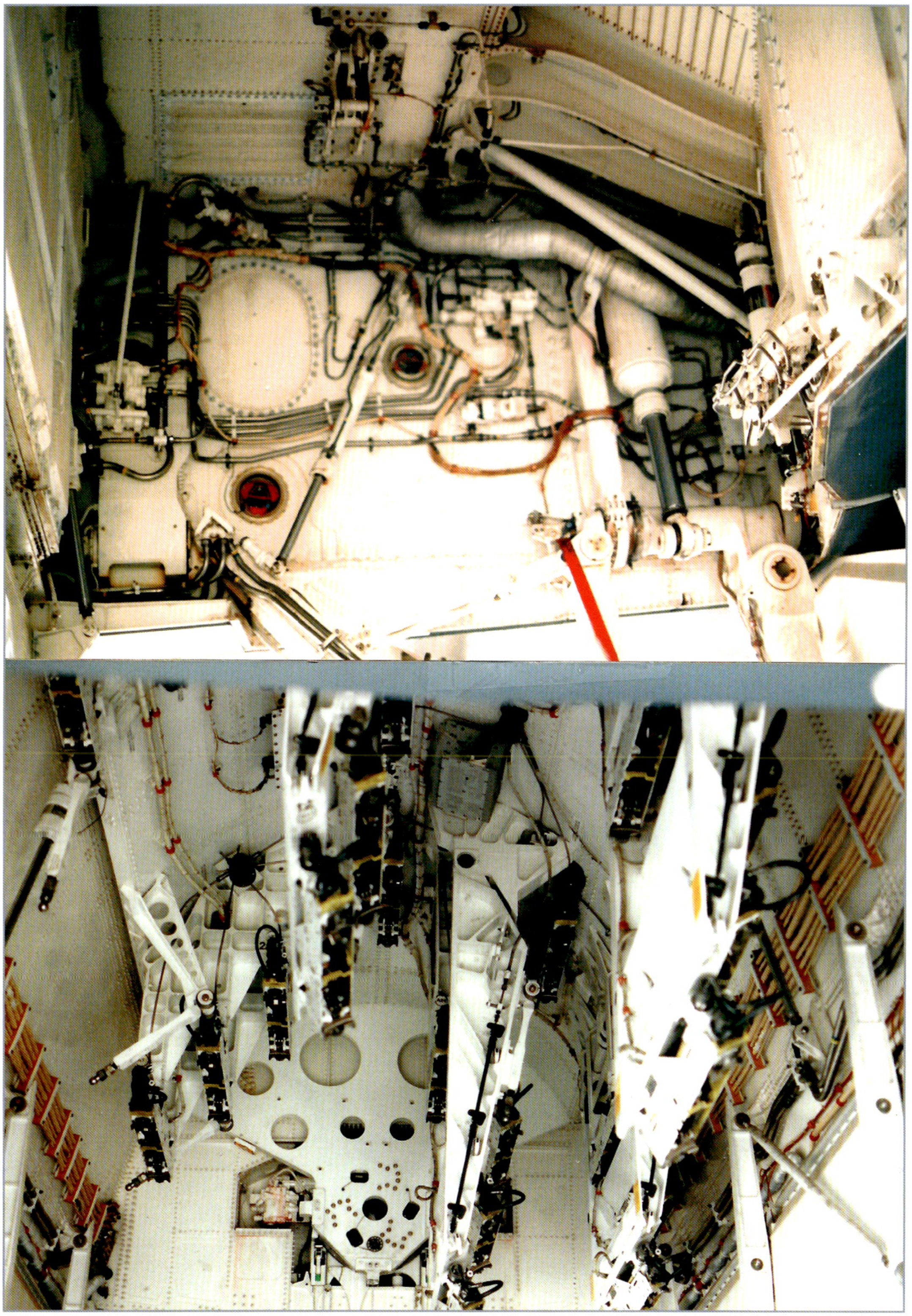

Top: The trunnion mounted on the bulkhead can support either the Conventional Weapons Module (CWM) or a rotary launcher. Bottom: This is an empty CVM. A perforated spoiler mounted on the bulkhead extends down when the bomb bay doors open in flight, reducing turbulence inside the weapons bay and ensuring clean weapons release. *Author*

There are eleven Vortex generators on either side of the aft fuselage section, under the horizontal stabilizer. The Vortex generators smooth airflow around the lower rudder, reducing fatigue and enhancing control surface effectiveness. If any of these Vortex generators is missing, the B-1B is limited to subsonic speed. *Author*

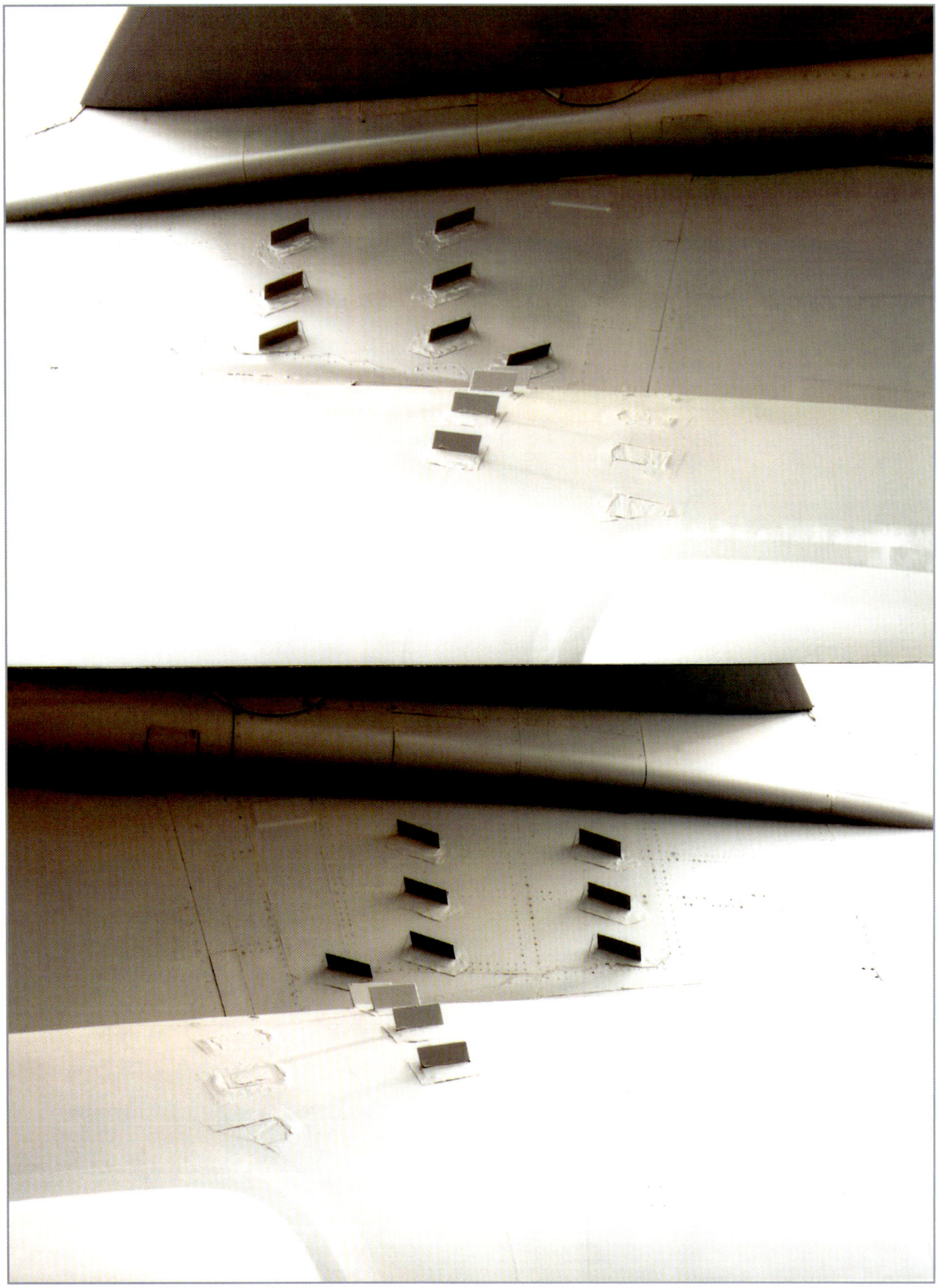

The right landing gear truck and fixed engine air intake. *Author*

The horizontal stabilizers operate collectively from plus ten degrees to minus twenty-five degrees for pitch control, as well as plus or minus twenty degrees for roll control. The pivot point is forward of the stabilizer cone. The horizontal stabilizers operate differentially to provide supersonic roll control and operate in tandem for pitch control throughout all flight regimes. *Author*

Fairings on either side of the tail cone house the Towed Decoy System (TDS). The TDS includes the Raytheon AN/ALE-50 Airborne Expendable System, a programmable, computer-controlled, expendable countermeasures system controlled by defense systems officers. The TDS displays an active Radio Frequency System (RFS) transmitter to redirect incoming missiles approaching the aircraft from the rear. The Air Force would neither confirm nor deny that TDS saved a B-1B operating on a combat mission over the Balkans supporting United Nations operations in 1999. *Author*

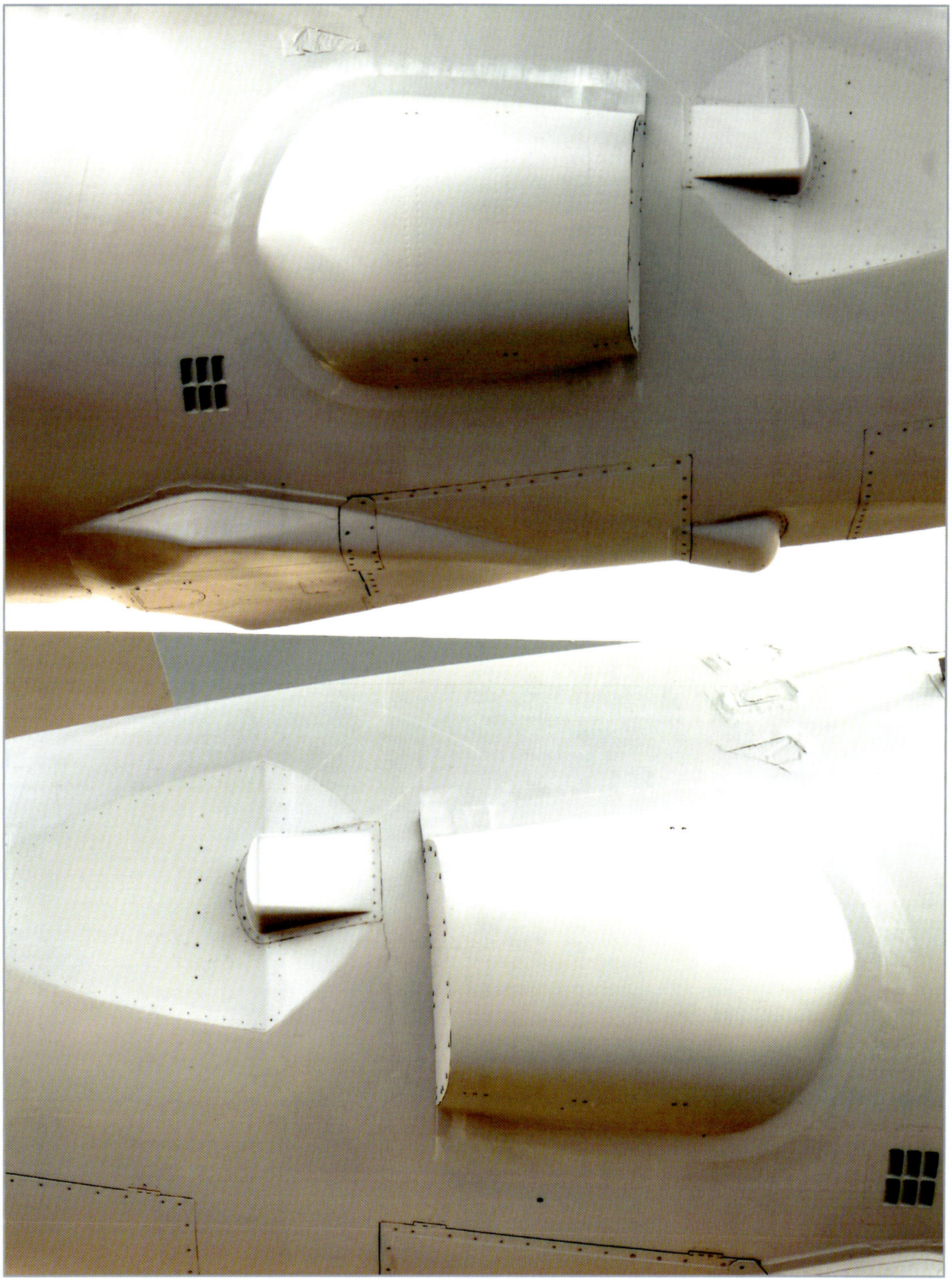

The rear, underside fuselage RFS/ECM antenna (top) and the forward, underside fuselage RFS/ECM antenna (bottom). *Author*

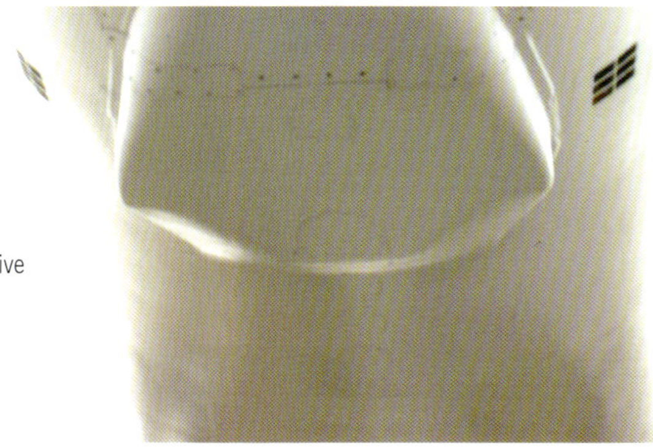

Rear mounted underside fuselage RFS/ECM defensive antenna. *Author*

To fulfill SIOP nuclear strike mission profiles, B-1Bs on nuclear alert awaited a crew launch under EWO procedures, launching to rapidly clear the Dyess runway and then climbing to altitude into a designated clear corridor (estimated to be outside any expected air or ground nuclear detonations). Sitting on alert, B-1Bs are equipped with a self-contained engine starting system using bleed air and mechanical power from the onboard APU. The aircraft's systems could also operate using power from the APUs. The Central Integrated Test System (CITS) allows maintenance troubleshooting without test equipment. All that is required is a runway with sufficient length for a fully combat loaded aircraft to become airborne. The eight thermonuclear bombs could be selected to destroy assigned SIOP targets, with SRAMs destroying static enemy defenses or threats along the B-1B's flight path to the target, neutralizing those ahead and to either side of the bomber's penetrating course.

On notification of a SAC initiated alert scramble, B-1B alert crews had to take off within three minutes. Once airborne, B-1Bs turned away from Dyess AFB, with the crew updating and aligning the aircraft's inertial navigation systems using GPS. The B-1B arrived at its SIOP refueling point with its assigned tanker for its first aerial refueling. A second programmed SIOP tanker would refuel the B-1B prior to penetrating Soviet air space. The B-1B would drop to low level—possibly as low as 200 feet—and increase speed to approximately 600 mph—just below the speed of sound, although a supersonic dash capability was available to evade Soviet fighters, anti-aircraft artillery fire, or SAM launches and active radar lock-ons.

> The B-1B's aircrew can use the aircraft's precision, terrain-following radar capability to mask detection from radar emitters using ground clutter and high terrain elevations to hide. Onboard SRAMs can be launched to destroy enemy defenses along the pre-programmed SIOP target route. The Defense Systems Officer can re-program the SRAM guidance package to destroy hostile, previously undetected threats to the aircraft, clearing the low-level approach to the SIOP target(s). This makes the B-1B a highly flexible and capable nuclear delivery system.

At this point, the Offensive Systems Officer updated the aircraft's position, pre-arming the on-board bomb's thermonuclear warheads as authorized by the president and confirmed by two officers in the aircraft by comparing received launch codes with those carried in the aircraft. With the bomb in its pre-armed condition it was still safe, meaning that it was still not fully armed. The bomb became "hot" or armed when it was released from the aircraft, with automatic arming functions occurring inside the warhead once it reached a programmed distance from the aircraft. This was an internal function shielded from EMP radiation or ECM jamming. If the bombing system was set to automatic and the required release consents were transmitted by the pilot or copilot and OSO, the navigation systems would fly the aircraft to the programmed target and the Avionics Control Unit Complex (ACUC) would release the selected bomb so it impacted the designated target. If the bombing system was set to manual mode, after the previous procedures were completed in automatic mode the bomb was released by the OSO by pressing the bomb's release switch. This was a fall back to a malfunctioning automatic release sequence or if battle damage degraded the automatic system's electronics. Once the bomb impacted the desired target, a timer in the warhead detonated the nuclear material after the timer reached zero. The timer function allowed the aircraft to reach a safe distance outside the detonation shock wave zone prior to the circuit closing. In a low-level mission profile, the crew proceeded to the next preprogrammed targets, exiting enemy airspace and recovering at the nearest survivable airfield.

In the cruise missile mission profile and armed with a thermonuclear warhead, the B-1B's stores bulkhead was moved forward with the CSRL installed; the payload consisted of eight ALCMs, as well as four Air to Ground Missiles (AGMS) on the external pylons. Refueling was

B-1Bs on Dyess Air Force Base's flight line. *Dyess Air Force Base, 7th Bomb Wing Public Affairs*

the same as during the low-level mission profile. In this option the missiles were launched at high altitude, without the aircraft attempting to penetrate Soviet air space. The launch aircraft then landed at its designated or emergency SIOP recovery base.[3]

In a less known and publicized event, on October 1, 1986, a Dyess AFB B-1B assumed nuclear alert "cocked" status while the Air Force continued flight testing the four B-1A prototypes at Edwards AFB's Flight Test Center. Flight testing indicated operational deficiencies in some of the aircraft's systems. Regardless, SAC pushed forward with placing B-1Bs on nuclear alert as they were delivered to the various SAC bomb wings. Because SAC allocated B-1Bs to SIOP nuclear sorties, it was not tasked to fly operational conventional ground attack support missions during the 1991 Gulf War.[4]

On October 1, 1993, the 96th BW's B-1Bs came under control of the 7th BW, with specific organizations to support the bomber and its conventional bombing attack mission in support of the US military. The host unit was assigned to the 12th Air Force Headquarters at Davis-Monthan AFB, Arizona. The wing is a component of Air Combat Command Headquarters at Joint Base Langley-Eustis, Virginia.

7th Bomb Wing Operations Group

Responsible for executing global conventional bombing. With no official confirmation by Air Force sources, by 2000, all nuclear bombs and warheads had been removed from Dyess AFB's Special Weapons Storage area and were shipped to Kirkland AFB's nuclear stockpile site in New Mexico. The munitions area at Dyess AFB now supports B-1B conventional weapons delivery responsibilities. It is the Air Force's largest B-1B operations group, comprising thirty-six B-1Bs and approximately 1,100 personnel. Exact personnel numbers and their assigned AFSC numbers are not confirmed. The Operations Group consists of four squadrons: the 9th BS, 28th BS, the 7th Operations Support Squadron, and the 436th Training Squadron. The Operations Group combines the skills and experience of these squadrons to provide the application of firepower world-wide at short notice.

9th Bomb Squadron

Maintains combat readiness to deliver rapid, decisive air power on a large scale in support of conventional weapons warfare tasks. Squadron experts provide war fighting commanders with the best operational aircrews and B-1B aircraft. The squadron repairs, services, launches, recovers, and inspects B-1B aircraft, making them capable of sustained intercontinental missions and world-wide deployments and employment from forward operating locations. This squadron is the oldest active bomb squadron in the Air Force and its most recent combat involvement was during Operation ENDURING FREEDOM. The squadron flew more than 300 combat sorties during its four-month deployment in the middle of 2006 in support of America's global war on terror.

28th Bomb Squadron

The largest in the Air Force and largest flying squadron. Its primary mission is to provide all B-1B initial qualifications, re-qualifications, and instructor upgrade training for ACC. The squadron determines, evaluates, and implements formal training requirements to qualify crew members in long-range, day or night, all-weather, and air to ground attack missions. Each year, the squadron trains over 200 B-1B crew members. The squadron also maintains conventional combat readiness, supporting higher headquarters contingency world-wide operational deployments.

7th Operations Support Squadron

The squadron is responsible for B-1B combat effectiveness. It directs the wing's higher headquarters' designated flight operations, conventional mission planning, combat tactics, airfield management, aircrew training, exercise scheduling, weapons and tactics standardization, intelligence integration, war plans, deployment planning, weather support, small computer support, simulator training, air traffic control, and wing life support functions.

436th Training Squadron

Provides formal training to ACC using fifteen schools at Dyess AFB and thirty-eight other programs exported directly for local training needs. Training includes command and control; air, ground, and weapons safety; Air Force Resource Management System; classroom instructor training; Air Force Mission Support Systems administration; mission planning cell training; life support and survival; and computer software use and development. The squadron also develops multi-media formal presentations used in training program development. Multi-media personnel are based at Dyess AFB and deploy world-wide to perform their mission. Unit products and services are used throughout the Department of Defense.

7th Maintenance Group

Provides maintenance support to the 7th BW, deployed units, and associate units assigned there. The five units assigned are: Maintenance Operations Squadron, Aircraft Maintenance Squadron, Equipment Maintenance Squadron, Component Maintenance Squadron, and Munitions Squadron.

7th Maintenance Operations Squadron

The squadron supports the B-1B mission by managing and controlling aircraft maintenance and coordination of support to ensure aircraft availability. It also manages the wing's ancillary maintenance training program. It provides scheduling and analysis of maintenance and flying indicators for wing-level decisions on aircraft reliability and ensuring aircraft integrity.

7th Aircraft Maintenance Squadron

Provides aircraft maintenance assuring mission readiness for assigned B-1Bs to meet local and higher headquarters' taskings. The unit manages aircraft cannibalization and inspection programs to keep the B-1B fleet mission ready.

7th Equipment Maintenance Squadron

Provides aircraft maintenance support for B-1B, C-130, transient, and special mission aircraft. It is responsible for B-1B Phase Inspections, aircraft parts fabrication, and maintenance of aerospace ground equipment at Dyess AFB.

7th Component Maintenance Squadron

The squadron performs on and off equipment maintenance on the B-1Bs and C-130J-30s at Dyess AFB. It is responsible for the F-101 Engine Regional Repair Center—the only one in ACC—performing all major engine repairs for the B-1B fleet (currently the 7th BW at Dyess AFB), the 28th BW at Ellsworth AFB, and supporting B-1B test aircraft at Edwards AFB, California, and Eglin AFB, Florida. Squadron experts repair avionics, computer drive-in-flight control, and navigation and radar/electronic warfare components. It also maintains all B-1B ejection seats and fuel systems, rebuilds hydraulic components, and overhauls selected electrical components on B-1B and C-130J-30 aircraft.

7th Munitions Squadron

The squadron provides all munitions support for Dyess AFB's B-1B fleet. The unit is responsible for storing, maintaining, processing, and preparing all conventional munitions requirements in support of training and combat warfare tasks. The squadron is also responsible for maintaining all weapons release systems.

7th Munitions Support Group

The group provides operations and support for the base's population, which is similar to any city and is home to thousands of military personnel and their dependents. From family services to construction and security, the group keeps the physical installation and its members performing at peak efficiency while also preparing and supporting the base for its military requirements within the Air Force's expeditionary role. Skilled craftsmen operate a power plant, water plant, and waste treatment plant, making base operations self-sufficient. The group provides required base administrative, educational, communications, and computer system requirements, as well as managing lodging, food service, mortuary affairs, and child development functions. It also provides recreational activities for base personnel, dependents, and civilian workers through the fitness center, base library, and skill centers and clubs that are considered vital to the morale, health, and off-duty relaxation of the base community. The group's squadrons consist of Logistics, Security Force, Services, Communications, Contracting, and Civil Engineering.

7th Logistics Readiness Squadron

Responsible for home base logistics support, as well as mobility support of deployed forces. It provides supplies, equipment, and fuel to all base units, receiving and storing more than 388,000 pieces of government property valued at over $211,000,000. It fulfills the base's transportation requirements and maintains approximately 600 vehicles, operates the base taxi fleet, aircrew transportation, personnel assistance in shipping of personal property to new base assignments, recalling and training ready augmentation duty for personnel to support deployment exercises, and inspections and contingencies.

7th Security Forces Squadron

The squadron protects operational resources on the flight line, as well as patrolling the entire base in a traditional law enforcement role. As of 2013, the squadron maintained a continuous presence in Southwest Asia at undisclosed forward operating locations and keeps several mobility teams in peak readiness for world-wide contingency deployment. The squadron also functions as a base and local community support agency, providing services such as pass and id, auto registration (currently not required by the Department of Defense, with entrance to military bases a function of a valid active duty or retired military identification card), combat arms training, armory operations, investigations, military working dogs, and drug abuse resistance education for students.

7th Service Squadron

The squadron is the most widely diverse organization at Dyess AFB, providing more than twenty-one different activities for the base's population. It manages programs for the betterment of the base personnel's health and welfare. It also maintains a strong military deployment contingency, providing world-wide support.

7th Communications Squadron

The squadron provides communications and electronics maintenance on meteorological and navigational aid systems, doppler weather, and land mobile and air traffic control radios. It provides information system services, including computer networking, telephone (unclassified and classified secure), mail support, and protection and planning for all communications and information services. It provides visual information services, including graphic, photographic, and video support.

7th Contracting Squadron

The squadron solicits and awards more than 20,000 contracts, with more than $35,000,000 allocated (2012) each year. The squadron's experts are responsible for handling contracts covering operations and maintenance construction, services, supplies, and environmental contracting for the 7th BW, including all deployed units and services. The squadron also supplies emergency contracting operations during global contingency deployments and responds to support combat missions world-wide.

7th Civil Engineering Squadron

Base civil engineers maintain and repair all base facilities, conduct disaster preparedness training, fire protection and prevention activities, manage environmental programs, and handle housing responsibilities for unaccompanied personnel (previous base housing units for accompanied personnel are under private management). In addition to operating shops with craftsmen skilled in building trades, the squadron is ready for world-wide deployment of its Prime Base Engineer Emergency Force Contingency Teams that are equipped for short-notice movement to sustain the deployed team in a battlefield environment and perform wartime repair and construction.

7th Medical Group

Provides personalized health care through five military TRICARE Prime Teams staffed by board-certified family practice physicians, flight surgeons, pediatricians, internists, general medical officers, physician assistants, and nurse practitioners. The medical facility boasts specialty clinics for optometry, mental health, and general surgery. Additional services include immunizations, laboratory, radiology, physical therapy, and a pharmacy. It consists of the following squadrons: Medical Support, Aeromedical/Dental, and Medical Operations.[5]

The 7th Bomb Wing staff includes the Wing Operations Center, Plans, Judge Advocate, Public Affairs, Protocol, Anti-Terrorism, Manpower, Chapel, Treaty Office, Comptroller, Military Equal Opportunity, Air Park and Visitors Center, Honor Guard, Wing Administration, and Wing Career Advisor. The Wing Inspector General's office handles call wing inspections, exercises, IG complaints (fraud, waste, and abuse allegations), and licensed military attorneys in the Dyess AFB legal office and professional military paralegals. They provide services such as legal assistance on wills, power of attorney, domestic affairs, landlord and off base military tenant issues, Soldiers and Sailors Civil Relief ACT issues, consumer issues, and tax assistance.

In October 1994, the 384th BW disbanded, with the 28th BS transferred and assigned to Dyess AFB, replacing the 337th BS. In June 1995, two of the wing's B-1Bs (serial numbers 85-0082 and 84-0052), supported by KC-135 and KC-10 tankers, completed a nonstop, around-the-world Power Project flight in thirty-six hours and thirteen minutes code named CORONET BAT. The flight demonstrated the B-1B's global reach as previously completed by SAC's B-50s, B-47Es, and B-52Bs. This highlighted long-range, conventional weapons delivery flexibility in support of America's global war on terror.

The B-1B dropped a conventional bomb in action during the air campaign against Iraqi military forces on December 17, 1998. Two B-1Bs (86-0096, Ellsworth AFB, 28th BW; and 37th BS, and serial number 86-0135, Dyess AFB, 7th BW, 9th BS) using conventional MK-82 bombs took off from Sheikh Isa Air Base, Bahrain, at 23:30. Their assigned (designated) target was the Iraqi Republican Guard barracks at Alkut, Baghdad. The attack demonstrated the B-1B's integration into the complete air battle scenario of the Air Force's target attack options. An orbiting E-8 JSTARS based at Prince Sultan Air Base, Saudi Arabia, provided updated, real-time targeting information to the airborne aircraft. The airborne support package also consisted of two Navy F-14 Tomcats for fighter top cap protection, warning of any approaching Iraqi fighters that might launch; a Navy EA-6B Prowler for electronic countermeasures to interfere with Iraqi ground radar identification and missile guidance radars detecting the B-1Bs; two Navy Wild Weasel F/A-18s to destroy active identified Iraqi radars; and six Navy F/A-18s with conventional weapons stores to attack any identified collateral targets. The B-1Bs safely landed at Sheikh AB at 0700 the next morning after a pre-midnight launch.

On June 14, 2000, the 13th BS was re-activated at Dyess AFB as a supplement to the 7th BW, providing combat-ready aircrews, aircraft, and maintenance personnel to support the Aerospace Expeditionary Force (AEF). To improve the B-1B's conventional bomb delivery accuracy, on August 14, 2001, two 9th BS B-1Bs dropped JDAMs from 31,000 feet over the Utah Air Force Test Range, the first live drop for the 7th BW. This was critical, because after the United States was attacked on September 11, 2001, B-1Bs were again called upon to protect the United States.

In late December, the 7th BW sent elements of the 9th, 13th, and 28th Bomb Squadrons to Thumrait Air Base, Oman. B-1Bs played an important role in combat operations during Operation ENDURING FREEDOM. Air combat continued for Dyess B-1Bs on January 14, 2002, with the 13th BS deploying to continue support in Southwest Asia. During Operations IRAQI FREEDOM and ENDURING FREEDOM, B-1Bs completed 497 combat mission sorties, dropping 4,560,000 pounds of ordnance, with many released bombs classified as JDAMs. As of June 3, 2005, Dyess' 13th BS was inactivated, leaving the 9th and 28th Bomb Squadrons operational. Under the Defense Realignment and Closure Commission's decision of August 26, 2005, B-1Bs would be stationed at Ellsworth AFB, SD, and Dyess AFB, Texas. It was decided not to station the entire B-1B fleet at Dyess AFB, instead maintaining two widely separated operating locations. In September 2006, B-1Bs were again tasked to support air operations in Southwest Asia, with air operations directed by the 379th AEW at Al Udeid AB.[6]

In a February 3, 2009, Air Force dispatch from Southwest Asia:

> Keeping Lancers constantly ready to assist Coalition forces defeating terrorists are Airmen assigned to Dyess AFB's 7th Aircraft Maintenance Squadron in Southwest Asia. The majority of missions for the B-1B are used for close air support in Afghanistan and limited operations in Iraq [at that time]. It is in a close air support role because of the Sniper Advanced Targeting Pod, which allows the B-1B to identify targets at long distances without additional aids from other aircraft or ground support installations. This increases the B-1B's flexibility in attacking real-time targets of opportunity while orbiting above a battlefield area to support ground troops.[7]

To maintain 6,000 feet of runway at Dyess AFB a section had to be closed for major repairs, requiring the temporary relocation of twenty 7th BW B-1Bs and 500 support personnel to Ellsworth AFB in mid-September 2007. The construction was conducted to keep deteriorating sections of the runway from breaking into small debris that could cause damage to B-1B and C-130J-30 engines. This was scheduled in coordination with the 7th BW's deployment to Southwest Asia. Necessary repairs were scheduled to take two months. The Air Force employed Rapid Engineer Deployable Heavy Operation Squadron engineers to complete the construction project. Under its more common name, the Red Horse Team applied its war-time training to this construction project, as if deployed to a combat location. While the main runway section was closed, the reconstruction plan permitted C-130J-30s to continue flight operations on the taxiway. In the interim, new paint and temporary lights were installed to assure the safety and well being of crew members and the surrounding community.[8]

The history of the B-1B is one of continued adaptation from a nuclear SIOP bomber to a conventional close-air support role. Operating at 20,000 feet over the battlefield, the B-1B can loiter with up to thirty-five tons of precision guided munitions. When ground troops encounter enemy resistance, the B-1B's four crew members can engage in minutes because of its combat readiness and speed to target. The aircraft has a "shock and awe" perspective as well: when the B-1B flies at low altitude and high speed over enemy combatants in a non-lethal show of force, the 200,000 pound aircraft intimidated the enemy below. The Sniper Advanced Targeting Pod was added to the B-1B at the request of ground combat commanders of US Central Command in Southwest Asia. In 2010, the B-1B reached an aviation milestone: after twenty-five years of Air Force operations it became a more deadly precision airborne weapon platform. The laser can precisely target and minimize unintended damage when the enemy places hostile forces near schools, mosques, and non-combatants. The B-1B is to be completely upgraded by 2014, depending on continued congressional funding for advanced Pentagon programs.[9]

On April 9, 2010, Boeing B-1B Bomber Program Team members joined 7th BW personnel to celebrate the twenty-fifth anniversary of Air Force aircraft operations for the B-1B Lancer. The question arose if the B-1B was following in the footsteps of another Boeing bomber, the B-52 Stratofortress. The B-1B has supported US and coalition military forces around the world and began its Air Force service on June 29, 1985, at Dyess AFB, Texas.[10]

B-1B landing at Dyess Air Force Base. The rear landing trucks touched down first, with the nose gear held off the runway until speed had bled off, then slowly came down to touch the runway. The smoke is from the wheels impacting the runway. The rear flats and slats provide lift for the aircraft at slow speeds. The leading edge slats are fully extended during landing. *Dyess Air Force Base, 7th Bomb Wing Public Affairs*

As missions for the B-1B expand, increased training is essential for aircrew proficiency. The Training System Support Center (TSSC) is in the 28th BS building; while the name seems self explanatory, there is much more to training support than most people realize. Inside the TSSC are engineers hard at work, without the presence of military uniforms. TSSC is comprised of civilian employees who support B-1B aircrew training through software and hardware upgrades and maintenance of B-1 simulators. The flight simulator organization is under Detachment 4, 29th Training System Squadron, 53rd Wing, at Eglin AFB, Florida. TSSC employees are employed by Rockwell Collins Simulation & Training Solutions, LCC. Taskings for simulator upgrades are based on B-1B aircrew write-ups and new software and hardware implementation. Rockwell Collins engineers keep the simulator software and supporting hardware current with what is in the B-1B. When an aircraft modification is made, the same change or upgrade modification is made in the simulators. This is very important, because if a pilot could not learn a new instrument or system in the simulator they would have to fly sorties to gain proficiency, which is more costly. There is more than just the B-1B flight simulator at Dyess AFB. TSSC engineers ensure timely upgrades to Dyess AFB's ten simulators: weapon systems trainers, cockpit procedure trainers, simulated maintenance training systems, avionics and armament maintenance training systems, and mission trainers. The Dyess trainers are valued at more than 740 million dollars. In addition to the aircrew simulators, TSSC ensures maintenance training systems are kept current with aircraft system software and hardware.

Maintenance technicians use mission trainers to learn troubleshooting procedures and new software and hardware processes similar to the way aircrew members learn new operating procedures in their simulators. There are times when an upgrade to the maintenance system software or hardware may mirror an aircrew's system upgrade and, in the past, these upgrades would have been done independently on the operator and maintenance sides of the engineering arena, even though the changes were nearly identical. It was because of these redundancies in aircrew and maintenance training system upgrades that ACC Program Management proposed combining engineering efforts in 2004. TSSC is significant because the consolidation of the maintenance and

A first-generation Rockwell-International B-1B forward crew station mock-up simulator for pilot and copilot, 1985, on display at the South Dakota Air and Space Museum. *Author*

Rockwell-International first generation simulator of a B-1B aft crew station mock-up for offensive and defensive weapons officers, 1985. On display at the South Dakota Air and Space Museum. *Author*

operator training systems engineering, administration, and overall structure will streamline how the organization does its training, ultimately saving the Air Force considerable funds. B-1B support organizations at Ellsworth and Dyess AFB perform essentially the same tasks, such as site management, network administration, configuration management, master library maintenance, and other administrative functions. All of the engineering processes are identical and the application of those processes differs only with respect to the specific training device being modified.

TSSC consolidation eliminated redundancies and streamlined the support functions. Combining site operations and key engineering staff from Ellsworth AFB, 28th BW, with the engineering staff at Dyess AFB reduced manning from forty-seven to thirty-six personnel. The combined improvements to TSSC efficiency and productivity will give the B-1B wings more effective, concurrent training capabilities through the coincident releases of aircrew simulator and maintenance trainer upgrades and enhancements. With increased emphasis on simulator training, the capabilities of the simulators will be constantly upgraded to meet training and mission requirements.[11]

In 2011, the Air Force continued to upgrade its B-1B flight simulator trainers at Dyess and Ellsworth AFB to maintain aircrew proficiency and increase aerial combat skills. The cost of the upgrade project was $18,400,000. The upgrades to the flight simulators provided fully updated visual and sensor databases, as well as updates to the simulators' projectors and display screens. This updated the 1995 simulator to 2011, allowing B-1B aircrews to train on what they are actually flying in an operational B-1B airborne flight training sortie or combat in Southwest Asia. These updates to the B-1B simulator training system include improved real-beam radar and high resolution mapping radar pictures that give those inside the simulator comparable operational B-1B radar imagery. Visual and sensor system upgrades provide imagery to the trainer's laptop-controlled targeting pod display in electro-optical and infrared modes, creating a real flight operational scenario. These upgrade benefits provide sustainability and ease of maintenance for weapon system trainers. The upgrades enhance training resources to be more effective in aircrew training, increasing their combat capability. In 2013, the Air Force was reducing flying hours and the use of simulators was increasing.[12]

On March 15, 2011, the last operational B-1B at Dyess AFB received modifications to operate the Sniper Advanced Targeting Pod. Beginning in November 2010, the 7th Maintenance Group "Maintainers" installed wiring throughout the B-1B so operators could control the Sniper Pod through a laptop onboard computer. The aircraft can carry the largest payload of precision-guided and unguided weapons in the Air Force inventory, as well as travel at speeds of more than 900 mph. The new system allows aircrews to look ahead with long-range video to determine what is happening on the ground. Instead of relying on radar to identify a target, aircrews and commanders will have eyes on the target. It stabilizes the image and allows them to use a laser beam to target and engage in real time. It also allows aircrews to give their own immediate BDA. The Sniper Pod has streaming capability, providing the B-1B crew with the ability to downlink the video recorded by the Sniper Pod to let personnel on the ground see exactly what the aircraft crew saw. The Air Force started developing the Sniper Pod in 2007. The system began operating in Southwest Asia in 2008. In October 2010, Boeing Aircraft completed the first of two modifications making the Sniper Pod initially operationally capable. Additional or following modifications were made to the B-1B's Central Integrated Test System and Vertical Situation Display Unit under Air Force FY 2012 budget appropriations.[13]

As the sophistication of the B-1B flight simulator developed it became full motion, with complete external visual displays fully duplicating what pilots encounter when airborne. The simulator is in use at Ellsworth AFB (28th BW) and Dyess AFB (7th BW). The simulator shown here is at Dyess Air Force Base. *Dyess Air Force Base, 7th BW Public Affairs*

On March 22, 2011, the 337th Test and Evaluation Squadron began the first phase of testing of a Multiple Ejector Rack (MER) on a Dyess AFB B-1B. The modified rotary launcher will increase the number of 500-pound JDAMs and laser guided JDAMs that can be carried by the B-1B from fifteen to forty-eight. With this upgrade, one B-1B can carry and deliver up to four times as many precision-guided weapons as the B-52H. The B-1B's MER has a mixed load capability, meaning each bomb bay can hold an assortment of JASSMs, precision-guided 2,000-pound, and the now 500-pound JDAMs. The capability to carry so many different weapons on the same bomb rack gives B-1B aircrews greater targeting flexibility during combat support missions. Aircrews from the 337th TES and 419th Flight Test Squadron at Edwards AFB flew a Dyess AFB 7th BW B-1B on March 22 equipped with a MER and successfully released two dummy 500-pound JDAMs over the China Lake Missile Test Range, California. The aircrew flew another successful mission on March 24 to validate the release and separation safe distance from the aircraft's bomb bay of a 500-pound JDAM from the modified rotary launcher. The upgrade enables the B-1B to attack and destroy twice the number of targets, saving the Air Force money, and also places fewer airmen at risk.[14]

In early June 2012, Dyess AFB began an advanced hardware and software upgrades as part of the Sustainment Block 16 Program. This program consists of a fully integrated data link in the aft station and a vertical situation display upgrade in the front station, as well as updates to navigation, radar, and diagnostic systems. The aft crew station received five new color displays, all capable of providing moving maps and data link integration. Weapon System Officers received full "querty" keyboards and new controllers to interface with the Integrated Battle Station software.

A new MIDS LVT-1 radio using Integrated Battle Station capabilities provides the B-1B access to the Link-16 network, allowing the B-1B to send and receive text messages, imagery, and mission assignments. Fully integrated data link assignments interface directly with the aircraft, allowing combat commanders to transmit target sets directly to weapons onboard the B-1B. The fully integrated data link upgrades primarily support the weapon systems officers in the aft station. Sustainment Block-16 includes vertical situation display upgrades for the front station. Pilots received a new digital flight instrument display, providing more precise flight parameters. The pilot (aircraft commander) and copilot stations received new eight by ten inch multi-function displays and the cursor control that was installed in the aft station. The new situation displays provide independent moving maps and link information to the front station, supplying identical information available to the aft station. Fully integrated data link and vertical situation display upgrades completed the developmental testing at Edwards AFB. Development testing for the entire Sustainment Block-16 package started in March 2013, with the 337th TES operationally testing in September 2013.[15]

President Obama chartered a new direction in US military strategy under Secretary of Defense Leon Panetta (who resigned in 2013), shifting western Pacific air power responsibilities to the B-1Bs assigned to the 28th BW and 7th BW at Ellsworth and Dyess AFB, respectively.

The B-1B has become the aerial workhorse of the Southwest Asia aerial campaign, supporting US and coalition troops up until 2014.

More than 400 Dyess AFB airmen returned from an undisclosed location in Southwest Asia on July 25-26, 2012, after being deployed there for six months in support of Operation ENDURING FREEDOM. This marked the largest deployment of B-1Bs and supporting personnel since 2002. Families and friends waited, holding signs and banners, while others waived and screamed as airmen came off their aircraft and down the stairs to the parking apron. The 9th EBS and 9th Expeditionary Aircraft Maintenance Unit (EAMU) provided more than twenty-five percent of the total fixed-wing, close-air support for coalition ground forces in Afghanistan every day by launching the most B-1B sorties executed on a single deployment in the last ten years of sustained operations. Over the course of the six-plus month deployment, the Dyess AFB squadron flew more than 770 in-country combat sorties—over 9,500 hours of B-1B flight time—providing twenty-four hour coverage, seven days a week, to coalition ground forces. The 9th EBS and 9th EAMU completed a complex B-1B Sustainment Block upgrade while maintaining combat operations and avoided degradation and support of ongoing close air, ground support missions. The upgrade was completed to all nine deployed Dyess AFB B-1Bs in six days, fulfilling an Air Force operational requirement to fully integrate the Sniper Targeting Pod onto the bomber and thereby providing machine to machine electronic interface between the carried Sniper Targeting Pod and onboard weapons, reducing time on target by one-third. The modifications ensured full operational capability for the B-1B to employ the GBU-5L Laser JDAM, providing the combined forces air component commander with the first ever B-1B capability to engage and destroy moving targets on the ground.[16]

In September 2013, Dyess AFB B-1B aircrews took to the skies with aspirations of representing the 7th BW as the premier bomb wing during the third annual Global Strike Challenge (GSC). The challenge is the world's premier bomber, ICBM, and security forces competition, with units participating from Air Force Global Strike Command, Air Combat Command, Air Force Reserve, and Air National Guard. Through competition and team work the event fosters esprit de corps, recognizes outstanding personnel and teams, and improves combat capabilities. The bomber portions of GSC had three main components for aircrews to earn points:

1. Bomb score. Aircrews are judged on how close bombs are dropped to the targets.
2. Timing Control. Aircrews are penalized for every second—early or late—the bombs hit the targets.
3. Real world combat bombing scenario for scoring.

The challenge increases real-world combat capabilities for the 9th BS, 28th BS, Operations Support Squadron, and the 337th Test and Evaluation Squadron.[17]

From October 15 through 17, 2012, Team Dyess was tested on their ability to deploy personnel and assets to a deployed location in support of combatant commanders during an Operational Readiness Exercise (ORE). During this exercise known as "Phase I ORE," Dyess was evaluated on the wing's ability to prepare and mobilize from peacetime readiness to wartime posture on short notice. Areas included command and control, deployment processing, employment readiness, information operations, and force protection. Preparing for the October 2014 Operational Readiness Inspection (ORI) gave wing leadership the opportunity to observe the state of readiness and the base's ability to rapidly deploy to a down range location.[18]

On January 18, 2013, the 7th Bomb Wing was awarded an overall "Excellent" grade following the Headquarters Air Combat Command inspector general's first Consolidated Unit Inspection. The comprehensive inspection began on January 13, combining numerous evaluations and assessments from multiple agencies to accomplish a comprehensive and consolidated look at a wing's compliance with their peacetime and wartime mission directives. During the inspection, more than 160 inspectors closely examined how well the 7th BW's programs, plans, and procedures follow Air Force instructions and Department of Defense directives. The inspection results are graded on the Air Force five-tier grading scale: outstanding, excellent, satisfactory, marginal, and unsatisfactory. During the IG's out-briefing, 157 airmen were recognized as superior performers, as well as twenty-six superior performing teams.[19]

From January 24 through 29, 2013, B-1Bs from the 7th BW participated in a combined training exercise called COMPTUEX in support of the USS *Harry S. Truman* (CVN 75) Strike Group (HSTSG). COMPTUEX was a series of training scenarios designed to certify the HSTSG as a deployment ready fighting force capable of operations in overseas theaters (such as the Western Pacific, in the Sea of Japan, and South China Sea). The exercise incorporated a myriad of missions, including air defense, maritime interdiction, and anti-submarine warfare. 7th BW aircrews participated in the exercise by providing joint maritime defense for the HSTSG. The COMPTUEX scenario involved a friendly ally at war in a highly volatile area prone to terrorism. Training vessels and personnel played the role of hostile forces within each scenario. The role of the B-1B during the exercise was providing a convoy armed over watch, this time a US Navy carrier strike group. The area B-1Bs protect in a Joint Maritime Defense (JMD) role is extremely vast, and part of that tactical problem is where threats are and protecting US Navy assets. The 337th TES wrote a bulletin on JMD tactics, techniques, and procedures, specifically using their current communications (pre-Link 16) structure and soon-to-be fully fielded Advanced Targeting Pod Sensor enhancement. This multi-service exercise is part of a new Department of Defense initiative referred to as the Air-Sea Battle (ASB) concept. The primary target is China, guaranteeing the US Navy's presence in the Western Pacific in the Sea of Japan, especially along the Korean Peninsula and the South China Sea. The ASB concept guides US military forces as they work together to maintain the US advantage against the global proliferation of advanced military technologies and anti-access/area denial capabilities. ASB is designed to leverage military and technological capabilities that reflect US Navy, Marine Corps, and Air Force collaboration.[20]

On February 12 through 13, 2013, budget, Air Force culture, and comprehensive airmen fitness were the main themes during the Air Combat Command commander's first visit to Dyess AFB, 7th BW. US Air Force Gen. G. Michael Hostage III (assumed command of ACC on September 13, 2011) told members of the 7th BW:

> The fact that we continue to live like this is because one-tenth of one percent of our society is willing to fight and die for our freedom. We all grew up free to make our own choices because generations ago someone put on a uniform and fought and died to protect that freedom for us. I have kids and grandchildren who will grow up with that freedom because each one of you chose to put on a uniform. It doesn't matter how long you serve, every bit of service is important because you are preserving something that really is unique in the history of humanity and freedom.[21]

On February 22, 2013, Dyess AFB maintainers learned hot pit refueling from airmen assigned to Ellsworth AFB, 28th BW, 28th Maintenance Group. Hot pit refueling is a procedure that rapidly refuels an aircraft as maintenance crews perform safety checks while the aircrew remains in the cockpit with the aircraft running. This is a new procedure for the B-1B, and this aircraft refueling tactic increases the longevity of the aircraft and decreases the time spent on the ground. In the past few months, 28th MXG maintainers have incorporated hot pit refueling B-1B bombers and are now passing on the knowledge to Dyess AFB airmen. During the first training a B-1B landed, taxied to the refueling area, and shut down the right side engines so the airmen could get on that side of the aircraft and fill it with fuel. This is helpful for the aircrew, as it allows them to keep systems running instead of shutting them off, decreasing the time it takes to re-launch the aircraft. While hot pit refueling decreases the time it takes to launch a sortie aircraft parts are preserved, with the aircraft requiring less maintenance. By saving time and putting less stress on the aircraft, money and man hours are being saved, both crucial for an aircraft that has been operating since 1985. This refueling process can be used to launch jets with lighter fuel loads, allowing less stress on the aircraft, which in turn also helps with the longevity of the B-1B. Though from separate bases, Dyess and Ellsworth AFB maintainers work together to ensure the B-1B stays current and mission ready.[22]

Aircrews from the 9th Bomb and 77th Weapons Squadrons partnered with Joint Terminal Attack Controllers (JTACs) from Fort Sill, Oklahoma, during a joint training exercise held April 29 through May 3 near Snyder, Texas. The exercise was conducted to prepare B-1B aircrews for future contingency operations and to keep JTAC* combat skills proficient. The exercise was composed of multiple realistic scenarios consisting of both day and night operations, where JTACs on the ground directed close air support and precision attacks of Dyess B-1Bs against simulated high-value targets attempting to evade detection and capture. Training scenarios included Dyess personnel portraying insurgents planting Improvised Explosive Devices (IEDs) along dirt roads to see if B-1B crews could locate them, report their behavior, and conduct simulated air strikes against their positions. B-1s were also directed to follow moving vehicle targets, giving aircrews a chance to test the aircraft's recent Sniper Advanced Target Sensor Enhancement modification. Throughout the simulated enemy engagements, JTACs were required to defend their position against enemy aggressors while maintaining contact and directing aircraft overhead.[23]

The 337th Test and Evaluation Squadron successfully completed their first captive carry test of a Long Range Anti-Ship Missile (LRASM) on board a B-1B bomber on June 17, 2013; a significant step forward in the B-1B's role in a maritime environment. Designed and developed by the Defense Advanced Research Projects Agency (DARPA) and the Office of Naval Research, the LRASM is based off the Joint Air to Surface Standoff Missile Extended Range (JASSM-ER) and was constructed as part of an effort to overcome challenges faced by current anti-ship missiles penetrating sophisticated enemy air defense systems. The point of this program is not to field a missile, but to demonstrate the new technologies the Department of Defense wants to put into an anti-surface warfare Joint Air to Surface Standoff Missile (JASSM) variant.

Because the LRASM leverages the state-of-the-art JASSM-ER airframe, it proved to be a seamless transition for the B-1B team in terms of compatibility, significantly reducing the time and costs of traditional weapons testing. When the B-1B looks at this missile it reads it as a JASSM-ER. In turn, DARPA was able to exploit that capability and simply add on the new technology to expedite cost. Currently (July 2013), JASSM officials are doing everything they can to take this missile's technology and move it into a program that would eventually become operational. However, while the LRASM does utilize the airframe of the JASSM-ER, it incorporates additional sensors and systems to achieve a stealthy and survivable subsonic cruise missile, as well as a weapon data link and an enhanced anti-jam GPS to detect and destroy specific targets within a group of ships. One of the biggest improvements of this weapon is its ability to receive target or coordinate updates in-flight. Unlike JASSMs "fire and forget" mentality, this new technology gives the crew

* JTACs are highly skilled military personnel who, from a forward position through radio communication, direct combat aircraft engaged in close air support operations against lawful targets and combatants.

the chance to "fire and change their mind." Because of the standoff feature these weapons possess, they tend to be in-flight for some time. For B-1B crews to be able to change its coordinates on the fly provides them with greater flexibility.

The overarching concept behind the B-1B's rise in the maritime environment can be attributed to the Department of Defense's much discussed Air-Sea Battle (ASB), in which long range bombers serve as a key target. ASB is designed to guide the four branches of the armed forces as they work together to maintain a continued US advantage against global proliferation of advanced military technologies and anti-access/area denial capabilities. In preparing for this type of mission, a 9th Expeditionary Squadron B-1B, 379th Air Expeditionary Wing, participated in Exercise Spartan Kopis in the Arabian Gulf on August 13, 2013. Spartan Kopis was a US 5th Fleet training event that validates the effectiveness of using joint aviation assets in a maritime environment, as well as exercising joint force command and control structure and communications.[24]

Southwest Asia operations do not appear to be going away any time soon. The 9th Expeditionary Bomb Squadron, deployed from Dyess AFB, is airborne throughout the US Air Force Central Command area of responsibility in support of Operation ENDURING FREEDOM (OEF). Flying missions nearly 24/7/365, one of the B-1B's capabilities and key roles at the 379th Air Expeditionary Wing is to provide combat air support to troops on the ground through their long range bombing capability. Serving as the backbone of America's long range bomber force, the B-1B carries the largest payload of guided and unguided munitions in the Air Force.[25]

On January 21, 2014, the first operational B-1B equipped with the Integrated Battle Station (IBS) upgrade landed at Dyess AFB.

Real-time communication networks will allow for immediate mission planning and much quicker in-flight target changes. As the threat changes, so can coordination with allied forces, enabling the B-1B to reach and target new strike locations. With the Link-16 network, the B-1B crew can connect through FIDL, which is already being used on many other aircraft platforms, so integration with allied forces is nearly seamless. Full battlefield communication and information exchanges will greatly improve mission planning and provide real-time mission feedback. With the new IBS upgrade to the B-1B, the mission capabilities of the aircraft could evolve as new mission sets arise in the theater of operations. Although Dyess AFB received the first operational IBS upgraded B-1B, the upgrade program is scheduled to continue through 2019, with Ellsworth AFB, South Dakota, also receiving upgraded aircraft.[26]

A Dyess B-1B undergoing hot refueling with the right side engines turned off, leaving the left side engines running and powering all onboard aircraft systems. *Dyess Air Force Base, 7th BW Public Affairs*

To keep the B-1B Lancers ready to operate now and well into the integrated battlefield of the future, the 419th Test Squadron began testing Sustainment Block 16A (SB 16A) software upgrades at Dyess AFB starting on April 1, 2014. The SB 16A is considered "fielding" configuration software that will provide enhancements to the recently added glass cockpit configuration. The glass cockpit is part of the Lancer's Integrated Battle Station modification that increases Link 16 capabilities. The SB 16A configuration is expected to improve situational awareness for all B-1B aircrew members, increase the maintainability of the aircraft, and provide data link capabilities to the field. Major software enhancements include improved integration between the B-1B's offensive avionics system, various onboard sensors, and data link, resulting in improved battle space awareness for both the B-1B aircrew and fellow strike package assets.

The new displays and interface will have such a great impact on B-1B tactics and situational awareness that the team is learning and identifying how the new aircraft will be used. This has also changed the B-1B testing philosophy; the Air Force had to adapt B-1B testing to the new system. The 419th Flight Test Squadron plans to test the upgrades in four phases; the final phase will be the configuration that B-1B aircrews use during combat operations. SB 16A testing builds on and merges prior tests that included, but were not limited to, the IBS with new glass cockpit design, updated Inertial Navigation Systems (INS), and the B-1B Radar Reliability and Maintainability Improvement Program. The flight and ground tests will be accomplished in four phases, each relating to a different software drop and ultimately resulting in the first operational fielding of the new cockpit design. SB 16A testing is projected to end in February 2015.[27]

The pace of the B-1B's worldwide deployments is not without cost. Lt. Col. Shane Henderson, Chief, Air Combat Command's B-1B Weapons Sustainment Team, stated in October 2014 that the command's aging bombers need more money and maintainers to keep up the pace of operations:

Dyess airmen cleaning a Sniper Pod's forward optics prior to a B-1B takeoff. *Dyess Air Force Base, 7th Bomb Wing Public Affairs*

> The least ready aircraft in the Air Force's fleet in fiscal 2014 is also one of the busiest, the B-1B Lancer [Ellsworth and Dyess AFB]. The long-range strike bomber saw a mission capable rate of 47.7 percent in fiscal year 2014, down from 57.7 percent in 2013. The aircraft saw a 23.2 percent break rate in 2014, with 38.4 percent of those fixed within twenty-four hours. While these numbers might be staggering at first glance, there's a lot more to B-1 operations and how the Air Force handles its Lancer fleet. Just to give you an idea of the B-1, the average age of the fleet is twenty-seven years. It's over its designed life span. Each aircraft has 8,700 hours on it. Over the past ten years there's 23,000 hours per year on the fleet. They're doing a lot of flying, and a lot of flying in combat environments. We've done a good job adapting with our sixty-two aircraft. The aircraft have flown extensively in combat in every conflict the Air Force has seen, including recent operations in Iraq against terrorist captured territory in Syria and Iraq referred to as the Islamic State, or ISIS or ISIL. These are largely close air support missions, a type of combat the aircraft was never expected to be involved in when it was originally designed.
>
> The airplane's a little tired. It's been flying a long time past its designated life. Because of this, B-1s are finding new and inventive ways of breaking. To combat this, Air Combat Command has several upgrade, maintenance, and testing plans for the fleet. These plans take multiple B-1s out of service at a time, contributing to its low mission capable rate. The upgrades include a new wheel brake systems improvement program, which will make the aircraft's wheel and brake system 500 percent more reliable. Crews are inspecting and repairing the B-1s' wings after discovering cracks on the structure of the wings, along with preemptively fixing the skin on the aircraft's wings. These changes are taking place while the Air Force is upgrading the B-1's integrated battle station, which is the largest modification ever done to the aircraft's weapon systems. The Air Force is also doing full-scale fatigue testing on the B-1s, shaking the aircraft to try to get in front of structural breaks and plan around what problems can arise.

B-1s are flying hard and we have diminishing sources of repair. They are breaking in ways we haven't seen in the past. Because of these modifications, over the next couple of years you'll see a decrease in mission capable rates by design. Currently [October 2014] there are eleven B-1s in depot maintenance at Tinker Air Force Base, Oklahoma, with an average stay of between 180 and 200 days. The wing modifications are done together to maximize the amount of work we're doing while the aircraft is down. We absolutely look for every effort we can to consolidate maintenance. The idea is short-term pain for long-term gain by having B-1s stand down for maintenance so they can keep flying at a high operational tempo.[28]

Working to reinvigorate its nuclear force after missteps and scandal, the Air Force has put a four-star general in charge for the first time in the post-Cold War era. His mission is to restore institutional muscle and assert more influence on the force's behalf. Gen. Robin Rand takes over amid optimism that the Air Force has put its nuclear force back on track after reports revealed the force had atrophied and morale had suffered, in part because of a lack of resources. The days of having a four-star nuclear command ended at the close of the Cold War when the United States dismantled the Strategic Air Command; the Air Force's strategic bombers were reassigned to the Air Combat Command and the Air Force Space Command took control of the ICBM forces. (This was corrected when the Air Force Global Strike Command consolidated control of all bombers effective October 1, 2015, for B-1Bs at Ellsworth AFB, South Dakota, and Dyess AFB, Texas; B-52Hs at Minot AFB, North Dakota, and Barksdale AFB, Louisiana; and B-2s at Whiteman AFB, Missouri.) AFGSC also controls the nation's 450 Minuteman III ICBMs. If required, the conventional mission B-1Bs can now seamlessly integrate into an increased nuclear deterrent mission as directed by the president of the United States. General Rand has been tasked with maintaining a credible nuclear force.[29]

DYESS AIR FORCE BASE LINEAR AIR PARK

The Dyess AFB Linear Air Park originated from the Texas Museum of Military History, founded in 1981. The air park was dedicated at Dyess AFB on June 12, 1991, by Lieutenant Gen.Robert D. Beckel, Commander, 15th Air Force. The historic aircraft on display represent the success and untold sacrifices of the members of the US armed forces since WWII. Each aircraft has earned its status in the annals of Air Force history with a special place in the hearts of men and women who served with them. Dyess AFB is the permanent home for these aircraft. Dyess AFB's air power warriors have preserved America's freedom during war, peace, and currently, the global war on terrorism. The majority of aircraft on display are on custody loan from the National Museum of the United States Air Force, Wright-Patterson AFB, Dayton, Ohio. The air park is a 1.2 mile long outdoor aircraft static display area showing a wide variety of Air Force air power. Each aircraft on static display is assigned a sponsor. These sponsors volunteered and continue to volunteer countless hours restoring and maintaining these aircraft to museum display quality. Aircraft color schemes and markings show the squadron and era in which the aircraft flew in an attempt to display the far-ranging history of that particular make and type of aircraft—not necessarily the particular aircraft itself. There are thirty-two aircraft and missiles on display. There is one additional aircraft on display at the Dyess AFB front gate and another at the Dyess elementary school. A memorial wall in the air park is designed to display historical and heroic actions by Air Force units and personnel. Additional information on the air park is available from 7th BW public affairs (1-915-696-2196).

Dyess Air Force Base Linear Air Park Aircraft

- Curtis P-40 Warhawk (replica) (on display at Dyess AFB front gate)
- Douglas A-26C Invader
- Boeing B-52D Stratofortress
- North American Rockwell Hound Dog Air to Surface Missile
- Boeing B-17G Flying Fortress
- Boeing EB-47E Stratojet
- Douglas Aircraft Company EB-66 Destroyer
- Glen L. Martin EB-57B Canberra
- North-American Rockwell International B-1B Lancer
- Lockheed Corporation F-104A Starfighter
- McDonnell Aircraft F-101B Voodoo
- North American Aviation F-100C Super Sabre
- North American Aviation F-86L Sabre Jet
- Northrop Aircraft F-89H Scorpion
- Douglas Aircraft Company MB1/AIR-2 Genie Air to Air missile
- Republic Aviation F-105D Thunderjet
- Republic Aviation RF-84F Thunderflash
- Republic Aviation F-84F Thunderstreak
- McDonnell Aircraft F-4D Phantom (on display at the William Dyess Elementary School)
- General Dynamics F-111 Aardvark
- North American Aviation T-6F Texan
- Cessna Aircraft O-2A Skymaster
- Beechcraft Aircraft T-34B Mentor
- Cessna Aircraft T-37B Tweety
- Convair T-29C Flying Classroom
- Lockheed Aircraft T-33A Shooting Star
- Northrop Corporation T-38A Talon
- North American T-39A Saberliner
- Boeing Aircraft KC-135A Stratotanker
- Boeing Aircraft KC-97L Stratofreighter
- Douglas Aircraft C-47A Skytrain
- Fairchild Aircraft Industries C-123K Provider
- Lockheed Aircraft C-130A Hercules
- DeHavilland C-7A Caribou
- Grumman Aircraft Corporation HU-16E Albatross[1]

Over 14,000 Warhawks were built by the end of production in 1944. On March 17, 2006, an honorary piece of Dyess AFB history made its final flight home when a replica of Lt. Col. William A. Dyess' P-40 Warhawk "Kibosh" was flown to base in the cargo hold of a Hercules C-130 from a Southern California Air Force base. Because the original P-40 was destroyed in a crash in 1942 while being flown by Lt. Jack Donnalson—who survived the crash—the Abilene Chamber of Commerce, in coordination with Dyess AFB, commissioned a replica built for display just outside the main Dyess AFB gate. Like the original, it is painted to represent Lt. Col. Dyess' P-40 as it would have appeared in WWII, adorned in olive drab military color with "US Army" painted on the wings' underside.

Curtis P-40 Warhawk (replica) at the front gate to Dyess Air Force Base, Texas. *7th Bomb Wing Public Affairs*

In 1942, Lt. Col. Dyess was stationed in the Philippines with the 21st Pursuit Squadron and made himself a name by leading an outnumbered and severely under-supplied group of aviators that terrorized the Japanese first from the air and then, when supplies ran so low they could no longer fly, from the ground. It was during these months that Lt. Col. Dyess earned his reputation as a "one man scourge." By April 8, 1942, the unit was starving and could no longer resist Japanese attacks. Rather than abandon his men, Lt. Col. Dyess ordered Lt. Donnalson to fly to safety in "Kibosh." Dyess stayed with the surviving members of the squadron, eventually surrendering to the Japanese. Lt. Donnalson crash-landed the P-40 on the island of Cebu because the landing gear was inoperative. Lt. Col. Dyess' decision to surrender led to his forced participation in the eighty-five-mile Bataan Death March, which he was lucky to survive. Later, he managed to escape from prison camp and fought alongside Filipino forces before eventually returning to the United States. While airborne in a Lockheed P-38 Lightning, it caught fire over a heavily populated area. Instead of bailing out and allowing the P-38 to crash and possibly harm civilians below he turned the fighter away from the area before it crashed, killing him.

The replica P-40 was built by Ron (father) and Leon (son) Starr, requiring a year of careful labor. These two have been building aircraft together for the past thirty years and have built airplanes for museums and Air Force bases around the world, including for the movie *The Aviator*. Starr Aircraft is the only company that still builds replica aircraft from metal, only building three to five aircraft per year. The replica is mounted on a concrete pedestal in front of the "Welcome to Dyess AFB" sign at the front gate.[2]

★ Douglas Aircraft A-26C Invader

Douglas A-26C Invader at the Dyess Air Force Base Linear Air Park, Texas. *7th Bomb Wing Public Affairs*

The Invader was one of the most unheralded US aircraft during its many years of military and civilian service. It was often overshadowed by more glamorous types or assigned combat roles that kept it out of public view. It amassed an operational combat record the likes of which few other US aircraft have achieved. It is one of the few American aviation designs to be developed, evaluated, and produced during WWII. It has the distinction of being one of the few US combat aircraft to serve in WWII, the Korean War, and the Vietnam War.

The A-26 first flew in 1942, and by 1945, it was used throughout the European and Pacific theaters of operation. Modified A-26s saw duty as night intruders against pin-point targets, as well as night fighters. They also served as armed intruders during the Korean War, providing ground support to US, Republic of South Korea Army, and United Nations troops. In 1948, the Air Force Intruder was re-designated the B-26. The Air Force wanted it classified as a light bomber instead of an attack aircraft. The Vietnam War resulted in more roles for the B-26. It was equipped with new radar and other modifications allowing it to support special forces during night missions. Some B-26s accompanied jet fighters in daylight attacks, bombing ground targets the jets could not reach.

The air park's A-26 was delivered to the Air Force on July 9, 1948, assigned to Biggs AFB, Texas. It was removed from the Air Force inventory in April 1958 and was later modified into a civil transport and flying test bed.

DOUGLAS AIRCRAFT A-26C
Specifications and Performance Information

Manufacturer	Douglas Aircraft
Designation	A-26
Version (variant)	"C"
Serial number	44-35913
Nickname	Invader
Equivalent	B-26C
Type	Light attack bomber
Crew	Pilot, copilot/bombardier, gunner
7th Bomb Wing sponsor	28th Bomb Squadron
Length	51 feet 3 inches
Tail height	18 feet 6 inches
Wingspan	70 feet
Wing area	540 square feet
Empty weight	22,850 pounds
Gross weight	27,600 pounds
Maximum weight	35,000 pounds
Power plant	(two) Pratt & Whitney 2,000 hp R-2800-27 engines
Maximum range	1,400 miles
Cruising speed	284 mph
Maximum speed	337 mph
Service ceiling	22,100 feet
Armament	(8) .50-caliber machine guns
Bombs (internal)	4,000 pounds
External	Under wing mounted rockets

★ Boeing B-52D Stratofortress

The B-52 began its life in 1946, the same year the Strategic Air Command (SAC) was formed. It was designed to deliver atomic and then thermonuclear bombs to targets at intercontinental range. The Air Force needed a long-range, heavy, strategic bomber to meet this mission. Boeing was awarded a contract to begin engineering studies and preliminary design on a long-range turbojet bomber. A pair of experimental XB-52s was funded in September 1947. On November 29, 1951, the XB-52 prototype was pulled out of Boeing's production building. It was followed by the rollout of the YB-52 on March 15, 1952. Interestingly, the YB-52 flew before the XB-52, on April 15, 1952. The XB-52 prototype made its first flight in October.

During the Vietnam War, Dyess AFB deployed nineteen B-52Ds to support US and South Vietnamese Army troops in Southeast Asia. The final Stratofortress Linebacker II missions were flown on December 29, 1972. During Linebacker II, SAC's B-52s dropped more than 49,000 bombs and destroyed or damaged more than 1,600 military structures and 373 pieces of railroad equipment. An estimated three million gallons of North Vietnamese petroleum products were destroyed. B-52 rear gunners were credited with two confirmed MiG kills. This success came at a great cost: the loss of fifteen B-52s. After the Vietnam War, the 96th BW continued to fly the B-52D before converting to the B-52H and then transitioning to the B-1B Lancer.

The air park's B-52D saw extensive combat in Southeast Asia and was damaged by a North Vietnamese SA-2 SAM on April 9, 1972. It was repaired and the aircraft flew four more combat missions during Linebacker II. It is displayed on a concrete slab cut from Dyess AFB's original runway.

Boeing B-52D Stratofortress at the Dyess Air Force Base Linear Air Park, Texas. *7th Bomb Wing Public Affairs*

BOEING B-52D STRATOFORTRESS
Specifications and Performance Information

Manufacturer	Boeing Aircraft
Designation	B-52
Version (variant)	"D"
Serial number	56-0685
Type	Heavy bomber
Crew	Pilot, co-pilot, navigator, radar navigator, Electronic Warfare officer, gunner
7th Bomb Wing sponsor	28th Bomb Squadron
Length	156 feet 6 inches
Tail height	48 feet 4 inches
Wingspan	185 feet
Wing area	4,000 square feet
Gross weight	180,000 pounds
Maximum weight	450,000 pounds
Power plant	(8) Pratt & Whitney 8,000 pound thrust J-57-P-19W engines
Cruising speed	521 mph
Maximum speed	660 mph
Combat ceiling	46,350 feet
Range (unrefueled)	6,200 miles (combat loaded), 10,000 miles (ferry)
Armament	(4) .50-caliber machine guns in tail turret
Bomb load (internal)	(84) 500 pound bombs -or- (42) 750 pound bombs
External	(24) 750 pound bombs

North American Rockwell Hound Dog Air-to-Surface Missile at the Dyess Air Force Base Linear Air Park, Texas. *7th Bomb Wing Public Affairs*

★ North American Rockwell AGM-28A Hound Dog

An air to ground, air-breathing missile designed as a long-range, stand-off nuclear armed warhead strategic weapon. It was carried on an underwing pylon on each side of the B-52's fuselage, inboard of the engines. SAC armed its alert B-52s with the Hound Dog as an increased capability under the SIOP and EWO. Its development was started by the Air Force in 1957, realizing that Soviet air defenses would improve and become more lethal to SAC penetrating bombers. It was intended to provide a long-range capability, destroying heavily defended targets ahead or to either side of the low-level, penetrating bomber and allowing the aircrew to reach and attack its primary targets with free-fall gravity thermonuclear bombs. The missile's first test launch was in 1959, from a B-52G. A unique feature of the Hound Dog was that its single turbo-jet engine could be used to supplement the available thrust of the B-52's eight engines on heavy combat-loaded missions or to increase speed during evasive maneuvers to counter enemy defenses. The missile could be refueled from the B-52 mother ship's fuel cells prior to launch, enabling it to sustain its maximum launch range and speed profile. Six hundred Hound Dogs were manufactured from 1957 to 1963, with the last missile removed from Air Force inventory in 1978.

NORTH AMERICAN ROCKWELL AGM-28 HOUND DOG
Specifications and Performance Information

Manufacturer	North American Rockwell
Designation	AGM-28
Version (variant)	"A"
Nickname	Hound Dog
Type	Strategic Air to Ground missile
7th Bomb Wing Sponsor	7th Bomb Wing Equipment Maintenance Squadron
Wingspan	12 feet
Length	42.5 feet
Diameter	28 inches
Weight	10,000 pounds
Power plant	(1) Pratt & Whitney 7,500 pound thrust J-52-6 turbojet engine
Maximum speed	Mach 2.1
Range (low-level)	500 miles
High-level	700 miles
Maximum altitude	55,000 feet
Electronics	Anti-radar terrain-following onboard guidance
Warhead	W-28
Yield	One megaton
Operational with SAC	1961 to 1967

Originally, it was designated as Model 299. It first flew on July 28, 1935. Early flight testing was promising, but on October 20, 1935, the prototype crashed. The Air Corps was sufficiently impressed with the results of the flight testing program, ordering thirteen aircraft designated Y1B-17. The name "Flying Fortress" was penned by a newspaper reporter covering the formal rollout ceremonies. Later models had improved engines, armor plate protection for the aircrew, and the installation of added defensive guns. Over 13,000 B-17s of all variants were built before the end of WWII. It became the mainstay of the Eighth Air Force's daylight, high-altitude precision bombing raids against Germany.

The air park's B-17G was built by Lockheed Aircraft Corporation, one of the additional production plants Boeing sub-contracted to build the bomber. It was delivered to the Army Air Force on March 31, 1945, modified into a DB-17P. This modified aircraft was used as a mother ship to remotely control pilotless aircraft for special test programs. After WWII, this type of modified aircraft guided unmanned aircraft penetrations through atomic cloud test detonation series to measure radiation levels actual SAC combat aircrews might encounter during a nuclear attack on the Soviet Union. These modified aircraft were retired in October 1960. The air park's B-17G never flew in combat, although it proudly displays WWII aircraft markings of the 337th BS, Eighth Air Force.

BOEING B-17G FLYING FORTRESS
Specifications and Performance Information

Manufacturer	Lockheed Aircraft Corporation (Boeing Aircraft sub-contractor)
Designation	B-17
Version (variant)	"G"
Serial number	44-85599
Nickname	Flying Fortress
Operational Use	Director-type aircraft (DB-17P) for unmanned aircraft
Crew	Pilot, co-pilot, navigator, radio operator
7th Bomb Wing sponsor	9th Bomb Squadron
Length	74 feet 4 inches
Tail height	19 feet 1-inch
Wingspan	103 feet 10 inches
Wing area	1,420 square feet
Empty weight	36,135 pounds
Gross weight	65,500 pounds
Power plant	(4) Wright Cyclone 1,200 hp R-1820-97 radial piston engines
Maximum range	2,000 miles
Cruising speed	160 mph
Maximum speed	302 mph
Service ceiling	35,600 feet
Armament	Removed in its role/mission as director for unmanned aircraft
Bomb load	None

Boeing B-17G Flying Fortress at the Dyess Air Force Base Linear Air Park, Texas. *7th Bomb Wing Public Affairs*

The B-47 was the first production all turbojet medium-bomber in the Air Force and was the backbone of SAC's bomber fleet in the 1950s. The Air Force liked Boeing's design and ordered two prototypes. The initial prototype (XB-47) rolled out of Boeing's Seattle production facility on September 12, 1947. It made its first test flight on December 17, 1947. The B-47 was classified as a medium bomber. With aerial refueling and forward basing options it could reach and attack targets inside the Soviet Union. The B-47 proved versatile, undergoing many modifications that extended its life with SAC. The B-47A had a clear Plexiglas bombardier nose and two .50-caliber machine guns mounted in a remotely controlled tail turret. The B-47E's defensive armament was increased by replacing the two .50-caliber machine guns with two 20mm cannon, the Plexiglas nose was eliminated, and an optical dome was installed for the horizontal periscope bombsight. The B-47E had an alcohol/water injector system to provide maximum takeoff thrust augmented by JATO rockets, since the bomber's weight had increased from 125,000 to 221,000 pounds.

The air park's EB-47E was delivered to the Air Force on September 21, 1953. It was originally assigned to the 376th BW at Barksdale AFB, Louisiana. The 376th BW later moved to Lockbourne AFB (renamed Rickenbacker AFB) in 1957. It was used as an electronic test bed aircraft and was transferred to the Navy in 1965 for use as an Electronic Counter Measure (ECM) test aircraft. The aircraft was retired in 1977, outliving the majority of B-47Es used in a bomber role.

Boeing EB-47E at the Dyess Air Force Base Linear Air Park, Texas. *7th Bomb Wing Public Affairs*

BOEING EB-47E STRATOJET

Specifications and Performance Information

Manufacturer	Boeing Aircraft
Additional	Douglas Aircraft, Lockheed Aircraft
Designation	EB-47
Version (variant)	"E"
Serial number	52-0412
Nickname	Stratojet
Type	Electronic warfare/special electronics
Crew	Pilot, copilot, navigator
7th Bomb Wing sponsor	7th Operations Support Squadron
Gross weight	206,700 pounds
Power plant	(6) General Electric 7,200 pound thrust J-47-GE-25 engines
Auxiliary power	(33) jettisonable 1,000 pound thrust JATOs (Jet-Assisted-Takeoff rockets)
Cruising speed	557 mph at 38,500 feet
Maximum speed	600 mph
Service ceiling	40,500 feet
Maximum range	4,000 miles (unrefueled)
Bomb load	20,000 pounds

Douglas Aircraft Company EB-66 Destroyer at the Dyess Air Force Base Linear Air Park, Texas. *7th Bomb Wing Public Affairs*

Douglas Aircraft RB-66 Destroyer

The B-66 was developed by the Air Force from the Navy A-3D Sky Warrior as a light tactical bomber and photo-reconnaissance aircraft. The B-66 was operational in 1956, with production ending in 1958. The RB-66 reconnaissance variant was the first serial production of the B-66, with 155 built out of a total of 294. The B-66 was the last tactical bomber built and purchased by the Air Force. Only the B-66 was designed and produced as a light tactical bomber. The final variant (WB-66D) was designed for electronic weather reconnaissance missions.

The air park's RB-66B was modified for service in Southeast Asia during the Vietnam War, carrying high-speed cameras mounted along the bottom of the fuselage and a chaff dispenser replacing the rear tail gun. The aircraft ended its operational service at Bergstrom AFB, Texas. It is one of seven surviving Douglas Destroyers.

DOUGLAS AIRCRAFT RB-66B DESTROYER
Specifications and Performance Information

Manufacturer	Douglas Aircraft Company
Designation	RB-66
Version (variant)	"B"
Serial number	53-0466
Nickname	Destroyer
Type	Reconnaissance
Crew	Pilot, copilot, Electronic Warfare officer
7th Bomb Wing sponsor	7th Transportation Squadron
Length	75 feet 2 inches
Tail height	23 feet 7 inches
Wingspan	72 feet 6 inches
Empty weight	43,476 pounds
Gross weight	59,550 pounds
Maximum weight	83,000 pounds
Power plant	(2) Allison 10,000 pound thrust J71-A-13 turbojet engines
Auxiliary thrust	(12) 1,000 pound thrust JATO rockets
Cruising speed	525 mph
Maximum speed	585 mph
Service ceiling	43,000 feet
Range	1,800 miles
Armament	(2) 20mm cannons in tail turret
Bombs	8,044 pounds, -or- Photo flash bombs for night photo reconnaissance

In 1951, the United States broke a self-imposed and long-standing policy of not purchasing foreign military aircraft for quantity manufacture for the US Air Force, deciding to purchase the British B-57 Canberra, licensed for production in the United States. The first Canberra with American markings flew in 1951, followed by the first flight of an American-built Canberra in 1953. The B-57 served as a light tactical bomber and reconnaissance aircraft. American produced Canberras were exported to Turkey and other US allies. One version (RB-37) was modified with larger wings for high-altitude reconnaissance operations—providing aerodynamic lift in thinner air—and larger engine air intakes to maintain engine thrust at higher altitudes. Other B-57s served as tactical bombers during the Vietnam War. A unique feature of the B-57 was its rotating bomb bay door. Bombs were loaded on the door assembly itself, which would rotate completely inside the bomb bay prior to bomb release.

The EB-57B on display is an electronic warfare version nicknamed "Night Intruder." It dispensed chaff to jam enemy radar transmissions. Other B-57s were used to tow aerial target sleeves and as transitional trainers for single engine pilots to move to multi-engine aircraft. It was delivered to the Air Force on November 5, 1954, and was retired on December 3, 1981.

GLEN L. MARTIN EB-57B CANBERRA
Specifications and Performance Information

Manufacturer	Glen L. Martin
Designation	EB-57
Version (variant)	"B"
Serial number	52-1504
Nickname	Canberra and Night Intruder
Type	Electronic warfare/special electronics
Crew	Pilot, weapons/radar operator
7th Bomb Wing sponsor	7th Security Police Squadron
Length	65 feet 6 inches
Tail height	15 feet 6 inches
Wingspan	64 feet
Empty weight	26,000 pounds
Maximum weight	55,000 pounds
Power plant	(2) Wright turbojet 7,200 pound thrust J-65-W-5 engines
Cruising speed	450 mph
Maximum speed	582 mph
Service ceiling	48,000 feet
Range	2,300 miles
Armament	(4) 20mm cannons -or- (8) .50 caliber machine guns
Bombs	5,000 pounds (internal)
External	Four under wing weapons pylons for bombs or rockets

Glen L. Martin EB-57B Canberra at the Dyess Air Force Base Linear Air Park, Texas. *7th Bomb Wing Public Affairs*

★ Rockwell International, North American Aircraft, and Boeing Aircraft B-1B Lancer

The B-1B was developed in the 1970s as a replacement for the Boeing B-52 Stratofortress. The air park's B-1B "Star of Abilene" was initially flown to Edwards AFB for development of maintenance procedures under Air Force technical orders to validate and verify aircraft upkeep in May 1985. On June 17, 1985, the aircraft was flown to Offutt AFB (SAC headquarters) for formal command acceptance ceremonies and inspection by senior SAC officers. On July 14, 1985, the aircraft was delivered to Dyess AFB. On March 1, 2003, the aircraft completed its final operational flight. Once the aircraft's salvageable equipment was removed for spare parts it was towed to the air park for display.

North American Rockwell International B-1B Lancer at the Dyess Air Force Base Linear Air Park, Texas. *7th Bomb Wing Public Affairs*

ROCKWELL INTERNATIONAL B-1B LANCER
Specifications and Performance Information

Manufacturer .... Rockwell International
Designation B-1
Version (variant) .... "B"
Serial number 83-00068
Nickname .... Bone
Type .... Bomber
Crew .... Aircraft Commander (pilot), copilot, Offensive Systems officer, Defensive Systems officer
7th Bomb Wing sponsor .... 7th Bomb Wing
Length .... 146 feet
Tail height .... 34 feet
Wingspan .... 137 feet (full forward swept position), 79 feet (full retracted position to create delta wing shape)
Wing area .... 1,950 square feet
Empty weight .... 192,000 pounds
Maximum weight .... 477,000 pounds
Power plant .... (4) General Electric 30,000 pound thrust F101-GE-102 turbofan engines
Maximum speed .... 900 mph
Service ceiling .... 30,000 feet
Maximum ceiling .... 60,000 feet
Range .... 6,450 miles (high-altitude, unrefueled), 1,730 miles (low-altitude, unrefueled)
Armament .... 48,000 pounds

B-1B "Star of Abilene" nose art. *Dyess Air Force Base, 7th Bomb Wing Public Affairs*

B-1B "Texas Raider" nose art. *Dyess Air Force Base, 7th Bomb Wing Public Affairs*

B-1B "7 Wishes" nose art. *Dyess Air Force Base, 7th Bomb Wing Public Affairs*

B-1B Lancers Assigned to Dyess Air Force Base and Current Disposition at Museums

Star of Abilene **(83-0065, museum display aircraft)**
Delivered to Edwards AFB, California, for use during aircraft technical evaluation and verification during May through June 1985. It was scheduled to be flown to Dyess AFB with its nose art displayed as the "Star of Abilene," but did not reach Dyess on the date scheduled for the base's official B-1B activation ceremonies. It finally landed at Dyess AFB on June 17, 1985. After a production flying career it was moved to Dyess Linear Air Park on March 1, 2003, for static display.

Ole Puss **(83-0066, museum display aircraft)**
Delivered to Dyess AFB on October 16, 1985. It was flown to Mountain Hone AFB, Idaho, as a static display aircraft.

Texas Raider **(83-0067, museum display aircraft)**
Delivered to Dyess AFB on January 13, 1986. It was flown to Ellsworth AFB, South Dakota, for display at the South Dakota Air and Space Museum.

Spuds **(83-0068, museum display aircraft)**
Delivered to Dyess AFB on February 18, 1986. It was flown to McConnell AFB, Kansas, and renamed "Kansas Tail Wind" on February 28, 2002, for static display.

Rebe **(83-0069, museum display aircraft)**
Delivered to Dyess AFB on March 13, 1986. It was flown to Robins AFB, Georgia, for static Display.

7 Wishes **(83-0070, museum display aircraft)**
Delivered to Dyess AFB on May 6, 1986. It was flown to Hill AFB, Utah, on February 3, 2003, for display at Hill Air Force Base Museum.

Grand Illusion **(83-0071)**
Delivered to Dyess AFB on May 24, 1986. It was flown to Tinker AFB, Oklahoma, for display at the Major Charles B. Hall Memorial Air Park.

Surprise Attack (85-0050, Aircraft Maintenance and Regeneration Center or AMARC storage)
Delivered to Dyess AFB on October 1, 1986. It was flown to Davis Monthan AFB, Arizona, and moved to storage at the Aircraft Maintenance and Regeneration Center (AMARC) on January 11, 2002.

Boss Hawg (84-0051, museum display aircraft)
Delivered to Dyess AFB on July 9, 1986. It was flown to Wright-Patterson AFB, Dayton, Ohio, for display at the National Museum of the United States Air Force.

B-1B "Boss Haug" nose art. *Dyess Air Force Base, 7th Bomb Wing Public Affairs*

No Name (84-0052) (lost due to aircraft crash)
Delivered to Dyess AFB on July 11, 1986. On September 28, 1987, the aircraft crashed near La Junta, Colorado, because of heavy (repeated) bird strikes, killing three of the six aircrew members. The larger crew was part of an airborne training flight.

Tasmanian Terror (84-0054, AMARC storage)
Delivered to Dyess AFB on July 26, 1986. It was flown to AMARC on September 18, 2002.

B-1B "Sweet Sixteen" nose art. *Dyess Air Force Base, 7th Bomb Wing Public Affairs*

Sweet Sixteen (84-0056, AMARC storage)
Delivered to Dyess AFB on August 27, 1986. It was flown to AMARC on August 20, 2002.

The Hellion (84-0057) (lost due to aircraft crash)
Delivered to Dyess AFB on April 30, 1987. It crashed on February 18, 1998, due to an electrical failure near Mattoon, Kentucky, with no resulting fatalities.

Master of Disaster (84-0058, AMARC storage)
Delivered to Dyess AFB on March 26, 1987. It was flown to AMARC on August 26, 2002.

B-1B "Hellion" nose art. *Dyess Air Force Base, 7th Bomb Wing Public Affairs*

Better Duck (85-0059) (9th Bomb Squadron or BS)
Delivered to Dyess AFB on September 26, 1986.

Night Hawk (85-0060) (transferred)
Delivered to Dyess AFB on October 31, 1986. It was transferred to Ellsworth AFB, 28th BW, in January 1991.

French Connection (85-0061, 28th BS)
Delivered to Dyess AFB on March 18, 1987. It was transferred to Ellsworth AFB, 28th BW, and then back to Dyess AFB.

B-1B "Polarized" nose art. *Dyess Air Force Base, 7th Bomb Wing Public Affairs*

Sky Dancer **(85-0062, AMARC storage)**
Delivered to Dyess AFB on November 4, 1986. It was flown to AMARC on August 21, 2002.

No Name **(85-0063) (lost due to aircraft crash)**
Delivered to Dyess AFB on November 30, 1986. On November 8, 1988, after takeoff the aircraft crashed because of an engine fire.

Eliminator **(85-0064, 28th BS)**
Delivered to Dyess AFB on February 3, 1986. It was transferred to Ellsworth AFB, 28th BW, on May 31, 1992, and later back to Dyess AFB.

Texas Armor **(85-0065, 28th BS)**
Delivered to Dyess AFB on November 30, 1986.

Missouri Miss **(85-0066) (transferred)**
Delivered to Dyess AFB on December 31, 1986. It was transferred to Ellsworth AFB, 28th BW, in January 1991.

Miss Behavin **(85-0067, AMARC storage)**
Delivered to Dyess AFB on December 30, 1986. The Aircraft was transferred to Ellsworth AFB, 28th BW, and was flown to AMARC on March 25, 2003.

Daisy Mae **(85-0069, 9th BS)**
Delivered to Dyess AFB on December 23, 1986.

Excalibur **(85-0070, AMARC storage)**
Delivered to Dyess AFB on January 7, 1987. It was flown to AMARC on August 26, 2002.

Liberator **(85-0071, AMARC storage)**
Delivered to Ellsworth AFB, 28th BW, on February 4, 1987, then transferred to Dyess AFB, and was later flown to AMARC on August 23, 2002.

Polarized **(85-0072, 9th BS)**
Delivered to Dyess AFB on February 27, 1987.

Cerberus **(85-0073, 9th BS)**
Delivered to Ellsworth AFB, 28th BW, on January 21, 1987, then transferred to Dyess AFB in January 1991.

Penetrator (85-0074, 9th BS)
Delivered to Ellsworth AFB, 28th BW, on February 18, 1987, then transferred to Dyess AFB in January 1991.

Screamin Demon (85-0080, 9th BS)
Delivered to Ellsworth AFB, 28th BW, on March 13, 1987, then transferred to Dyess AFB in January 1991.

Gunsmoke (85-0082, AMARC storage)
Delivered to Ellsworth AFB on March 23, 1987, then transferred to Dyess AFB in January 1991. It was transferred to AMARC on September 19, 2003.

Phoenix (85-0088, 28th BS)
Delivered to Ellsworth AFB, 28th BW, on February 22, 1987, then transferred to Dyess AFB in January 1991.

B-1B "Phoenix" nose art. *Dyess Air Force Base, 7th Bomb Wing Public Affairs*

Midnight Prowler (85-0089, 28th BS)
Delivered to Ellsworth AFB, 28th BW, on June 22, 1987, then transferred to Dyess AFB in January 1991.

Trail Blazer (85-0090, 28th BS)
Delivered to Ellsworth AFB, 28th BW, on May 14, 1987, then transferred to Dyess AFB in January 1991.

Undecided (86-0095, 28th BS)
Delivered to Ellsworth AFB, 28th BW, on July 2, 1987, then transferred to Dyess AFB in January 1991.

Iron Eagle (86-0097, 9th BS)
Delivered to Ellsworth AFB, 28th BW, on June 25, 1987. In 1991, it was transferred to Grand Forks AFB, 319th BW. It was then transferred to Dyess AFB. It was flown to AMARC on April 3, 2003, and regenerated to Dyess AFB on September 2, 2004.

Freedom I (86-0098, 9th BS)
Delivered to Ellsworth AFB, 28th BW, on July 15, 1987, then transferred to Dyess AFB in January 1991.

Night Hawk (86-100, 28th BS)
Delivered to Ellsworth AFB, 28th BW, on July 20, 1987, then transferred to Dyess AFB in January 1991.

Low-Level Devil **(86-0101, 28th BS)**
Delivered to Ellsworth AFB, 28th BW, on August 21, 1987, then transferred to Dyess AFB in January 1991.

Lovely-Lady **(86-0103, 28th BS)**
Delivered to Ellsworth AFB, 28th BW, on September 8, 1987, then transferred to Dyess AFB in January 1991.

Snake Eyes **(86-0105, 28th BS)**
Delivered to Ellsworth AFB, 28th BW, on September 24, 1987, then transferred to Grand Forks AFB, 319th BW, in 1990. It was transferred to Dyess AFB in January 1991.

Lone Wolf **(86-0106, lost due to aircraft crash)**
Delivered to Ellsworth AFB, 28th BW, on September 5, 1987. The aircraft was transferred to Dyess AFB in January 1991. The B-1B was lost in a mid-air collision with a KC-135 tanker over Nebraska on March 24, 1992. It was repaired, but was in a second crash near Van Horn, Texas, on November 30, 1992. Unfortunately, all four crew members were killed.

Valkyer (86-0107, 28th BS)
The B-1B was transferred to Grand Forks AFB, 319th BW, on October 26, 1987, then to Ellsworth AFB, 28th BW, and was later transferred to Dyess AFB in January 1991.

Hawk **(86-0108, 28th BS)**
Delivered to Grand Forks AFB, 319th BW, on November 30, 1987, then transferred to Dyess AFB in January 1991.

Spectre **(86-0109, 9th BS)**
Delivered to Ellsworth AFB, 28th BW, on October 1, 1987, then transferred to Dyess AFB in late 1990.

Vanna **(86-0112, 9th BS)**
Delivered to Grand Forks AFB, 319th BW, on October 28, 1987, transferred to Dyess AFB in January 1991.

Pride of North Dakota **(86-0117, 9th BS)**
Delivered to Grand Forks AFB, 319th BW, on December 4, 1987, then transferred to Dyess AFB in January 1991.

Christine **(0119, 28th BS)**
Delivered to Grand Forks AFB, 319th BW, on December 2, 1987, then transferred to Dyess AFB in January 1991.

Mad Dawg (86-0120, 28th BS)
Delivered to Grand Forks AFB, 319th BW, on December 22, 1987, then transferred to Dyess AFB in January 1991.

Excalibure (86-0122, 9th BS)
Delivered to Grand Forks, AFB, 319th BW, on January 12, 1988, then transferred to Dyess AFB in January 1991.

High Noon (86-0123, 28th BS)
Delivered to Grand Forks AFB, 319th BW, on January 8, 1988, then transferred to Dyess AFB in January 1991.

Penetrator (86-0124, 28th BS)
Delivered to McConnell AFB, Kansas, 384th BW, on February 29, 1988, then transferred to Dyess AFB in January 1991.

Bad Company (86-130, 28th BS)
Delivered to McConnell AFB, Kansas, 384th BW, on March 3, 1988, then transferred to Dyess AFB in January 1991.

Oh! Hardluck (86-0132, 28th BS)
Delivered to McConnell AFB, Kansas, 384th BW, on August 20, 1988, then transferred to Dyess AFB on February 21, 1989.

B-1B "Oh! Hardluck" nose art. *Dyess Air Force Base, 7th Bomb Wing Public Affairs*

The Outlaw (86-0133, 9th BS)
Delivered to McConnell AFB, Kansas, 384th BW, on April 14, 1988; transferred to Ellsworth AFB, 28th BW, on October 16, 1990; and transferred to Dyess AFB in January 1991.

Special Delivery (86-0136, 28th BS)
Delivered to McConnell AFB, Kansas, 384th BW, on April 15, 1988, then transferred to Dyess AFB in January 1991.

Wichita Express (86-0137, 28th BS)
Delivered to McConnell AFB, Kansas, 384th BW, on April 29, 1988, then transferred to Dyess AFB in January 1991.

Peace Warrior (86-0140, 9th BS)
Delivered to Dyess AFB on May 2, 1988.[2]

Caption 13-10 [DAFB-210] Lockheed Corporation F-104A Starfighter at the Dyess Air Force Base Linear Air Park, Texas. *7th Bomb Wing Public Affairs*

★ Lockheed F-104A Starfighter

C. L. "Kelly" Johnson designed the F-104 in 1952, and it became one of the most successful fighters produced. It was the first aircraft to fly at twice the speed of sound (Mach 2.0), along with holding many air speed and altitude records. The air park's F-104 was a test aircraft at Edwards AFB Flight Test Center from June 1957 to October 1967. It was used as a supersonic chase plane during X-15 launches from a B-52B and landings on the dry lake bed runway. Because of its physical appearance, the F-104 was nicknamed the "missile with a man in it." Like the F-84 Thunderstreak and the F-16 Fighting Falcon, the F-104 was purchased by US NATO allies. The design was a by-product of air combat lessons of the Korean War and was developed as a point defense interceptor. However, its range was sacrificed for spectacular full-afterburner thrust and rate of climb to altitude. Range was improved by adding auxiliary wing tip fuel tanks and a nose-mounted aerial refueling probe. A few F-104s remain flying around the world. The air park's F-104 was retired at the Edwards Flight Test Center in December 1972.

LOCKHEED AIRCRAFT CORPORATION F-104A STARFIGHTER
Specifications and Performance Information

Manufacturer.................................. Lockheed Aircraft Corporation
Designation.. F-104
Version (variant).. "A"
Serial number.. 56-0748
Nickname ....Starfighter
Type .... Point interceptor
Crew .... Pilot
7th Bomb Wing Sponsor........7th Equipment Maintenance Squadron
Length.. 54 feet 8 inches
Tail height... 13 feet 5 inches
Wingspan.. 21 feet 9 inches
Empty weight .... 14,082 pounds
Maximum weight .... 28,779 pounds
Power plant......(1) General Electric 14,800 pound thrust J-79-GE-3 engine, equipped with afterburner to increase thrust to 18,000 pounds
Cruising speed.. 519 mph
Maximum speed .... 1,450 mph
Climb rate.....................................50,000 feet in one minute
Service ceiling .... 58,000 feet
Maximum range.. 1,000 miles
Armament.................................(1) M-61 Vulcan 20mm cannon
Bombs.... 4,000 pounds on external under wing pylons -or- (2) Air to Air missiles

McDonnell Aircraft F-101B Voodoo at the Dyess Air Force Base Linear Air Park, Texas. *7th Bomb Wing Public Affairs*

★ McDonnell Aircraft Company F-101B Voodoo

The F-101 was one of the "century series" fighters that entered the Air Force in the 1950s. The development of the F-101B took place at a time when the Air Force was going through radical changes in development and procurement policies. The F-101 was originally conceived for bomber escort operations for SAC bombers prior to target penetration. The three commands that participated in the fighter's development were Air Research and Development Command, Air Material Command, and Air Defense Command. The F-101 flew for the first time on September 29, 1954. It held numerous speed and endurance records in the 1950s and 1960s. In 1954, an F-101C established a world speed record of 1,206.7 mph. The F-101 was the workhorse and design prototype for the McDonnell-Douglas F-4 Phantom, which remains operational in limited numbers. The F-101 had an important intelligence collection role during the Cuban Missile Crisis and Vietnam War. It remains in service with the Canadian and Taiwanese Air Forces, but is scheduled for replacement. The air park's TB-101B was delivered to the Air Force, serving with the Air Defense Command as a trainer and interceptor.

MCDONNELL AIRCRAFT F-101B VOODOO
Specifications and Performance Information

Manufacturer	McDonnell Aircraft Company, later McDonnell-Douglas Aircraft Company
Designation	F-101
Version (variant)	"B"
Serial number	57-0287
Nickname	Voodoo
Type	(this aircraft) trainer
Crew	Pilot
7th Bomb Wing sponsor	7th Security Policy Squadron
Length	67 feet 5 inches
Tail height	18 feet
Wingspan	39 feet 8 inches
Empty weight	28,000 pounds
Maximum weight	46,700 pounds
Power plant	(2) Pratt & Whitney 18,880 pound thrust J-57-P-55 turbojet engines, each fitted with an afterburner
Maximum speed	1,220 mph
Climb rate	17,000 feet per minute
Service ceiling	52,000 feet
Range	1,943 miles
Armament	20mm cannons
External	(2) AIR-2A Genie nuclear warhead tipped un-guided air to air missile

The F-100 began life as a North American project to improve on the basic F-86 Sabre design. The program did not receive any Department of Defense interest until F-86s engaged in fierce aerial combat against Russian-produced MiG-15 Fagots in "MiG alley," in northwest North Korea. Early Korean War aerial combat experiences made it evident that communist bloc countries had brought their air forces close to the technical capabilities of the United States and Western nations. The US Air Force recognized the danger and awarded North American Aviation a contract to design and build two YF-100A prototypes, with series production ordered in November 1951. The Super Sabre became the first fighter to attain level supersonic flight on October 29, 1953. The F-100 reached operational Air Force units in 1954, after the end of the Korean War. With this new Air Force fighter operational, Russian aviation engineers developed and designed the MiG-17 Fresco, MiG-19 Farmer, and the MiG-12 Fishbed.

NORTH AMERICAN AVIATION F-100C SUPER SABRE
Specifications and Performance Information

Manufacturer	North American Aviation
Designation	F-100
Version (variant)	"C"
Serial number	54-1752
Nickname	Super Sabre
Type	Fighter
Crew	Pilot
7th Bomb Wing sponsor	7th Bomb Wing
Length	46 feet 1-inch
Tail height	15 feet 6 inches
Wingspan	38 feet 10 inches
Empty weight	21,000 pounds
Maximum weight	34,832 pounds
Power plant	(1) Pratt & Whitney 17,000 pound thrust J-57-P-21A turbojet engine, equipped with afterburner for increased thrust
Cruising speed	565 mph
Maximum speed	864 mph
Climb rate	21,600 feet per minute
Service ceiling	49,100 feet
Combat radius	530 miles
Range	1,350 miles
Armament	(4) M-39 20mm cannons
External	(6) under wing pylons for bombs, rockets, auxiliary fuel tanks

The F-100 was originally designed as an air superiority fighter, but the F-100A was the only pure variant. The F-100B was an all-weather fighter/interceptor (to match the Russian MiG-21). As the Air Force realized the F-84 fighter-bomber fleet was becoming obsolete, the logical choice was to modify the F-100A into the F-100C. The F-100D was the definitive version of this fighter, with 1,274 produced (Mach 1.3 speed). It had improvements in aerodynamics and weapons delivery and was capable of carrying and delivering tactical nuclear weapons.

The F-100D was used by the Thunderbirds. The air park's F-100C on display was delivered to the Air Force on September 14, 1955, and served with the 450th Fighter Day Group and the 322nd Fighter Day Group, Foster AFB, Texas, from September 1955 to June 1958. It was retired in January 1975. It carries the paint scheme and markings of the wing commander of the 322nd Fighter Day Group.

North American Aviation F-100C Super Sabre at the Dyess Air Force Base Linear Air Park, Texas. *7th Bomb Wing Public Affairs*

★ North American Aviation F-86L Sabre Jet

In 1944, North American Aviation started a design study for a high-performance fighter powered by a single turbojet engine. Its design was submitted to the Air Force on May 8, 1945, and the design was designated the XP-86. On August 8, 1947, the XP-86 rolled out of North American's production hangar, flying for the first time on October 1, 1947. The first production Sabre flew on May 20, 1948. In 1948, the F-86 was the first production fighter to break the speed of sound in a dive.

The F-86 became the mainstay of Air Force fighter forces during the Korean War, where its pilots drove MiG-15s out of "MiG alley" but were not allowed "hot pursuit" into Manchuria or attacking fighter air bases across the Yalu River. North American Aviation Company produced 9,502 F-86 fighters. There are a few of these remarkable planes flying today, most with the Republic of South Korea Air Force as transitional jet trainers. The F-86 D/L was the first Air Force fighter armed only with unguided, air to air rockets and the first all-weather fighter-interceptor to carry one pilot to fly and operate the onboard, integrated fire control system.

The air park's F-86D was delivered to the Air Force on August 15, 1955. It flew with the 331st Fighter Interceptor Squadron (FIS), ADC, at Webb AFB, Texas. In November 1956, the aircraft was upgraded with a wing tip extension into the F-86L. It was retired in June 1960.

North American Aviation F-86L Sabre Jet at the Dyess Air Force Base Linear Air Park, Texas. *7th Bomb Wing Public Affairs*

NORTH AMERICAN AVIATION F-86L SABRE JET
Specifications and Performance Information

Manufacturer	North American Aviation
Designation	F-86
Version (variant)	"L"
Serial number	53-4035
Nickname	Sabre Jet
Type	Fighter
Crew	Pilot
7th Bomb Wing sponsor	7th Equipment Maintenance Squadron
Length	40 feet 3 inches
Tail height	15 feet
Wingspan	39 feet 1-inch
Empty weight	13,125 pounds
Maximum weight	20, 171 pounds
Power plant	(1) General Electric 7,500 pound thrust J-47-GE-17B turbojet engine, equipped with afterburner for additional thrust
Cruising speed	550 mph
Maximum speed	707 mph
Climb rate	17,800 feet per minutes
Service ceiling	49,600 feet
Maximum range	750 miles
Armament	(24) 2.75-inch unguided rockets

One of the most heavily armed US fighters. The F-89 was the backbone of the North American Air Defense (NORAD) Command for more than seventeen years. The F-89 was the first multi-seat, all-weather jet interceptor. It was the first fighter designed to carry an all-rocket armament and the first to carry the Hughes Falcon air to air missile (AIR 2A Genie) armed with a thermonuclear warhead. The F-89 could carry two Genie nuclear AAMs or four of the lighter, conventionally armed Genie AAM. On May 3, 1946, Northrop was awarded a production contract to build two prototypes designated XP-89. The first prototype rolled out of Northrop's California production facility in the summer of 1948. After a number of taxi and brake tests the XP-89 was transported to the high desert north of Los Angeles at Muroc Dry Lake, soon to be Edwards AFB. Air and ground crews at Muroc Dry Lake test area remarked the new aircraft looked like a Scorpion ready to strike out in anger and the nickname stuck, then was officially recognized by the Air Force.

The F-89 made its maiden flight on August 16, 1948, with the first production aircraft accepted by the Air Force on September 28, 1950. At the time of its production, the F-89 was equipped with the most advanced radar system, enabling the two-man flight crew to track and engage hostile enemy bombers at all altitudes and in all weather. The Scorpion never launched a missile in anger, but was a major deterrent against any possible Russian Cold War attacks on the United States.

The air park has a F-89H, but with wing tip fuel tanks retrieved from an operational F-89J (the nuclear equipped Genie warhead). The F-89H was delivered to the Air Force on April 6, 1956, flying its entire operational Air Force service with the 3320th Technical Training Wing at Amarillo AFB, Texas, until retirement in August 1959.

Northrop Aircraft F-89H Scorpion at the Dyess Air Force Base Linear Air Park, Texas. *7th Bomb Wing Public Affairs*

NORTHROP AIRCRAFT F-89H SCORPION
Specifications and Performance Information

Manufacturer.......... Northrop Aircraft
Designation.......... F-89
Version (variant).......... "H"
Serial number.......... 54-0298
Nickname.......... Scorpion
Type.......... Fighter
Crew.......... Pilot
Radar operator
7th Bomb Wing Sponsor.......... 7th Communications Squadron
Empty weight.......... 25,194 pounds
Maximum weight.......... 42,241 pounds
Power plant....(2) Allison 7,200 pound thrust J-35-A-35 turbojet engines, equipped with afterburner for additional thrust
Cruising speed.......... 523 mph
Maximum speed.......... 636 mph
Climb rate.......... 8,360 feet per minute
Service ceiling.......... 49,200 feet
Maximum range.......... 1,370 miles
Armament..(4) .50 caliber machine guns in tail, (52) unguided 2.75-inch folding fin rockets, -or- (4) conventional warhead armed AIM-4 Falcon AAMs, -or- (2) nuclear warhead armed Genie AIR-2 AAMs

★ Douglas MB-1/AIR-2 Genie Air-to-Air Missile

In 1954, Douglas Aircraft Company began design work on a large, unguided, air to air missile. The missile was live fired from an F-89D during 1955 and 1956, with the missile becoming operational in 1957. It could be armed with a conventional or nuclear warhead. It armed the Air Force F-89J/H, F-101B, and F-106A. It remained operational until 1982.

Douglas Aircraft MB1/AIR-2 Genie Air-to-Air Missile at the Dyess Air Force Base Linear Air Park, Texas. *7th Bomb Wing Public Affairs*

DOUGLAS AIRCRAFT MB-1/AIR-2 GENIE AIR-TO-AIR MISSILE
Specifications and Performance Information

Manufacturer.......... Douglas Aircraft Company
Designation.......... MB-1/AIR-2
Nickname.......... Genie
Type.......... Unguided air to air missile
Length.......... 9 feet 8 inches
Diameter.......... 17.5 inches
Fin span (extended).......... 3 feet 4 inches
Weight.......... 820 pounds
Maximum speed.......... Mach 3.0
Maximum range.......... (launch to target) 6-miles
Propulsion system....... SR49-TC-1 (Thiokol TU-289) solid fuel rocket, with 36,000 pounds of thrust
Warhead.......... 1.5 kiloton nuclear warhead, -or- conventional warhead

The F-105 was the first Air Force heavy, supersonic fighter-bomber and the largest single-seat combat aircraft produced. The first production model flew on May 27, 1958, and was able to go Mach 2.0. It could also drop bombs from an internal bomb bay at supersonic speeds. The F-105D was heavily committed to the US air campaign during the Vietnam War in Southeast Asia. It was nicknamed the "Thud." The aircraft flew deep bomb strikes into heavily defended North Vietnam, penetrating the most overlapping and sophisticated anti-aircraft defenses ever encountered to deliver dumb iron bombs and later, the first generation of laser-guided munitions.

Republic Aviation F-105D Thunderchief at the Dyess Air Force Base Linear Air Park, Texas. *7th Bomb Wing Public Affairs*

Modified, two-seat F-105Gs called "Wild Weasels" were used to jam and attack North Vietnamese radars. After the Vietnam War, many Thunderchiefs served in the Air Force Reserve and Air National Guard. The F-105 was built around a large engine and internal bomb bay, initially as a tactical nuclear bomber to be used against the Soviet Union. The first production F-105 broke the speed of sound barrier in 1955, powered by a smaller, interim engine. When the final operational F-105 was retired, it was the only Air Force aircraft to receive a formal retirement ceremony attended by hundreds who had flown and maintained the fighter. The air park's F-105 was delivered to the Air Force on November 12, 1960, and retired in August 1981.

REPUBLIC AVIATION F-105D THUNDERCHIEF
Specifications and Performance Information

Manufacturer	Republic Aviation
Designation	F-105
Version (variant)	"D"
Serial number	59-1738
Nickname	Thunderchief
Type	Fighter-bomber
Crew	Pilot
7th Bomb Wing sponsor	7th Communications Squadron
Length	64 feet 5 inches
Tail height	19 feet 8 inches
Wingspan	34 feet 11 inches
Empty weight	27,500 pounds
Maximum weight	52,546 pounds
Power plant	(1) Pratt & Whitney 25,000 pound thrust J-75-P-19W turbojet, with afterburner for additional thrust
Cruising speed	778 mph
Maximum speed	1,420 mph
Climb rate	32,000 feet per minute
Service ceiling	52,000 feet
Maximum range	2,000 miles
Armament	(1) General Electric M-16 20mm Vulcan cannon
Bomb load	13,970 pounds, (4) external, under wing pylons (standard) each with four 750 pound bombs
Fuel	Auxiliary fuel tank inside bomb for strikes into North Vietnam

Republic Aviation RF-84F Thunderflash at the Dyess Air Force Base Linear Air Park, Texas. *7th Bomb Wing Public Affairs*

★ Republic Aviation RF-84 Thunderflash

On August 15, 1949, Republic Aviation presented the Air Force a proposal defining a design for a reconnaissance version of the F-84F. The prototype (YRF-84F) flew for the first time in early February 1952. The aircraft was fitted with six cameras mounted in the nose and lower front fuselage. Its primary mission was tactical air reconnaissance, including target assessment and ground coverage of B-29 Superfortress bombing missions. The most obvious change was the splitting of the single engine air intake, creating one to either side of the fuselage at the wing roots. This variant was used in the Fighter Conveyer (FICON) project, during which it was modified so it could be carried underneath and partially in the Convair B-36's bomb bay. The RF-84F was connected to a trapeze lowered below the B-36 for launch. The FICON project experiment was to test the operational feasibility of the B-36 mother ship carrying an RF-84F to its intended reconnaissance search area. This reconnaissance run was outside the Thunderflash's ground takeoff range. The RF-84F returned to the waiting B-36, attached onto the lowered trapeze on the aircraft's nose-mounted hook, and was raised into the bomber's bomb-bay. Twenty-eight RF-84Fs were modified with nose-mounted hooks for expected SAC reconnaissance missions. However, flight testing indicated this was not a viable option due to the danger of the launch and recovery, along with the aircraft's susceptibility to intercept by Russian Air Force fighters.

REPUBLIC AVIATION RF-84F THUNDERFLASH
Specifications and Performance Information

Manufacturer	Republic Aviation and General Motors Corporation
Designation	RF-84
Version (variant)	"F"
Serial Number	51-11293
Nickname	Thunderflash
Type	Fighter
Crew	Pilot
7th Bomb Wing sponsor	7th Logistics Squadron
Length	41 feet 8 inches
Tail height	15 feet
Wingspan	33 feet 7 inches
Empty weight	14,014 pounds
Maximum weight	25,390 pounds
Power plant	(1) Wright 7,800 pound thrust J-65-W-7 turbojet engine
Cruising speed	542 mph
Maximum speed	679 mph
Climb rate	5,820 feet per minute
Service ceiling	33,300 feet
Maximum range	2,200 miles
Armament	(4) .50 caliber machine guns

The air park's RF-84F was delivered to the Air Force on July 18, 1955. It flew with the 71st Strategic Reconnaissance Wing at Larson AFB, Washington, until transferred to the Air National Guard. It was retired in December 1971.

REPUBLIC AVIATION F-84F THUNDERSTREAK
Specifications and Performance Information

Manufacturer	Republic Aviation and General Motors Corporation
Designation	F-84
Version (variant)	"F"
Serial number	51-9364
Nickname	Thunderstreak
Type	Fighter
Crew	Pilot
7th Bomb Wing sponsor	436th Training Squadron
Length	43 feet 5 inches
Tail height	14 feet 5 inches
Wingspan	33 feet 7 inches
Empty weight	13,645 pounds
Combat weight	20,313 pounds
Gross weight	26,995 pounds
Power plant	(1) Wright 7,800 pound J-65-W-7 turbojet engine
Cruising speed	539 mph
Maximum speed	695 mph
Service ceiling	44,450 feet
Range	2,000 miles
Armament	(6) .50-caliber machine guns
Bombs	600 pounds

★ Republic Aviation F-84F Thunderstreak ★

The origins of Republic Aircraft Corporation's swept-wing F-84 variants can be traced back to the summer of 1944. The US Army Air Force proposed converting the piston-powered Republic P-47 Thunderbolt to a turbojet powered fighter by installing two General Electric TG-180 axial flow turbojets in the fuselage. Through several years of engineering changes this eventually became one of Republic Aviation's most famous early turbojet fighters, the straight-wing PF-84 Thunderjet. It made its first flight on February 28, 1946. Preliminary design work on a swept-wing version began on March 1947. This variant flew on June 3, 1950, and was a more capable and reliable aircraft. The F-84 was the first US Air Force single-seat fighter capable of carrying a tactical nuclear bomb, and 2,711 came out of Republic Aviation's production plant. The F-84 was the first turbojet fighter to fly across the North Atlantic nonstop, refueled by Air Force KC-97G Stratofreighters. In 1946, a Thunderjet established a world speed record of 611 mph. Different versions of the F-84 saw service during the Korean War. A small number of F-84s remained in service during the 1970s. The air park's F-84F was delivered to Bergstrom AFB, Texas, on July 1, 1954. Later, it served with the Texas Air National Guard at Kelly AFB, where it remained until pulled from active status in March 1971.

Republic Aviation F-84F Thunderstreak at the Dyess Air Force Base Linear Air Park, Texas. *7th Bomb Wing Public Affairs*

McDonnell Aircraft Corporation began studies on an all-weather attack fighter in August 1954. The basic version was a single-seat aircraft with a forty-five degree swept wing. The Navy sponsored the development of a two-seat fighter instead, which it ordered in September 1955. In compliance with a secretary of defense directive the Air Force evaluated the Navy's F-4B, concluding it was a flexible fighter more capable than its Republic F-105D Thunderchief. Although the F-105D was an outstanding heavy fighter-bomber, it was under-powered for its bomb loads and was not an air superiority fighter. On January 17, 1962, the Air Force ordered the F-4 phantom variant, the F-4C. The first prototype of the F-4C flew on May 27, 1963. The F-4C had only the basic requirements the Air Force needed and the modified variant became the F-4D. The first production F-4D flew on December 9, 1965, at Lambert Field, St. Louis, Missouri. The F-4D entered combat operations in Southeast Asia in May 1967. It proved its worthiness in aerial combat on June 5, 1967, when a crew assigned to the 555th Tactical Fighter Squadron shot down a North Vietnamese Air Force MiG-17 Fresco with an AIM-7 missile. At this time the F-4D, in accordance with Air Force tactical operations, was only armed with air to air missiles, but was later modified with a pylon mounted Gatling gun. Following production aircraft had an integral Gatling gun in the nose of the aircraft, improving close-in aerial dog-fighting against the smaller and very maneuverable MiG-17 and MiG-21. The F-4D was the first Air Force fighter to drop laser guided bombs, using the GBU-10/B MK-84 in May 1968. It allowed one F-4D to destroy pinpoint targets during one sortie.

The F-4D on display is not at Dyess AFB, but in front of the William E. Dyess Elementary School. The school is outside the base's fenced area. This F-4D was credited with shooting down a North Vietnamese Air Force MiG-21 Fishbed on January 8, 1973. This was the final (official) Air Force MiG kill of the war in Southeast Asia.

McDonnell Aircraft F-4D Phantom. On Display at the William Dyess Elementary School, outside Dyess Air Force Base. *7th Bomb Wing Public Affairs*

MCDONNELL AIRCRAFT COMPANY F-4D PHANTOM
Specifications and Performance Information

Manufacturer	McDonnell Aircraft Company
Designation	F-4
Version (variant)	"D"
Serial number	65-0796
Nickname	Phantom
Type	Fighter
Crew	Pilot, pilot/rear-observer
Sponsor	The City of Abilene, Texas
Length	62 feet 10 inches
Tail height	16 feet 6 inches
Wingspan	38 feet 5 inches
Wing area	530 square feet
Empty weight	25,598 pounds
Gross weight	50,341 pounds
Maximum weight	59,380 pounds
Power plant	(2) General Electric 17,000 pound thrust J-79-GE-15 Axial Flow turbojet engines (each with afterburner for additional thrust)
Cruising speed	587 mph
Maximum speed	1,466 mph (with full afterburners)
Climb rate	49,000 feet per minute
Service ceiling	59,600 feet
Range	2,300 miles
Armament	Wide variety (air defense and ground attack roles)

General Dynamics F-111 Aardvark, On display at the Dyess Air Force Base Linear Air Park, Texas. *7th Bomb Wing Public Affairs*

★ General Dynamics F-111A Aardvark ★

This large fighter was conceived as a Joint Defense Fighter (JDF) under the Department of Defense's Tactical Fighter Experiment (TFX) Program in 1960, designated the F-111B. The F-111's first flight was on December 1, 1964. The Air Force decided to continue testing, development, and production, even though the Navy dropped out of the joint program. Tactical Air Command introduced the fighter into the Vietnam War for combat testing, but due to crashes withdrew it from combat. An Air Force crash investigation team determined the automatic terrain following radar had been shut off by the aircrew and they could not respond fast enough at low level and high speeds to clear terrain. The aircrew believed they were in danger of crashing if they allowed the aircraft to actually fly the aircraft. This was corrected and the aircraft resumed combat sorties in Southeast Asia in 1972. It served with distinction during intense air combat during Linebacker II in December 1973, particularly in and around Hanoi and Haiphong. It was also modified into the EF-111 ECM jammer aircraft. SAC took the F-111 airframe, modified it with longer wings and fuel capacity for longer range, and it became the medium SIOP/EWO FB-111 bomber.

GENERAL DYNAMICS F-111A AARDVARK
Specifications and Performance Information

Manufacturer	General Dynamics
Designation	F-111
Version (variant)	"F"
Serial number	67-0057
Type	(final designation) Ground force trainer, (original) Variable-wing fighter-ground attack
Crew	Pilot, copilot
7th Bomb Wing sponsor	Not listed
Empty weight	47,481 pounds
Maximum weight	100,000 pounds
Power plant	(2) Pratt & Whitney 25,100 pound thrust TF30-P-9 turbofan engines
Maximum speed	Mach 2.5 (with afterburners engaged)
Service ceiling	59,000 feet
Range	3,000 miles
Armament	(1) 20mm multi-barrel cannon
Bombs	25,000 pounds, mounted on under wing pylons

The air park's F-111A/GF-111A was delivered to the Air Force on November 13, 1968, assigned to the 474th Fighter Tactical Wing (FTW). On November 6, 1969, the aircraft's crew experienced a nacelle ejector duct failure that required extensive repairs. After the aircraft was repaired it returned to wing flight operations. The fighter was retired from flying operations at Mountain Home AFB, Idaho, on August 31, 1990. It was transferred to Sheppard AFB, Texas, for use as a static ground force trainer until it was trucked to Dyess AFB on February 4, 2000, for static display.

Whether you call it the Texan, Harvard, Yale, Mosquito, or simply the T-6, the North American T-6 trainer was one of the most important aircraft designs of WWII. The T-6 was built in greater numbers than most of the aircraft it trained pilots for. There were 15,495 Texans built by North American Aviation and foreign countries under license. Although designed as a basic trainer, the T-6 was used in a number of roles: advanced trainer, fighter, interceptor, fighter-bomber, forward air control, and counter-insurgency. The Texan served with at least fifty-five air forces throughout the world. It served in WWII and during the Korean War. The Texan saw action in dozens of brush fires around the world: Algeria, Congo, Biafra, Middle East, and Latin America. Despite its impressive war record, the Texan is best known as a trainer. There have been many other aircraft developed for training, but only the Texan is known by the name "Pilot Maker." The North American trainer design (NA-16) was a blend of the traditional and the innovative. The NA-16 rolled out of North American and flew for the first time on April 1, 1935. The US Army liked the aircraft, but wanted some changes before it would approve the aircraft for production. Once changes were completed the Army inspected the prototype (NA-18) and ordered forty-two under the designation BT-9 (it was not until 1940 that it was designated the T-6).

The air park's AT-6F was built in Dallas, Texas, and was delivered to Love Field, Texas, on March 11, 1945. It was retired from service in September 1955 and sold as surplus to a civilian owner who flew the aircraft in several movies, including *Tora, Tora, Tora* and *Midway*, painted to resemble a Japanese fighter. The aircraft was donated to the National Museum of the United States Air Force and currently wears colors and markings as if assigned to Avenger Field, Sweetwater, Texas, a WWII training base for Woman Air Force Service Pilots (WASPs).

NORTH AMERICAN T-6F TEXAN
Specifications and Performance Information

Manufacturer	North American Aviation
Designation	T-6
Version (variant)	"F"
Serial number	44-81819
Nickname	Texan
Type	Trainer
Crew	Student pilot, instructor pilot
7th Bomb Wing sponsor	7th Bomb Wing
Length	29 feet
Tail height	11 feet 9 inches
Wingspan	42 feet
Wing area	254 square feet
Empty weight	3,900 pounds
Maximum weight	5,617 pounds
Power plant	(1) Pratt & Whitney 600 hp air-cooled, radial engine
Maximum speed	210 mph
Service ceiling	23,500 feet
Range	770 miles
Armament (possible)	Under wing mounted guns, rocket pods

North American Aviation T-6F Texan at the Dyess Air Force Base Linear Air Park, Texas. *7th Bomb Wing Public Affairs*

Originally this aircraft started as the Cessna 337 Super Skymaster. This unorthodox, all-metal business aircraft resulted from several years of study by Cessna aimed at producing a twin-engine aircraft that would be simple to fly, low cost, and comfortable, while offering the traditional advantages of twin-engine reliability and survivability if selected by the Pentagon. The Air Force selected and purchased the twin-engine aircraft right off the Cessna production line to fly in South Vietnam as a Forward Air Controller (FAC) aircraft, beginning combat operations in 1967 designated as the O-2. The air park's "A" model was used as a FAC. The "B" models were used for low-level propaganda broadcasts over communist occupied and operational areas in South Vietnam. After the war, North Vietnamese officials indicated these aircraft-borne broadcasts were ineffective. The air park's aircraft was stationed at Da Nang Air Base and Cam Ranh Air Base, South Vietnam, from December 1967 until March 1971. The aircraft suffered extensive damage from communist ground fire, landing safely at Cam Ranh AB; gunfire holes are visible along the rear engine's lower coiling, the left side bottom of the aircraft's fuselage, and its vertical stabilizer. Ground personnel used metal patches pop-riveted over the shell holes to repair cosmetic damage. The aircraft continued to fly in support of US special forces operations.

Cessna Aircraft O-2A Skymaster at the Dyess Air Force Base Linear Air Park, Texas. *7th Bomb Wing Public Affairs*

The aircraft's survivability stems from its front and rear engine combination. If one engine received battle damage it could remain flying, safely exiting the combat area. Also, two engines allowed the pilot to not have to compensate for off-center thrust should one of the engines stop functioning. Originally, Cessna intended this feature as an aid to civilian and military pilot transition from single-engine trainer aircraft to twin-engine piston powered aircraft. In South Vietnam, tactical air operations relied on the O-2 to provide pilots flying low over enemy positions a margin of safety not otherwise available in the single engine O-1. When used either as a FAC or propaganda broadcast aircraft, the O-2 spent most of its combat operations flying over heavy jungle canopy, under constant threat from small arms and automatic weapons fire. As a FAC, the O-2 was responsible for visual reconnaissance, target identification, target marking for orbiting fighter-bombers, and ground to air coordination of multiple attack aircraft, as well as bomb damage assessment. The air park's O-2 was delivered to the Air Force on June 27, 1967, and retired in 1982.

CESSNA AIRCRAFT O-2 SKYMASTER
Specifications and Performance Information

Manufacturer	Cessna Aircraft Corporation
Designation	O-2
Version (variant)	"A"
Serial number	67-21326
Nickname	Skymaster
Type	Observation/propaganda
Crew	Pilot, observer
7th Wing bomb sponsor	Company Grade Officers Council
Length	29 feet 9 inches
Tail height	9 feet 2 inches
Wingspan	38 feet 2 inches
Empty weight	2,705 pounds
Maximum weight	4,630 pounds
Power plant	(2) Continental 210 HP 10-360 flat, six-piston engines
Cruising speed	196 mph
Maximum speed	205 mph
Service ceiling	19,300 feet
Range	1,325 miles
Armament	Wing gun pods, flares, marker rockets

The T-34 Mentor began as a private venture by Walter Beech after WWII. Beech felt there would be a future market for a military trainer based on the Model 35 Bonanza, which had been flying for one year. Beach used the Bonanza as a starting point to begin design work on the Model 45. The first two prototypes were powered by a 205 hp Continental engine, with the third prototype having a more powerful 225 hp engine. The first flight was on December 2, 1948. The aircraft was demonstrated to the Air Force, which was sufficiently impressed to proceed with testing three prototypes under the designation UT-34. It took until late 1952 for Air Force order production of the T-34. There was a need for a trainer to prepare pilots to advance into turbojet aircraft (F-84 and F-86). The T-34 was used for thirty-five years as a pilot trainer. The first production run of 350 aircraft was delivered to the Air Force in 1953, with the Navy accepting its first T-34 production run of 423 in 1954. The T-34's design was rugged and reliable due to its all-metal composition. The T-34 retained many common parts with production models of the civilian Beech Bonanza and Debonair, reducing military maintenance costs. In 1973, a few T-34s were upgraded with turboprop engines, twice as powerful as the former piston Continental engine. It was used as a trainer and light attack aircraft.

The air park's T-34B was delivered to the US Navy on February 21, 1956, and retired from active service on September 30, 1960. It accumulated a total of 1,123 flying hours. It has been restored to a standard T-34B paint scheme that the Air Force operated.

BEECHCRAFT AIRCRAFT T-34B MENTOR
Specifications and Performance Information

Manufacturer	Beechcraft Aircraft Company
Designation	T-34
Version (variant)	"B"
Serial number	140810
Nickname	Mentor
Type	Training
7th Bomb Wing Sponsor	7th Medical Group
Length	25 feet 11 inches
Tail height	9 feet 7 inches
Wingspan	32 feet 10 inches
Empty weight	2,254 pounds
Maximum weight	3,000 pounds
Power plant	(1) Continental 225 hp piston engine
Range	975 miles
Cruising speed	173 mph
Maximum speed	189 mph
Climb rate	1,200 feet per minute
Service ceiling	19,500 feet
Crew	Student pilot, instructor pilot

Beechcraft Aircraft T-34B Mentor at the Dyess Air Force Base Linear Air Park, Texas. *7th Bomb Wing Public Affairs*

Cessna Aircraft T-37B Tweety at the Dyess Air Force Base Linear Air Park, Texas. *7th Bomb Wing Public Affairs*

CESSNA AIRCRAFT T-37B TWEETY BIRD
Specifications and Performance Information

Manufacturer	Cessna Aircraft Corporation
Designation	T-37
Version (variant)	"B"
Serial number	54-2734
Nickname	Tweety Bird
Type	Training
Crew	Student pilot, instructor pilot
7th Bomb Wing sponsor	7th Component Repair Squadron
Length	29 feet 3 inches
Tail height	8 feet 10 inches
Wingspan	32 feet 9 inches
Wing area	184 square feet
Empty weight	3,860 pounds
Maximum weight	6,453 pounds
Climb rate	3,370 feet per minute
Power plant	(2) Continental 1,025-pound thrust J69-T-25 turbojet engines
Range	600 miles
Cruising speed	379 mph
Maximum speed	425 mph
Service ceiling	35,000 feet

Cessna Aircraft T-37B Tweety Bird

The T-37 was a twin-engine, primary trainer used to instruct student pilots on the fundamentals of jet aircraft handling characteristics and formation and night flying. It became known as the "Tweety Bird." It was the first Air Force jet aircraft designed as a trainer. The aircraft's flying characteristics helped prepare student pilots to handle the larger, faster T-38 Talon they would later fly during training. The T-37's side-by-side seating made pilot training more effective, allowing the instructor pilot to better observe and teach the student pilot. The production T-37A first flew in 1955, entering operational Air Force training service in 1957. Cessna produced 1,300 T-37As, T-37Bs, and T-37Cs by the late 1970s.

The air park's T-37B on display was built in 1954, with less than 1,500 flying hours. This T-37B was the sixth T-37A produced, and was originally used as a research and test aircraft at Edwards AFB Flight Test Center. It was transferred to James Connally AFB, Texas, and on to Sheppard AFB, Texas, as a ground maintenance trainer. It was converted to a T-37B in 1960. The air park's T-37B has never been painted and appears as it would have in 1954.

The T-29/C-131 series of aircraft was one of the US military's many cost saving examples for its utility and transport needs. The first military Convair Liner was accepted on March 8, 1950. Military production eclipsed civilian production with the final Convair, a military modification called the Canadair CL-66B Military Convair Liner. A total of 472 Military Convair Liners were produced. The variant remains operational with civilian airliners and in the US armed forces. Some were used as navigation trainers, other as transports. Many T-29s served as staff transports. C-131s performed as airborne ambulances designated the Samaritan. It could carry four crew members and forty-eight passengers.

The air park's T-29 was delivered to the Air Force on October 26, 1954, operationally serving at Harlington Air Force Base and Connally AFB, Texas, as a navigation trainer. It was equipped with individual student navigation stations for ten students who took turns navigating the airborne aircraft under the constant supervision of instructors on board. The display aircraft served as a navigation trainer at these two bases from March 1960 to October 1965, then transferred to the Navy. It was retired in March 1975.

CONVAIR T-29C FLYING CLASSROOM
Specifications and Performance Information

Manufacturer................ Consolidated Vultee Aircraft Corporation (Convair), later- Convair Division of General Dynamics
Designation T-29
Version (variant)........ "C"
Serial number........ 52-2275
Nickname .... Flying Classroom
Type .... Cargo, transport, navigation trainer
Crew 4
Passengers........ 48
Trainer........... Four crew/plus navigation instructors, ten navigator students
7th Bomb Wing sponsor .... 7th Medical Group
Empty weight .... 29,248 pounds
Maximum weight .... 47,000 pounds
Power plant........ (2) Pratt & Whitney 2,500 hp R-2800-99W, 18-cylinder, Double Wasp piston engines
Cruising speed .... 245 mph
Maximum speed .... 296 mph
Service ceiling .... 24,500 feet
Range........ 1,500 miles

Convair T-29C Flying Classroom at the Dyess Air Force Base Linear Air Park, Texas. *7th Bomb Wing Public Affairs*

Lockheed Aircraft T-33A Shooting Star at the Dyess Air Force Base Linear Air Park, Texas. *7th Bomb Wing Public Affairs*

★ Lockheed Aircraft T-33A Shooting Star

The T-33 trainer ("T-Bird") grew out of the F-80 fighter. By adding three feet to the fuselage the world's first jet trainer was born. Design work started in 1943, with the first flight on January 8, 1944. The P-80 was the first jet fighter to enter Air Force squadron service during the Korean War; although out-classed by the MiG-15, it became a superb ground attack aircraft, supporting US, South Korea, and UN troops. As more advanced turbojet aircraft entered service the F-80 became the perfect trainer, with a dual, in-line cockpit and its armament removed. Some T-33As were re-armed with two .50-caliber machine guns for student pilot gunnery training. A reconnaissance variant (RT-33) was manufactured for export sales and was licensed for production in Canada and Japan. The Navy's variant was the T-1A Sea Star.

The air park's T-33 was assigned to Big Springs, Texas, from March 1952 to February 1953. It was transferred to the 3560th Pilot Training Wing at Webb AFB, Texas, in 1954, remaining there until retiring from service in September 1961. Pylons under the wings were used to carry a variety of test equipment, including ECM pods and a chaff dispenser.

LOCKHEED AIRCRAFT T-33A SHOOTING STAR
Specifications and Performance Information

Manufacturer	Lockheed Aircraft Corporation
Designation	T-33
Version (variant)	"A"
Serial number	51-4300
Nickname	Shooting Star
Type	Trainer
Crew	Student pilot, instructor pilot
7th Bomb Wing sponsor	417th Field Training Detachment
Length	37 feet 9 inches
Tail height	11 feet 8 inches
Wingspan	38 feet 10 inches
Wing area	235 square feet
Empty weight	8,804 pounds
Maximum weight	14,442 pounds
Power plant	(1) Allison 5,200 pound thrust J-33-35 turbojet engine
Maximum speed	543 mph
Service ceiling	47,500 feet
Range	1,343 miles

In August 1956, North American Aviation began work on the NA-246 as a private venture in response to an Air Force requirement calling for a combat readiness trainer and utility aircraft. The first flight was on September 16, 1958, with the first production aircraft flying on June 30, 1960. By the end of 1963, the Air Force had accepted 143 T-39As. The majority of these aircraft were six-seat utility transports. They have been used by all Air Force major commands, as well as the Navy and Marine Corps. T-39s with the Air Training Command were used at Randolph Air Force Base, Texas. T-39Bs were used as radar systems trainers for F-105D Thunderchief pilots during the Vietnam War and for transition by Air National Guard and Air Force Reserve units that flew the F-105D. In 1968, three T-39s were modified into T-39Fs, equipped with the same electronics carried by the F-105G Wild Weasel, earning the nickname "Teeny Weeny Weasels." The air park's T-39A was delivered to the Air Force on February 4, 1962. It arrived at Dyess AFB from Randolph AFB, Texas, on October 5, 1985.

NORTH AMERICAN AVIATION T-39A SABERLINER
Specifications and Performance Information

Manufacturer	North American Aviation
Designation	T-39
Version (variant)	"A"
Serial number	61-0634
Nickname	Saberliner
Type	Trainer/utility
Crew	Pilot, copilot
Passengers	Six
7th Bomb Wing Sponsor	7th Transportation Squadron
Length	44 feet
Tail height	16 feet
Wingspan	44 feet 6 inches
Power plant	(2) Pratt & Whitney 3,000 pound thrust J60-P-3 engines
Cruising speed	452 mph
Maximum speed	595 mph
Service ceiling	39,000 feet
Range	1,725 miles

North American T-39A Saberliner at the Dyess Air Force Base Linear Air Park, Texas. *7th Bomb Wing Public Affairs*

The T-38A was produced for the Air Force as its first supersonic jet trainer. The T-38A was flown as an advanced trainer for upgrading pilots from the T-37 basic trainer to the more maneuverable and faster aircraft they would fly with operational Air Force units. Student pilots flying the T-38 gained experience in supersonic aircraft using its afterburner engines to attain a maximum 820 mph. The first prototype flew in 1959, with the first aircraft delivered to the Air Force in 1961. Series production ran from 1961 to 1972, with 1,100 built. As of May 2012, the Air Force operated fifty T-38As and 471 T-38Cs, with an estimated end of life cycle in 2020.

The air park's distinctive paint scheme reflects a potential aggressor's camouflage so Air Force pilots received near-real experience in aerial dog-fighting against simulated Soviet bloc fighters. The air park's aircraft was last assigned to Sheppard AFB, Texas, as a ground trainer for maintenance personnel.

NORTHROP CORPORATION T-38A TALON
Specification and Performance Information

Manufacturer................................ Northrop Corporation
Designation T-38
Version (variant).. "A"
Serial number..60-0592
Nickname ....Talon
Type (final use) ....Ground trainer
Crew (active trainer).............Student pilot, instructor pilot
7th Bomb Wing sponsor ....9th Bombardment Squadron
Length ....46 feet 4 inches
Tail height..12 feet 10 inches
Wingspan...25 feet 3 inches
Power plant.........(2) General Electric 3,850 pound thrust J-85-GE-5 turbojets, each with afterburner for additional thrust
Range...860 miles
Cruising speed..767 mph
Maximum speed ....820 mph
Service ceiling ....42,000 feet

Northrop Corporation T-38A Talon at the Dyess Air Force Base Linear Air Park, Texas. *7th Bomb Wing Public Affairs*

BOEING AIRCRAFT KC-135A STRATOTANKER
Specifications and Performance Information

Manufacturer	Boeing Aircraft Company
Designation	KC-135
Version (variant)	"A"
Serial number	56-3639
Nickname	Stratotanker
Type	Tanker
Crew	Pilot, copilot, navigator, boom operator
7th Bomb Wing sponsor	7th Logistics Support Squadron
Length	136 feet 3 inches
Tail height	38 feet 4 inches
Wingspan	130 feet 10 inches
Empty weight	98,466 pounds
Maximum weight	297,000 pounds
Power plant	(4) Pratt & Whitney 8,000 pound thrust J-57-P-59W turbojet engines, increased per engine to 11,000 pounds of thrust with water injection
Maximum speed	530 mph at 30,000 feet
Service ceiling	50,000 feet
Range	1,150 miles with 120,000 pounds of JP-4 fuel transferred
Ferry range	9,200 miles

Boeing Aircraft KC-135A Stratotanker at the Dyess Air Force Base Linear Air Park, Texas. *7th Bomb Wing Public Affairs*

★ Boeing Aircraft KC-135A Stratotanker

The air park's KC-135A arrived at Dyess AFB on May 26, 1981, assigned to the 917th Air Refueling Squadron. It was the third Dyess tanker sent to Incirlick Air Base, Turkey, in support of Operations DESERT SHIELD and DESERT STORM. This tanker completed thirty-eight combat sorties. Although originally assigned to SAC, the tanker flew its final operational mission with Air Combat Command on June 8, 1992.

Boeing Aircraft aviation engineers/designers fattened the B-29 Superfortress' fuselage—using the same wings, tail, and engines—to build the Stratofreighter. The prototype flew in 1944, with the first production C-97A in 1949. About the same time, Boeing Aircraft developed the flying boom for aerial refueling operations tested on a modified Superfortress (KB-29). Previously, the Air Force experimented with a trailing hose and drogue refueling system that is still used on certain types of aircraft (primarily helicopters). The C-97 Stratofreighter was modified into the KC-97 Stratofreighter (aerial tanker). Its mission was to provide aerial refueling for SAC bomber aircraft, primarily the Boeing B-47 Stratojet. The KC-97 provided pioneer operational work incorporated in the Boeing KC-135A Stratotanker. The KC-97 carried aviation gasoline (AVGAS) for its piston engines and JP-4 in separate fuel tanks for transfer to turbojet aircraft.

The air park's KC-97L was delivered to the Air Force on December 8, 1955. It was assigned to SAC and later transferred to the Air National Guard's 136th Air Refueling Wing, Dallas, Texas, from October 1976 to June 1978. It was retired from active service in July 1978.

BOEING AIRCRAFT KC-97L STRATOFREIGHTER
Specifications and Performance Information

Manufacturer	Boeing Aircraft Company
Designation	KC-97
Version (variant)	"L"
Serial number	56-3639
Nickname	Stratofreighter
Type	Tanker
Crew	Pilot, copilot, navigator, flight engineer, boom operator
7th Bomb Wing sponsor	7th Equipment Maintenance Squadron
Length	117 feet 5 inches
Tail height	38 feet 4 inches
Wingspan	141 feet 2 inches
Empty weight	82,500 pounds
Maximum weight	175,000 pounds
Power plant	(4) Pratt & Whitney 3,500 hp R-4360-59 Wasp Major radial piston engines
Auxiliary	(2) General Electric 7,200 pound thrust J-47-GE-23 turbojet engines
Cruising speed	300 mph
Maximum speed	375 mph
Service ceiling	30,000 feet
Range	2,300 miles

Boeing Aircraft KC-97L Stratofreighter at the Dyess Air Force Base Linear Air Park, Texas. *7th Bomb Wing Public Affairs*

⋆ Douglas Aircraft C-47A Skytrain

The C-47 (civilian designation DC-3) is apparently a fly-forever aircraft. Some are still operational around the world, carrying on where other newer aircraft have long been scrapped. First deliveries to the US Army Air Force occurred in 1938. The C-47 served as a passenger transport, cargo carrier, airborne/flying ambulance, paratroop delivery aircraft, glider tow and recovery aircraft, trainer, and sometimes an impromptu bomber. During WWII, float and glider variants existed, but only in small numbers; the twin-piston engine aircraft were too valuable to be siphoned off in other roles. During the Vietnam War, AC-47 gunships were armed with three 7.62mm Gatling guns aimed through the fuselage, delivering devastating, close-in artillery support for ground troops. The C-47 went by many different names, including Skytrain, Skytrooper, and Dakota, but most simply called it the "Gooney Bird." In many respects, the C-47 stands out as no other does, having served in WWII, the Korean War, the Vietnam War, and most recently with the Turkish Air Force in Operations DESERT SHIELD and DESERT STORM. The aircraft introduced practical commercial aviation to the world and is easily flown and maintained. Capable of operating from primitive, unimproved airstrips, it could deliver passengers and cargo where no other cargo transport could. It opened horizons for aviation and the people it served. The Russian Air Force built their own production copies of American WWII Lend Lease C-47s. Russian Air Force officers gave the C-47 the ultimate compliment, claiming their aviation designers and engineers developed the aircraft.

The air park's C-47 wears the paint scheme of Allied D-Day aircraft during the Normandy Invasion on June 6, 1944. Hundreds of C-47s flew on D-Day, towing gliders and dropping pre-invasion pathfinder paratroop teams the night before the dawn landings to mark paratroop jump zones. The air park's C-47 last flew with the US Customs Service.

Douglas Aircraft C-47A Skytrain at the Dyess Air Force Base Linear Air Park, Texas. *7th Bomb Wing Public Affairs*

DOUGLAS AIRCRAFT C-47A SKYTRAIN
Specifications and Performance Information

Manufacturer	Douglas Aircraft
Designation	C-47
Version (variant)	"A"
Serial number	41-108808
Nickname	Skytrain
Type	Cargo/transport
7th Bomb Wing sponsor	39th Airlift Squadron
Length	63 feet 9 inches
Tail height	17 feet
Wingspan	95 feet 6 inches
Wing area	987 square feet
Empty weight	16,970 pounds
Maximum weight	33,000 pounds
Power plant	(2) Pratt & Whitney 1,200 hp R-1830-92 Twin Wasp 14 cylinder radial piston engines
Cruising speed	207 mph
Maximum speed	230 mph
Service ceiling	23,000 feet
Range	1,600 miles

First flown in 1949, the C-123 design was initiated as a glider. By this time the Air Force had lost interest in gliders, so the design was modified with two piston engines, making its first powered flight in 1953. It was very maneuverable at low speed and was ideal for short field operations in its role as a tactical transport. During its early career, C-123s were used as paratroop transports. During the Vietnam War the aircraft became an all-purpose tactical aircraft, usually used in support of US special forces operating out of isolated armed camps in South Vietnam along or blocking North Vietnamese and Viet Cong supply lines. The C-123 was the US aircraft used in Operation RANCH HAND.

The air park's C-123K was delivered to the Air Force as a C-123B—the first production series—and was later modified into a C-123K. The upgrade added two 2,850-pound thrust turbojet engines—one outboard of each piston engine—to improve takeoff performance from very short jungle runways in South Vietnam. The air park's aircraft was delivered to the Air Force in November 1955. After the Vietnam War the aircraft served with Florida, Georgia, and Pennsylvania Air National Guard units. It was retired from active service in August 1981.

Fairchild Aircraft Industries C-123K Provider at the Dyess Air Force Base Linear Air Park, Texas. *7th Bomb Wing Public Affairs*

FAIRCHILD AIRCRAFT INDUSTRIES C-123K PROVIDER
Specifications and Performance Information

Manufacturer .... Chase/Kaiser-Frazier, Fairchild Aircraft Industries
Designation C-123
Version (variant) .... "K"
Serial number 54-604
Nickname .... Provider
Type .... Tactical cargo/transport
Crew .... Pilot, copilot
Passengers .... 61 troops, -or- 50 litter patients with six sitting wounded and six medical personnel to take care of the wounded
7th Bomb Wing sponsor .... 40th Airlift Squadron
Length .... 76 feet 3 inches
Tail height .... 34 feet 6 inches
Wingspan .... 110 feet
Wing area .... 1,223 square feet
Empty weight .... 25,367 pounds
Maximum weight .... 40,318 pounds
Cargo weight limitation ...... 15,000 pounds -or- 61 troops in cargo compartment
Power plant .... (2) Pratt & Whitney 2,300 hp R-2800-99W 18-cylinder Double Wasp Major engines
Auxiliary .... (2) General Electric 2,850 pound thrust J-85-17 turbojet engines
Cruising speed .... 170 mph
Maximum speed .... 245 mph
Service ceiling .... 29,000 feet
Range .... 1,420 miles

The first operational C-130A Hercules was delivered to the 463rd Troop Carrier Wing—not the 463rd Airlift Wing—at Ardmore, Oklahoma, on December 9, 1956. The air park's C-130A was the first Hercules delivered to the 463rd Tactical Carrier Wing. C-130s served with the Air Force, Navy, Marine Corps, Coast Guard, and many air forces around the world. There are no plans to retire Hercules from active service, with the latest variant, the C-130J-30, currently operating at Dyess AFB with the 317th Airlift Group. C-130s have been used in many different roles: troop carrier, radio relay airborne station, aerial refueling tanker for helicopters, and aerial firefighting bombers to fight US forest fires in remote and rugged areas not easily accessible from the ground. The US Navy tested a C-130 for aircraft carrier operations. Tests proved it could take off and land on the deck of Navy carriers. However, it was determined the aircraft's size limited the number of combat aircraft that could be operated from the carrier. Also, the Hercules could not fit on the carrier's elevators for storage in the hangar deck to allow for continuous air operations.

The air park's C-130A "City of Ardmore" saw service during Air Force operational deployments to Europe, Japan, Okinawa, and South Vietnam during the Vietnam War. It flew in support of President Dwight Eisenhower's 1958 US peacekeeper forces sent to Lebanon and also to Taiwan. During its combat tour with the 374th Tactical Airlift Wing, the aircraft was hit by communist small arms ground fire while delivering troops in South Vietnam. The damage caused fuel to leak from its ruptured tanks into the cargo ramp area, catching fire and crippling the aircraft. The Loadmaster was wounded, but the aircraft safely returned to its launch base. The Loadmaster designated his Purple Heart to be permanently mounted on the interior of the aircraft, where it remains. After repairs, the Hercules was flown back to the United States for extensive depot maintenance repair. Lockheed workers located holes on the Hercules underneath the fuselage and on the jump doors and engine hoods. The C-130A returned to operational status after six months of Lockheed repairs. It was retired from active service on October 9, 1989.

Lockheed Aircraft C-130A Hercules at the Dyess Air Force Base Linear Air Park, Texas. *7th Bomb Wing Public Affairs*

LOCKHEED C-130A HERCULES
Specifications and Performance Information

Manufacturer	Lockheed Aircraft Corporation
Designation	C-130
Version (variant)	"A"
Serial number	55-0023
Nickname	Hercules
Type	Cargo/transport
Crew	Pilot, copilot, navigator, flight engineer, loadmaster
7th Bomb Wing sponsor	Airlifter Association
Length	97 feet 9 inches
Tail height	38 feet 3 inches
Wingspan	132 feet 7 inches
Wing area	1,745 square feet
Empty weight	57,892 pounds
Maximum weight	108,000 pounds
Overload weight	124,200 pounds
Aviation fuel capacity	5,080 gallons
Power plant	(4) Allison 3,750 hp T-56-A-9 turboprop engines
Propellers	(4) Constant speed, fully feathered, reversible pitch
Auxiliary power	(8) Aerojet General Electric 1,000 pound thrust 15KS-1000 JATOs
Cruising speed	345 mph
Maximum speed	245 mph
Service ceiling	33,000 feet
Range	3,400 miles

The air park's Caribou began its long career as the fourth aircraft of the first five YAC-1s built for the US Army. The aircraft's records indicate the Air Force initially accepted the aircraft before it could be transferred to the US Army. The first three of five C-7As for the Army were delivered in an official ceremony on November 8, 1959, at the DeHavilland production plant outside Toronto, Canada. The Army accepted serial number 57-3082 three weeks later. That aircraft, along with the other four prototypes, went through official evaluation/acceptance trials at different US bases. Serial number 57-3082 was re-designated YC-7A. In early 1966, the Army and Air Force chiefs of staff agreed to transfer the Army Caribou force, along with their control and operations, to the Air Force. Aircraft and equipment were officially transferred on December 31, 1966. The Air Force, in return, agreed not to press for a helicopter airlift arm, thus removing that force from Army control. The aircraft was transferred to headquarters Air Force Logistics Command at Wright Patterson AFB, Dayton, Ohio, where it remained until March 13, 1975. The aircraft was then flown to Fort Bragg, North Carolina. The aircraft remained under Air Force control, but was assigned to support the US Army's Golden Knights parachute team. The Caribou was used to transport the Golden Knights around the United States. On March 2, 1980, the aircraft was transferred to US Army control, at which time the Golden Knights continued to use the aircraft for parachute demonstrations until transitioning to the more capable Fokker C-31 in 1985.

DeHavilland C-7A Caribou at the Dyess Air Force Base Linear Air Park, Texas. *7th Bomb Wing Public Affairs*

Dyess AFB's 463rd Airlift Wing decided to add a C-7A for static display when Operations DESERT SHIELD and DESERT STORM began. A year later, personnel from the 463rd Maintenance Squadron deployed to Pope AFB, North Carolina, to dissemble the aircraft so it could be loaded into a C-5B Galaxy transport for air movement to Dyess AFB. It was officially dedicated on May 2, 1992.

DEHAVILLAND C-7A CARIBOU
Specifications and Performance Information

Manufacturer	DeHavilland of Canada
Designation	C-7
Version (variant)	"A"
Serial number	57-3082
Nickname	Caribou
Type (initial)	Prototype
Final	US Army Golden Knights parachute team aircraft
Crew	Pilot, copilot, flight engineer/loadmaster
7th Bomb Wing sponsor	39th Airlift Squadron
Length	72 feet 7 inches
Tail height	31 feet 8 inches
Wingspan	95 feet 7 inches
Empty weight	18,380 pounds
Maximum weight	26,000 pounds
Power plant	(2) Pratt & Whitney 1,450 hp R-2000-7M2 14-cylinder two-row radial air-cooled engines
Propellers	(2) Hamilton Standard, three-blade, fully featherable, hydromantic
Range	1,400 miles
Cruising speed	182 mph
Maximum speed	216 mph
Service ceiling	27,700 feet

Grumman Aircraft Corporation HU-16E Albatross at the Dyess Air Force Base Linear Air Park, Texas. *7th Bomb Wing Public Affairs*

★ Grumman Aircraft Corporation HU-16E Albatross

The Albatross first flew on October 1, 1947, entering military service in July 1949. A total of 305 were delivered to the Air Force, Navy, and Coast Guard. The aircraft could land on land, water, and ice. Many crewmen referred to the aircraft as the "unique tri-a mphibian." It served in many roles, including anti-submarine patrol, search and rescue, utility transport, and coastal surveillance. The aircraft is credited with over 1,000 rescue missions during the Korean War. A few Albatrosses were adapted as civilian commercial transports. Periodically, an Albatross landed on ice or snow using their hulls and not deploying the landing gear, which would rip off on the rough and uneven surface. The aircraft could be based at a traditional airport using its landing gear for hard surface operations, taxi on the concrete surface to a ramp into the water, and then take off. The Albatross ended its long military service in 1976, but civilian operators continue to fly it. The air park's Albatross was delivered to the Air Force in December 1949, ended operations in 1959, then transferred to the Coast Guard, remaining in search and rescue service into July 1982.

GRUMMAN AIRCRAFT CORPORATION HU-16E ALBATROSS
Specifications and Performance Information

Manufacturer	Grumman Aircraft Corporation
Designation	HU-16
Version (variant)	"E"
Serial number	51-7251
Nickname	Albatross
Type	General purpose/utility amphibian
Crew	Pilot, copilot, navigator, radio operator, one to two observers
7th Bomb Wing sponsor	40th Airlift Squadron
Length	61 feet 3 inches
Tail height	25 feet 10 inches
Wingspan	96 feet 8 inches
Empty weight	22,883 pounds
Maximum weight (land)	29,500 pounds
Water operations	37,000 pounds
Cargo	5,000 pounds
Combinations	10 passengers and 12 stretchers -or- 22 troops
Power plant	(2) Cyclone 1,425 hp R-1820-76A 9-cylinder radial piston engines
Auxiliary power	JATOs
Cruising speed	225 mph
Maximum speed	264miles
Service ceiling	25,000 feet
Range	1,150 miles[3]

CHAPTER 14

PHOTOGRAPHIC TOUR OF DYESS AIR FORCE BASE

Main gate of Dyess Air Force Base. *7th Bomb Wing Public Affairs*

The United States Marine Corps Reserve Center. *7th Bomb Wing Public Affairs*

Aerial view of Dyess Air Force. *7th Bomb Wing Public Affairs*

7th BW headquarters building. The wing is the host unit at Dyess Air Force Base and is assigned to the 12th Air Force at Davis-Monthan Air Force Base, Arizona. The wing is a component of Air Combat Command, headquartered at Langley Air Force Base, Virginia. *7th Bomb Wing Public Affairs*

Dyess Air Force Base control tower.
7th Bomb Wing Public Affairs

The 28th Bomb Squadron is the largest bomb squadron in the Air Force and the largest flying squadron in Air Combat Command. *7th Bomb Wing Public Affairs*

B-1Bs on the flight line. *7th Bomb Wing Public Affairs*

A B-1B on a taxiway. *7th Bomb Wing Public Affairs*

A line of C-130Js on the taxiway. *7th Bomb Wing Public Affairs*

Fire truck in front of the bays of the Dyess Air Force Base Fire Station. *7th Bomb Wing Public Affairs*

Two bay maintenance hangar for B-1Bs or C-130Js operating at Dyess Air Force Base. *7th Bomb Wing Public Affairs*

317th Airlift Group Headquarters. *7th Bomb Wing Public Affairs*

Army-Air Force Exchange Service Exchange.
7th Bomb Wing Public Affairs

Child Development Center.
7th Bomb Wing Public Affairs

The United States Army National Guard building. *7th Bomb Wing Public Affairs*

Dyess Air Force Base Commissary. *7th Bomb Wing Public Affairs*

Base chapel. *7th Bomb Wing Public Affairs*

Base Theater. *7th Bomb Wing Public Affairs*

Fitness Center. *7th Bomb Wing Public Affairs*

Dyess Inn. *7th Bomb Wing Public Affairs*

Education Center. *7th Bomb Wing Public Affairs*

Three of the eleven on-base dormitories. *7th Bomb Wing Public Affairs*

7th Medical Group (hospital). *7th Bomb Wing Public Affairs*

Contract (privatized) base personnel housing units. *7th Bomb Wing Public Affairs*

Thrift shop. *7th Bomb Wing Public Affairs*

On base golf course and pro shop.
7th Bomb Wing Public Affairs

Longhorn Dining Facility. *7th Bomb Wing Public Affairs*

Dyess Air Force Base Museum. *7th Bomb Wing Public Affairs*

APPENDIX I

NUCLEAR WEAPONS AND AIRCRAFT OF DYESS

Nuclear Weapons for the Boeing B-47 Stratojet

Mark-6 thermonuclear bomb at the National Museum of Nuclear Science and Technology, Albuquerque, New Mexico. *Author, March 1997*

Mark-6 or MK-6

It was an improved high-yield, lightweight, updated variant of the earlier MK-4, which was an updated, post-WWII plutonium "Fat Man" bomb. This weapon was produced on an assembly line to acquire sufficient weapons for a growing SAC bomber fleet. The MK-6 could be configured to deliver a weapon with a varying yield of 8, 26, 80, 154, or 160 kilotons. Its fusing could also be adjusted (programmed) for an air burst or contact detonation (surface). The weapon weighed 7,600 to 8,500 pounds and was twenty-eight inches long and sixty-one inches in diameter. It was produced from June 1951 through early 1955 and retired from active inventory in 1962.

Mark-15 thermonuclear bomb at the National Museum of Nuclear Science and Technology at Albuquerque, New Mexico. *Author, March 1997*

MK-15

This was the first lightweight thermonuclear bomb. Its detonation was delayed after release from the aircraft by three parachutes, allowing the bomber sufficient time to reach a safe distance from the point of detonation. It had a yield of sixteen to thirty-nine megatons, was 140 inches long and thirty-four and one third inches in diameter, and weighed 7,600 pounds. The weapon was designed to detonate with an airburst for maximum destructive power; a great leap in effectiveness of target destruction over the MK-6. This allowed the B-47E to destroy more individual targets in a large area and make up for the weapon's delivery Circular Error Probable (CEP).

MK-21

The weapon weighed between 15,000 to 17,700 pounds, which was toward the upper end of the B-47E's capacity, limiting it to one bomb in the bomb bay. As with any increase in weight, the aircraft paid the cost in reduced range. Production ran from 1955 to 1956. SAC decided not to operationally deploy this weapon with the B-47E. In the last half of 1957, engineers modified and converted the weapon to the MK-36, with a yield of four to five megatons and options for airburst, contact, or laydown detonation. It was 150 inches long and fifty-eight inches in diameter.

The Mark-21 thermonuclear bomb was not active with SAC until upgraded to the Mark-36. On display at the National Museum of Nuclear Science and Technology, Albuquerque, New Mexico. *Author, March 1997*

MK-28

This became SAC's primary Cold War thermonuclear bomb. Its production began in January 1958, but a serious problem was discovered with the weapon's safety mechanism, resulting in a five-month delay that impacted operational alert deployment. Engineers corrected the deficiency and production continued through May 1966. The weapon turned out to be a highly dependable, multi-purpose tactical and strategic bomb carried by almost all SAC bombers. Now the B-47E could carry four MK-28s on a preloaded clip inside the bomb bay. The weapon remained in SAC's inventory from 1958 to 1991. It weighed 1,700 to 2,320 pounds, so the B-47E could easily carry four of these bombs without sacrificing range on thermonuclear SIOP Emergency War Operations (EWO) Plan strike packages. The bomb was 170 inches long and twenty-two inches in diameter, giving it a slim aeronautic ballistic shape that improved accuracy; it had a variable yield of seventy kilotons to 1.1 megatons. The bomb could be delivered in an airburst or contact mode. The MK-28 was initially developed as an entirely new weapon to meet SAC's requirements for a lightweight and lethal thermonuclear weapon carried by the B-47E and follow-on B-52, B-58, B-70, and FB-111.[1]

Mark-28 thermonuclear bomb at the National Museum of Nuclear Science and Technology, Albuquerque, New Mexico. *Author, March 1997*

KC-97G (left side, forward view). *Aircraft at the Strategic Air Command Museum, Ashland, Nebraska. Author, July 13, 2009*

Atlas F with a re-entry cone that would protect the thermonuclear warhead on an operational missile on alert. This missile is on display outside the entrance to the Strategic Air Command Museum, Ashland, Nebraska. *Author, July 2009*

CONVAIR DIVISION OF GENERAL DYNAMICS ATLAS F (SM-65/HGM-16) INTERCONTINENTAL BALLISTIC MISSILE
Specifications and Performance Information

Classification .... Intercontinental Ballistic Missile (ICBM)
Air Force designation .... SM-65/HGM-16 (strategic missile/silo-stored surface attack missile)
Manufacturer .... Convair Division of General Dynamics
Length .... 82 feet 6 inches (with MK-4 re-entry vehicle)
Span of outboard engine fairings .... 16 feet
Diameter .... 10 feet
Launch weight .... 268,000 pounds
Range .... 10,360 miles
Maximum speed .... 18,000 mph
Propulsion. (2) LR 89 booster engines of 165,000 pounds of thrust, (2) LR101 vernier engines, each with 1,000 pounds of thrust
Fuel .... Liquid oxygen (LOX)/kerosene (RP-1)
Apogee .... 640 miles
Warhead W-38
Diameter .... 32 inches
Length .... 82.5 inches
Weight .... 3,080 pounds
Yield .... 3.75 megatons
Re-entry vehicle (RV) .... Avco Mk-4
Fuzing .... Airburst or contact
Penetration aids .... Mylar balloons deployed during re-entry to replicate RV
CEP .... 4,600 feet (not a pinpoint weapon depending on large warhead)
Number produced .... 200 plus
Number deployed on alert 72
Deployed missile squadrons 379th SMS (Walker AFB, New Mexico), 578th SMS (Dyess AFB, Texas), 550th SMS (Schilling AFB, Kansas), 551st SMS (Lincoln AFB, Nebraska), 556th SMS (Plattsburgh AFB, New York)[2]

NIKE-HERCULES SURFACE TO AIR MISSILE
Specifications and Performance Information

Designation	MIM-4
Overall length	41 feet 6 inches
Length without booster	27 feet
Wingspan	6 feet 2 inches
Diameter	2 feet 6 inches
Launch weight	10,560 pounds
Weight without booster	5,250 pounds
Maximum speed	Mach 3.5
Speed at burnout	2,597 mph
Maximum slant range	75 to 90 miles (depending on interception altitude)
Maximum ceiling	100,000 feet
Standard intercept altitude	40,000 to 50,000 feet
Booster	Cluster of four solid propellant rockets
Sustainer motor	Solid propellant
Warhead-conventional	T-45 high explosive (HE) fragmentation
Warhead-nuclear	Initial (W-7), Standard (W-31 thermonuclear-dial able or variable yield)
Variable yields	Low (two kilotons), medium (20 kilotons), high (30 to 40 kilotons)
Missile guidance	Alternate Battery Acquisition Radar (ABAR), High Power Acquisition Radar (HIPAR)[3]

Nike-Hercules MIM-4. *The Nike Historical Society*

C-133B at the Air Mobility Command Museum, Dover Air Force Base, Dover, Delaware. *Courtesy Air Mobility Command historian*

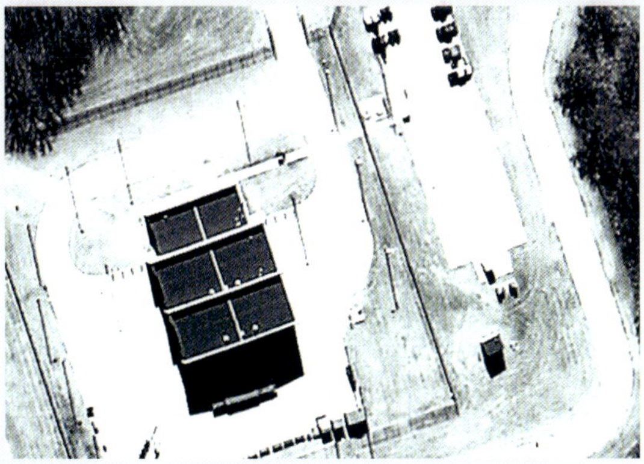

Former Atlas F missile assembly building equipped with a heavy overhead traveling crane. It is currently used for weapons assembly, inspection, and maintenance. *USGS*

Interior of C-133B's cargo compartment, with the two halves of the upper cargo deck secured to the ceiling. When lowered and secured they formed the aircraft's upper deck. Double overhead cargo rails supported the aircraft's two heavy cranes for the movement and securing of oversized cargo. Web fold down web personnel seats along both sides of the fuselage. *Courtesy Air Mobility Command Museum*

BOEING B-52C STRATOFORTRESS
Specifications and Performance Information

Designation .... Long-range, strategic bomber (conventional and nuclear)
Manufacturer .... Boeing Company
Wingspan .... 185 feet
Wing area .... 4,000 square feet
Length .... 156 feet 6 inches
Tail height .... 48 feet 3 inches
Power plant .... (8) 10,000 pound thrust J57-P-29WA turbojets with water injection
Maximum speed .... 630 mph at 19,800 feet
Service ceiling .... 47,300 feet
Combat radius .... 3,110 nautical miles
Empty weight .... 164,000 pounds
Combat weight .... 272,000 pounds
Maximum weight .... 450,000 pounds
Auxiliary fuel tanks .... (2) 3,000 gallon tanks, one under each wing, outboard of engines
Total fuel capacity .... 41,385 gallons
Weight .... 258,910 pounds
Payload capacity .... 43,000 pounds
Electronics ......AN/ASQ-48 Bomb-Nav System, A2/2G-11 Autopilot, N-1 compass, A-3A Fire Control System, ECM
Color-schemeTop surface-natural aluminum, under wing/bottom fuselage-SAC gloss white anti-radiation paint
Defensive armament.......... (2) 20mm M24AI cannons, each with 400 rounds of ammunition -or-(4) .50-caliber machine guns, each with 600 rounds of ammunition
Primary mission .... SAC transitional aircrew training aircrew from B-47E to B-52
Number built 35
Crew .... Aircraft commander, copilot, navigator, bombardier, Electronic Warfare Officer, Gunner[4]

Boeing B-52C at Boeing Aircraft Company, Seattle, Washington, November 1956. This Stratofortress was painted with SAC's new (at that time) gloss white anti-radiation paint on the underside of the fuselage, wings, and horizontal stabilizers. *Strategic Air Command photo archives*

BOEING B-52E STRATOFORTRESS
Specifications and Performance Information

Designation .... Long-range, strategic bomber (conventional and nuclear)
Manufacturer .... Boeing Aircraft
Wingspan .... 185 feet
Wing area .... 4,000 square feet
Length .... 156 feet 7 inches
Tail height .... 48 feet 4 inches
Landing gear .... (4) dual landing trucks, steerable, (2) outrigger landing gear wheels, outboard of engines
Power plant.... (8) Pratt & Whitney J57-P-18W turbojets, mounted in pairs underwing, Pylon mounts
Maximum takeoff thrust .... 12,100 pounds with water injection
Standard thrust .... 10,000 pounds
Maximum speed .... 585 mph at 20,000 feet
Cruising speed .... 554 mph
Initial rate-of-climb .... 2,460 feet per minute
Service ceiling .... 38,000 feet
Maximum ceiling .... 64,200 feet
Unrefueled combat range .... 3,000 miles
Refueled range .... Unlimited
Fuel capacity ... Fuselage fuel cells–15,378 gallons, internal wing cells–20,170 gallons, two auxiliary wing tanks (each) 3,000 gallons
Empty weight .... 177,816 pounds
Combat weight .... 293,100 pounds
Maximum weight .... 450,000 pounds
Bomb load (conventional) ....(84) MK-82 500 pound bombs -or-(42) MK-117 750 pound bombs
Thermonuclear .... (4) B-28 gravity, free-fall bombs
Yield .... 20 kilotons to 1.1 megatons
Maximum bomb load .... 60,000 pounds
Defensive armament ....(4) .50-caliber machine guns in rear-mounted tail turret
Electronics ....An/ASB-4 Bomb Navigation System, AN/APN-89A Doppler Radar System
Crew .... Aircraft Commander, copilot, navigator, bombardier, Electronic Warfare Officer, rear-gunner (enlisted)
Number built 100
Production cost .... $6,000,000.00[5]

Boeing B-52E. *National Museum of the United States Air Force*

B-57 THERMONUCLEAR BOMB
Specifications and Performance Information

Length	118 inches
Diameter	14 ¾ inches
Weight	490 pounds to 510 pounds
Yield	Five kilotons to 20 kilotons
Fusing	Parachute retarded airburst, contact burst, laydown detonation
Produced	1963 to 1967

B-57, a lightweight, multi-purpose thermonuclear bomb, on display in Albuquerque, New Mexico, in the National Museum of Nuclear Science and Technology. *Author*

B-28 THERMONUCLEAR BOMB
Specifications and Performance Information

Length .... 170 inches
Diameter .... 22 inches
Weight .... 1,700 pounds top 2,320 pounds
Yield .... 20 kilotons to 1.1 megatons
Fusing .... Airburst, contact
VariantsB28IN (1958), Ground detonation, airburst, B28RI (1960), retarded (parachute delayed), low-level delivery, B28FI (1962)
All of the above fusing options

B-53 THERMONUCLEAR BOMB
Specifications and Performance Information

Length .... 150 inches
Diameter .... 50 inches
Weight .... 8,850 pounds to 8,900 pounds
Yield .... 9 megatons
Fusing .... Retarded (parachute deployed), airburst, contact, laydown
Number produced 350
Retired 1967
Stockpile storage .... 1997 (removed)

The B-53 was adopted by SAC to attack and destroy hardened targets with a warhead yield of nine megatons. On display in the National Museum of Nuclear Science and Technology, Albuquerque, New Mexico. *Author*

B-61 THERMONUCLEAR BOMB
Specifications and Performance Information

Length	141 inches
Diameter	13 1/3 inches
Weight	695 pounds to 716 pounds
Yield	80 kilotons to 340 kilotons
Fusing	Retarded (parachute deployed), airburst, contact, laydown
Number produced	3,150
Produced	1966 to 1992
Retired	Early production weapons –no confirmation of numbers
Numbers remaining	No confirmation of remaining active inventory numbers

A B-61 thermonuclear bomb at the National Museum of Nuclear Science and Technology, Albuquerque, New Mexico. *Author*

NORTH AMERICAN-ROCKWELL AGM-28A HOUND DOG
Specifications and Performance Information

Wingspan	12 feet 2 inches
Length	46 feet 6 inches
Tail height	9 feet 4 inches
Weight	10,000 pounds
Power plant	(1) Pratt & Whitney J52-P-3 turbojet engine
Maximum speed	1,200 mph
Service ceiling	49,000 feet
Maximum ceiling	56,000 feet
Range	600 miles
Thermonuclear weapon	W-28
Yield	70 kilotons to 1.1 megatons
Fusing	Airburst, contact
Weight	1,700 pounds to 2,330 pounds
Length	170 inches
Diameter	22 inches
Number produced	4,500
Service	1958 to 1991[6]

A North American-Rockwell AGM-28 Hound Dog Air-to-Surface missile at the South Dakota Air and Space Museum outside Ellsworth Air Force Base, South Dakota.

BOEING B-52D STRATOFORTRESS
Specifications and Performance Information

Designation ....Long-range, strategic bomber (conventional and nuclear)
Manufacturer...Boeing Aircraft
Wingspan.. 185 feet
Wing area ....4,000 square feet
Length .... 156 feet 7 inches
Tail height.. 48 feet 4 inches
Landing gear .... (4) dual landing trucks, steerable, (2) outrigger type landing wheels, outboard of engines
Power plant.. (8) Pratt & Whitney J57-P-18W turbojets, mounted in pairs-underwing, Pylon positions
Maximum takeoff thrust.. 12,100 pounds with water injection
Standard thrust.. 10,000 pounds
Maximum speed .... 585 mph at 20,000 feet
Cruising speed.. 554 mph
Initial rate-of-climb... 2,460 feet per minute
Service ceiling .... 38,000 feet
Maximum ceiling .... 64,200 feet
Unrefueled combat range..3,000 miles
Refueled range...Unlimited
Fuel capacity..........................Fuselage fuel cells 5,378 gallons, internal wing cells 20,170 gallons
Two auxiliary wing tanks...(each) 3,000 gallons
Empty weight .... 177,816 pounds
Combat weight .... 293,100 pounds
Maximum weight .... 450,000 pounds
Bomb load (conventional) ....(84) MK-82 500 pound bombs -or-(42) MK-117 750 pound bombs
Thermonuclear ....(4) B-28 gravity, free-fall bombs
Yield.. 20 kilotons to 1.1 megatons
Maximum bomb load... 60,000 pounds
Defensive armament.................................(4) .50-caliber machine guns in rear mounted tail turret
Electronics ....An/ASB-15 Bomb Navigation System, AN/APN-108 Doppler Radar System, Updated Linebacker II, AN/ALR-18 Automated Receiver Set, AN/APR-25 Radar-Homing & Warning System, (4) AN/ALT-6B or AN/ALT-22 Continuous Wave Jamming transmitters, (2) AN/ALT-16 Barrage Jamming Systems, (2) AN/ALT-32H High-Band Jamming Sets, AN/ALT-32L Low-Band Jamming Set, (6) AN/ALE-20 Flare Dispensers with 16 flare capacity per dispenser, (8) AN/ALE-24 Chaff Dispensers-with 1125 bundles
Crew .... Aircraft Commander, copilot, navigator, bombardier, Electronic Warfare Officer, rear-gunner (enlisted)
Number built... 170
Boeing Seattle 101
Boeing Wichita 69
Years produced...1956 to 1957[7]

A B-52D at the South Dakota Air and Space Museum outside Ellsworth Air Force Base, South Dakota.

BOEING B-52H STRATOFORTRESS
Specifications and Performance Information

Designation .... Long-range, heavy strategic bomber
Manufacturer .... Boeing Military Aircraft Company
Wingspan .... 185 feet
Wing area .... 4,000 square feet
Length .... 154 feet 4 inches
Tail height .... 40 feet 8 inches
Height to top of fuselage .... 17 feet 6 inches
Tail span .... 52 feet
Power plant .... (8) 17,000 pound thrust Pratt & Whitney TF-33-P-33/103 fanjet engines
Cruising speed .... 509 mph
Maximum speed .... 650 mph
Unrefueled range .... 8,800 miles
Service ceiling .... 50,000 feet
Maximum ceiling .... 55,000 feet
Maximum fuel capacity .... 48,000 gallons
Empty weight .... 195,000 pounds
Maximum takeoff weight .... 488,000 pounds
Maximum bomb load .... 60,000 pounds
Combinations .... (24) 750 pound bombs on wing pylons, (84) 500 pound bombs in bomb bay
Nuclear combinations(4) gravity free-fall bombs in bomb bay, (20) AGM-69A SRAMs, (12) AGM-86B ALCMs, (12) SRAMs on wing pylons, (12) ALCMs on wing pylons
Defensive armament .... (1) 20mm Gatling gun (currently deleted)
Electronics ...... ASQ-38 Analog Bombing and Navigation Radar, APN-28 Doppler Navigation System, APN-224 Pulse Radar Altimeter, chin-mounted Electro-Optical Viewing System (EVS) with two AVQ-22, Low-Light Level Television (LLTV) with AAQ-6 Forward Looking Infrared (FLIR) System
Weapons electronics .... Sniper Targeting Pod (STP), Northrop Grumman LITENING II Advanced Targeting Pod (ATP)
Note: This is a self-contained, multi-sensor weapon arming system that enables the crew to Detect acquire, auto-track, and identify targets for highly accurate delivery of both conventional and precision guided munitions
Defensive electronics ..... ALQ-155 EW Power Management System, ALQ-122 Smart Noise Operation Equipment (SNOE) False Target Generator, ALR-46 Digital Radar Warning Receiver, ALQ-117 Tail Mounted Digital Deception Jammer (it provides active deception against radar guided missiles) upgraded for ALQ-117 to ALQ-172, ALQ-153 Tail Warning System
Active jammers .... Miniature Air Launch Decoys, Miniature Air Launch Decoy Jammers
Note: A small jet powered decoy designed to mislead enemy radars and deceive attacking fighter-interceptor tracking radars
Crew .... Aircraft Commander, copilot, navigator, radar operator, Electronic Warfare Officer
Inventory (2014) 76
Active 58
AFRC .... 18[22]

A B-52H assigned to the 5th Bomb Wing at Minot Air Force Base, North Dakota, at Ellsworth Air Force Base's "Dakota Thunder 2000" air show and open house. *Author*

BOEING KC-135A STRATOTANKER
Specifications and Performance Information

Designation .... KC-135A Stratotanker
Manufacturer .... Boeing Aircraft Company
Wingspan .... 130 feet 10 inches
Wing area .... 2,433 square feet
Overall length .... 136 feet 3 inches
Tail height .... 38 feet 4 inches
Power plant .... (4) Pratt & Whitney J-57-P-59W turbojet engines
Dry thrust .... 8,000 pounds
With water injection .... 11,000 pounds
Maximum speed .... 585 mph
Cruising speed .... 530 mph
Service ceiling .... 36,000 feet
Maximum ceiling .... 50,000 feet
Fuel load .... 189,702 pounds
Range.... 1,150 miles with 120,000 pound fuel transfer, 9,200 miles (maximum ferry range), 3,450 miles with 24,000 pound fuel transfer
Empty weight .... 98,466 pounds
Maximum weight .... 297,000 pounds
Maximum overload .... 301,600 pounds
Aerial refueling .... Boeing Flying Boom
Cargo capacity....... (6) standard 463L type cargo pallets (up to 83,000 pounds) -or- 80 passengers/troops
Cargo door .... Left side-forward of leading wing edge
Crew .... Aircraft commander, copilot, navigator, boom operator
Production cost .... $39,600,000[8]

A Boeing KC-135A assigned to an Air National Guard Air Refueling Squadron on display during Ellsworth Air Force Base's "Dakota Thunder" open house in 2000. *Author*

LOCKHEED C-130A HERCULES
Specifications and Performance Information

Designation	Cargo/transport
Manufacturer	Lockheed Aircraft Corporation
Wingspan	132 feet 7 inches
Wing area	1,745 square feet
Length	97 feet 9 inches
Tail height	38 feet 3 inches
Power plant	(4) 3,750 hp Allison T56-A-9 turboprop engines
Propellers	(4) Hamilton four-blade propellers with reversible pitch
Auxiliary thrust	(8) Aerojet General 1,000 pound thrust 15KS-1000 JATOs
Initial rate of climb	2,570 feet per minute
Maximum speed	382 mph
Cruising speed	327 mph
Service ceiling	33,000 feet
Maximum ceiling	41,300 feet
Empty weight	57,892 pounds
Loaded weight	107,770 pounds
Maximum weight	124,200 pounds
Payload	34,927 pounds
Fuel capacity	5,080 gallons
Combat range	2,086 miles
Maximum range	3,400 miles
Crew	Aircraft commander, copilot, navigator, flight engineer, load master
Number built	219[9]

A C-130D with skis added below the standard landing gear wheels for snow or ice operations. This was necessary for support flights to DEW Line construction sites and supply. *Washington, DC, Department of the Air Force Historical Photo Archives*

A C-130A/C-130D. *Dyess Air Force Base, 317th Airlift Group, Brian Smith, 317th Air Group historian to author, January 2012*

LOCKHEED C-130E HERCULES
Specifications and Performance Information

Designation .... Cargo/transport
Manufacturer .... Lockheed Aircraft Corporation
Wingspan .... 132 feet 7 inches
Wing area .... 1,745 square feet
Length .... 97 feet 9 inches
Tail height .... 38 feet 10 inches
Power plant .... (4) Allison T56-A-7 turboprops
Speed .... 345 mph at 20,000 feet
Service ceiling .... 19,000 feet with 42,000 pounds of cargo
Maximum takeoff weight .... 155,000 pounds
Maximum payload .... 42,000 pounds
Range with payload .... 1,150 miles
Normal payload .... 36,500 pounds
Range with payload .... 1,438 miles
Cargo combinations .... (6) pallets -or-(74) litters, (16) CDS bundles, (92) combat troops, (64) paratroops
Auxiliary fuel tanks .... (2) 1,290 gallon tank, under wing mounted
Crew (standard) .... Aircraft commander, navigator, flight engineer, loadmaster
Medical crew .... (2) Flight nurses, (3) medical technicians
Production cost $11,900.000.00
Number built .... 389[10]

A C-130E at the National Museum of the United States Air Force, Wright-Patterson Air Force Base, Dayton, Ohio.

DEHAVILLAND C-7A CARIBOU
Specifications and Performance Information

Designation	Cargo/transport
Manufacturer	DeHavilland of Canada
Wingspan	95 feet 7 inches
Length	72 feet 7 inches
Tail height	31 feet 8 inches
Power plant	(2) 1,450 hp Pratt & Whitney R-200-7M2 14-cylinder, two-row, air-cooled engines
Propellers	(2) Three-blade, Hamilton Standard, full-feathering hydromantic
Empty weight	18,380 pounds
Maximum weight	26,000 pounds
Cargo combinations	6,000 pounds capable, (26) paratroops, (20) litter patients
Combat range	1,175 miles
Maximum range	1,400 miles
Cruising speed	182 mph
Maximum speed	216 mph
Service ceiling	27,700 feet
Crew	Aircraft commander, copilot, crew chief
Production cost	$800,000.00
Number built	159[11]

C-7A. *Dyess Air Force Base, 317th Airlift Group, Brian Smith, 317th Air Group historian to author, January 2012*

LOCKHEED C-130H HERCULES
Specifications and Performance Information

Designation	Cargo/transport
Manufacturer	Lockheed-Martin Aeronautical Company
Wingspan	132 feet 7 inches
Wing area	1,745 square feet
Length	97 feet 9 inches
Tail height	38 feet 10 inches
Power plant	(4) Allison T56-A-15 turboprops
Speed	366 mph at 20,000 feet
Service ceiling	23,000 feet with 42,000 pounds of cargo
Cargo compartment	
Length	40 feet
Width	119 inches
Height	9 feet
Rear cargo ramp	
Length	123 inches
Width	119 inches
Cargo combinations	(6) pallets, (74) litters, (16) CDS bundles, (92) combat troops, (64) paratroops
Maximum takeoff weight	155,000 pounds
Maximum allowable payload	42,000 pounds
Maximum normal payload	36,500 pounds
Range	1,208 miles
Reduced payload	35,000 pounds
Range	1,496 miles
Auxiliary fuel tanks	(2) 1,290 gallon under wing mounted tanks
Crew	Aircraft commander, copilot, navigator, flight engineer, loadmaster
Aeromedical crew	(2) Flight nurses, (3) medical technicians
Number produced	308[12]

A C-130H (top) and a C-130J (below). *Dyess Air Force Base, 317th Airlift Group, Brian Smith, 317th Air Group historian to author, January 2012*

LOCKHEED C-130J-30 SUPER HERCULES
Specifications and Performance Information

Designation .... Cargo/transport
Manufacturer .... Lockheed-Martin Aeronautical Company
Wingspan .... 132 feet 7 inches
Wing area .... 1,745 square feet
Length .... 112 feet 9 inches
Tail height .... 38 feet 10 inches
Power plant .... (4) Rolls-Royce AE2100D3 turboprop
Propeller .... (4) six-blade composite
Maximum speed .... 410 mph at 22,000 feet
Service ceiling .... 28,000 feet with 42,000 pounds of cargo, 26,000 feet with 44,500 pounds of cargo
Maximum takeoff weight .... 164,000 pounds
Maximum payload .... 44,000 pounds
Range .... 1,956 miles
Standard payload .... 36,000 pounds
Range .... 2,417 miles
Cargo load combinations .... (8) pallets, (97) litters, (24) CDS bundles, (128) combat troops, (92) paratroops
Crew .... Aircraft commander, copilot, loadmaster
Aeromedical crew .... (1) Flight nurse, (2) medical technicians
Expanded medical .... (2) Flight nurses, (4) medical technicians
Unit Cost .... $48,500,000.00[13]

The first C-130J-30 delivered to Dyess Air Force Base. *Dyess Air Force Base, 317th Airlift Group, Brian Smith, 317th Air Group historian to author, January 2012*

B-83 THERMONUCLEAR BOMB
Specifications and Performance Information

Length	145 inches
Diameter	18 inches
Weight	2,400 pounds
Yield	Low kiloton range up to 1.2 kilotons
Fusing	Retarded-airburst, laydown-contact

A B-83 dummy training bomb used by munitions squadron personnel and aircrew for loading and operation of this type of thermonuclear weapon without handling an active bomb. Training did follow security and handling procedures to be certain personnel followed checklists. On display at the South Dakota Air and Space Museum. *Author*

BOEING AGM-69 SHORT-RANGE ATTACK MISSILE (SRAM)
Specifications and Performance Information

Length	14 feet, 15 feet 10 inches with tail fairing
Fin half spin	15 inches (fin tip to centerline)
Diameter	17.5 inches
Weight	2,230 pounds
Maximum speed	Mach 3.0
Maximum range	100 miles
Propulsion	Lockheed Propulsion Company, SR75-LP-1 two-stage, solid-fuel rocket
Range options	High-altitude flight profile (100 miles), low-altitude flight profile (35 miles)
CEP	1,400 feet
Warhead	W-69
Yield	200 kilotons

The W-69 was used to arm the AGM-28 Hound Dog on the B-52. SAC's two B-1B bomb wings (7th at Dyess AFB, Texas and 28th at Ellsworth AFB, South Dakota) could be armed with the AGM-69 until coming off nuclear alert in 1991.

A Boeing AGM-69 Short Range Attack Missile (SRAM) armed with a W-69 thermonuclear warhead at the National Museum of Nuclear Science and Technology, Albuquerque, New Mexico. *Author*

BOEING AGM-86B AIR LAUNCHED CRUISE MISSILE
Specifications and Performance Information

Length	20.5-feet
Diameter	20.9 inches
Wingspan	8.3 feet
Weight	3,200 pounds
Propulsion	(1) Williams F-107-WR-10 600-pound thrust turbofan engine
Speed	550 mph
Maximum range	2,300 miles
Warhead	W-80-1
Length	31 inches
Diameter	14 inches
Weight	300 pounds
Yield	5 to 150 kilotons
CEP	Precision due to INS/GPS updates
Production	(1000) W-80 (plutonium), (367) W-80-1 (fission fuel)[14]

A Boeing AGM-86B Air Launched Cruise Missile. *Dyess Air Force Base, 7th Bomb Wing Public Affairs*

APPENDIX II

CONVENTIONAL MUNITIONS STORED IN THE SPECIAL WEAPONS STORAGE AREA

An MK-82 500-pound bomb on a flat-bed munitions trailer on display next to a 28th BW B-1B, Ellsworth Air Force Base, South Dakota, Open House, 2011. *Author*

MK-82 (500-pound conventional dumb iron bomb)
This was the first conventional bomb certified for use on the B1-B. It is the smallest conventional bomb in the Air Force munitions inventory. The bomb has a streamlined casing and can be fused in many different options, including fin kits and retarders. It can be converted to a MK-82 Air Retarded bomb by adding a BSU-49/B high-drag assembly. The "ballute" air bag deploys from the bomb's tail to provide high-speed, low-altitude delivery capability by slowing the falling bomb, allowing the aircraft to sufficiently clear the blast zone's debris and fragmentation cone.

Two two-thousand pound inert (dummy) training bombs fitted with JDAM training kits on a munitions trailer next to a 28th BW B-1B, Ellsworth Air Force Base, South Dakota, Open House, 2011. *Author*

MK-84 (2,000-pound conventional dumb iron bomb)
Classified as a general purpose (GP) bomb. The basic bomb can be upgraded with the addition of a JDAM GBU-32 kit for precision accuracy.

CBU-87 (Combined Effects Munitions):
A free-fall bomblet, dispensing a ground impact detonation pattern 600 feet wide and 1,200 feet long. It is designed to attack lightly armored vehicles, as well as personnel, equipment, and support materials.

Dummy training CBU-87, -89, and -97 munitions next to a 28th BW B-1B, Ellsworth Air Force Base, South Dakota, Open House, 2011. *Author*

CBU-89 (Gator Mine)
An area denial cluster munitions weapon. It has a ground impact detonation pattern 600 feet wide and 1,950 feet long and is used as an anti-personnel attack weapon.

CBU-97 (Sensor Fused Weapon):
A ten sub-munitions size weapon set, with each containing four armor-penetrating projectiles equipped with infrared sensors to detect hit signature emitting targets. It is classified as an advanced weapon that at a preset altitude fires a rocket motor to spin the sub-munitions, starting the sequence for a rapid descent toward ground targets. The sub-munitions release its four projectiles, which are lofted over the designated target area. The projectiles' sensor detects a vehicle's signature and an explosively formed penetrator fires at the target heat source with great accuracy and efficiency.

Training CBU-103/CBU-105 Wind Corrected Munitions Dispenser (WCMD) next to a 28th BW B-1B, Ellsworth Air Force Base, South Dakota, Open House, 2011. *Author*

WCMD (Wind Corrected Munitions Dispenser)
The addition of this kit allows CBUs to be precision delivered from high altitudes, safe from small arms fire and light AAA. It is a low-cost glide weapon with a stand-off capability and a 1,000 pound warhead.

JSOW (Joint Stand Off Weapon)
It can be launched from the aircraft at a variable distance of fifteen to forty miles, depending on the altitude of release from the designated target. It is a launch-and-forget weapon, allowing the aircraft to turn away from enemy defenses. Once launched, the weapon's GPS/INS is engaged to conduct a day or night, all-weather attack. The weapon uses electronic inputs to conduct mid-course direction/navigator updates, including imaging infrared signature target identification, accomplished through a secure computer data link for terminal homing.

Joint Air-Surface Stand Off Missile (JASSM) next to a 28th BW B-1B, Ellsworth Air Force Base, South Dakota, Open House, 2011. *Author*

JASSM (Joint Air to Surface Stand Off Missile)
Consists of a 1,000-pound conventional warhead designed to be launched outside heavily defended areas. It has a CEP of less than eight feet using GPS/INS with built-in Bomb Damage Assessment (BDA), reporting on its position to target until the instant of detonation.

MK-65 (Quick Strike Mine)
A 2,000-pound weapon and a new generation of naval mines that can be dropped to detect and destroy submarines and surface vessels (warships, auxiliaries, and transports). It uses a variety of arming delay and sterilization (clearance of enemy naval assets within a designated area), and is fitted with a self-destruct system (selected operational time limit prior to weapon systems depredation due to electronics battery exhaustion and electrical components failure) and target detector systems (magnetic and seismic/pressure detection of nearby targets).

AGM-86C (Conventional Air Launched Cruise Missile):
A conventional weapon able to deliver either a 2,000-pound or 3,000-pound high-explosive blast and fragmentation warhead. It has a maximum range of 700 miles and is designed to attack and destroy hardened targets (including underground installations built to prevent surface attack and conceal sensitive military related facilities). It is considered a precision guided munitions weapon.

JDAM (Joint Direct Attack Munitions)
Can be used either as a 1,000- or 2,000-pound precision weapon. A kit is attached by munitions personnel consisting of: GPS (Global Positioning System) receiver, a guidance computer that coordinates GPS and INS inputs for great delivery/target impact accuracy, and adjustable airfoil fins to provide precision airborne guidance. It has a CEP of less than thirty-nine feet.[1]

Top to bottom: Boeing B-52H Stratofortress, Rockwell International B-1B Lancer, and a Northrop B-2 Advanced Technology Bomber. *Joint Base Langley-Eustis, Virginia, Air Combat Headquarters, Public Affairs*

APPENDIX III

BOEING, NORTH AMERICAN B-1B LANCER SPECIFICATIONS AND PERFORMANCE INFORMATION

Manufacturer..............................Rockwell International, North American Aircraft, Boeing Company
Designation B-1
Version (variant).."B"
Type ....Long-range, multi-role, heavy bomber
Wingspan................... 137 feet (extended-full forward wing sweep), 79 feet (full-aft swept position)
Wing area .... 1,950 square feet
Length .... 146 feet
Tail height .... 34 feet
Power plant.....(4) General Electric 30,780 pound thrust F101-GE-102 turbofan engines, each fitted with afterburner
Maximum speed .... 900 mph
Maximum range....... 6,450 miles (un-refueled), 1,730 miles (low-altitude mission profile), unlimited (aerial refueling)

Normal fuel capacity ....40,000 gallons
Service ceiling .... 30,000 feet
Maximum ceiling .... 60,000 feet
Empty weight .... 192,000 pounds
Maximum takeoff weight.. 477,000 pounds
Internal bomb capacity .... 75,000 pounds
External bomb capacity.. 59,000 pounds
Nuclear weapons ....(12) B-28 free-fall thermonuclear bombs
Combinations (internal)..(24) B-61 free-fall thermonuclear bombs
....(24) B-82 free-fall thermonuclear bombs
.... (24) AGM-69 Short Range Attack Missiles (SRAMs)
.... (8) AGM-86B Air Launched Cruise Missiles (ALCMs)
(external) ....(8) B-28 free-fall thermonuclear bombs
....(14) B-43 free-fall thermonuclear bombs
....(14) B-61 free-fall thermonuclear bombs
.... (14) SRAMs
.... (14) ALCMs
Conventional (internal)... (84) MK-82 500 pound dumb bombs
.... (84) MK-82 500 pounds JDAMs
.... (24) Mk-84 2,000 pound dumb bombs
....(24) MK-84 2,000 pound JDAMS (Joint Direct Munitions)
.... (30) CBU-87 Combined Effects Munitions
.... (30) CBU-89 Gator Mine
....(30) CBU-97 Sensor Fuzzed Weapons
.... (30) WCMDs (Wind Corrected Munitions Dispenser)
.... (12) JSOWs (Joint Stand Off Weapons)
.... (24) JASSMs (Joint Air to Surface Stand Off Missiles)
.... (12) MK-65 Quick Strike Mines
Note: The B-1B completed modifications to increase its internal, conventional bomb carrying capacity.

The B-1B's forward cockpit. The pilots' instrument panels are dominated by two large Cathode Ray Tubes (CRTs) incorporating the Visual Situation Display (VSD). VSDs show all flight data, including horizon, vertical speed, airspeed, ground speed, altitude, heading, and steering commands. Instrument Landing System (ILS) information is also displayed on the VSD. Backup steam gauges or analog instruments are grouped starboard of the pilot's VSD. The pilot and copilot have duplicate controls and instruments. Both have the wing sweep control lever. They have large vertical displays flanking the VSD to provide additional airspeed or Mach number and altitude/vertical velocity information. In the center, overhead instrument panels between the pilots provide access to the Air Refueling Control Panel, Auxiliary Power Unit (APU) Control and Indicator Panel, main lighting control panel, and crew compartment pressure altimeter. A standard compass is mounted at the vertical panel's center section, between the two air vents. *Joint Base Langley-Eustis, Virginia, Air Combat Headquarters, Public Affairs*

Conventional (external)	(44) MK-82 500 pound dumb bombs
	(44) MK-82 JDAMs
	(14) MK-84 2,000 pound dumb bombs
	(14) MK- 84 JDAMs
	(14) AGM-86C (conventional warhead) ACLMs
Electronics (as of 2012)	APQ Forward Looking Radar, (continually updated)
	ALQ-161 All Systems Inc., Defensive Avionics System
	APQ-164 Dual-Channel, Multi-Mode, Offensive Radar System
	APN-224 Radar Altimeter
	ALR-56M Warning Radar
	(2) 5-inch by 7-inch Rockwell Collins (color), Multi-Function displays.
	Installed at Offensive and Defensive System Officers' consoles in aft cabin. (each consists of active matrix liquid crystal operations)
	AN/AAQ-33 Lockheed Martin Sniper Advanced targeting Pod (ATP)
	IBM AP-101F Digital Computer
	AN/ALR-55 Radar Warning
	ASN-131 Radar Altimeter
	Kearfott Inertial Navigation System
	Northrop Grumman (Teledyne Ryan) APN-218 Doppler Radar Velocity Sensor or DVS
	Honeywell APN-224 Radar Altimeter
	Rockwell Collins APN-118 TACAN (Tactical Air Navigation System)
	Rockwell Collins APN-108 Instrument Landing System
	ASC-19 AFSATCOM satellite communications
	Rockwell Collins Long-Range ARC-190 HF radio
	Honeywell KY-58 Secure Voice, line-of-sight, encryption device
	Rockwell Collins ARC-177 UFF, line-of-sight communications radio system
	ARR-85 Secure or open line-of-sight system
	APX-101 IFF (Identification Friend of Foe)
	GPS (Global Position System)
	Line-of-Sight Link-16 Data Link
	FIDL (Fully Integrated Data Link)
	B-1 Laptop Controlled Targeting Pod
Defensive systems	Expendable Counter Measures consisting of chaff and flares
	ALE-50 Towed Decoy System
Crew	Aircraft Commander
	Copilot
	Offensive Systems Officer
	Defensive Systems Officer
Manufacturing cost	(FY 98 dollars) $283,100,000
Number built	(4) B-1A prototypes, (100) B-1Bs
Active inventory (2014)	63[1]

ENDNOTES

Chapter One

1. Texas Historical Commission, *Texas in World War II* (Austin, Texas: The State Agency for Historic Preservation, 2012).
2. John H. Hatcher, "Camp Barkeley," *Texas Military History* 3, no. 4 (winter 1963), 219-220. Courtesy Hardin-Simmons University, Richardson Library, Austin, Texas, November 9, 2012.
3. James M. Meyers, "Camp Barkeley," Handbook of Texas Online, accessed October 5, 2012. Published by the Texas State Historical Association.
4. James M. Meyers, "Barkley, David Bennes," Handbook of Texas Online, accessed October 5, 2012. Published by the Texas State Historical Association.
5. "Camp Barkeley," Handbook of Texas Online, accessed August 30, 2009. Published by the Texas State Historical Association.
6. Hatcher, 222.
7. "Camp Barkeley."
8. Hatcher, 225–226.
9. Ibid., 222.
10. "WW2 US Medical Replacement Training Centers (MRTC)."
11. "12th Armored Division."
12. "Camp Barkeley."
13. Krammer
14. "Camp Barkeley."
15. "12th Armored Division."
16. Proctor
17. "The Army Air Base," Texas Historical Commission, Military Sites Program, History Programs Division, Austin, Texas.
18. Mark Odintz, "Tye, TX," Handbook of Texas Online, September 20, 2012. Published by the Texas State Historical Association.
19. Wesley Frank Craven and James Lea Cate, ed., *The Army Air Forces in World War II*, Volume One, *Plans and Early Operations, January 1939 to August 1942* (Washington, DC: Office of Air Force History, US Government Printing Office, 1983), 112-114.
20. Odintz
21. US Army Corps of Engineers, Engineering Branch, War Construction Section, to Operations Branch, Air Forces Project Section, "Proposed Air Support Command Base, Camp Barkeley, Abilene, Texas," July 3, 1942. Courtesy US Army Corps of Engineers, Historical Archives Section, Washington, DC.
22. "Dyess Air Force Base, Texas," *The Military Standard-Air Force Bases.*
23. "Dyess History," *US Air Force Fact Sheet.*
24. "Summary History of Abilene Army Airfield, 1942-1946." Montgomery, Alabama: Maxwell Air force Base, Air Force Historical Research Agency, to author, November 13, 2012.

Chapter Two

1. Colonel Harry G. Summers, Jr., US Army (Ret.), *Korean War Almanac* (New York: Facts on File, 1990), 17.
2. "Dyess History."
3. United States House of Representatives, Military Appropriations Committee, "Operational Support for the United States Air Force, Fiscal Year 1953." Witness, Colonel J.C. Jensen, Directorate of Operations, Deputy Chief of Staff for Operations, March 12, 1952. Courtesy of the office of United States Senator John Thune, South Dakota via Dindi Robinson, Information Research Specialist, Foreign Affairs, Defense & Trade Section, Knowledge Service Group, Congressional Research Service, Library of Congress, Washington, DC, to author, November 14, 2012.

4. United States House of Representatives, Military Appropriations Committee, "Operational Support for the United States Air Force, Fiscal Year 1953." Witness, Lieutenant Colonel C.M. Turner, Directorate of Installations, Deputy Chief of Staff for Operations, March 12, 1952. Courtesy of the office of United States Senator John Thune, South Dakota via Dindi Robinson, Information Research Specialist, Foreign Affairs, Defense & Trade Section, Knowledge Service Group, Congressional Research Service, Library of Congress, Washington, DC, to author, November 14, 2012.
5. United States House of Representatives, Military Appropriations Committee, Mr. Mahon, Chairman, "Request for funds for bases not yet authorized for the United States Air Force, fiscal year 1953," March 12, 1952. Courtesy of the office of United States Senator John Thune, South Dakota via Dindi Robinson, Information Research Specialist, Foreign Affairs, Defense & Trade Section, Knowledge Service Group, Congressional Research Service, Library of Congress, Washington, DC, to author, November 14, 2012.
6. United States Senate and House of Representatives of the United States of America, "Public Law 534, Title III, Continental United States, Strategic Air Command," Washington, DC, July 14, 1952. Courtesy of the office of United States Senator John Thune, South Dakota via Dindi Robinson, Information Research Specialist, Foreign Affairs, Defense & Trade Section, Knowledge Service Group, Congressional Research Service, Library of Congress, Washington, DC, to author, November 14, 2012.
7. "Dyess Air Force Base, Texas."
8. Lt. Col. George A. Larson, USAF, Deputy Commander for Resource Management, Offutt Air Force Base, Nebraska. "History of Capehart Housing, Offutt Air Force Base," October 1989.
9. "Dyess Air Force Base."
10. "The Dyess Story," accessed September 20, 2012. Published by the Texas State Historical Association.
11. "Housing options at Dyess AFB."
12. "Installation overview—Dyess Air Force Base, Texas."
13. "Welcome to Dyess AFB Housing."
14. "Dyess Air Force Base-Abilene, Texas."
15. "AirNav: KDYS-Dyess Air Force Base."
16. "The History of Dyess Air Force, Texas."
17. "Welcome to Dyess AFB Housing."
18. "Dyess Air Force Base."

Chapter Three

1. "SAC bases: Abilene/Dyess Air Force Base."
2. "96th Bombardment Wing."
3. "Nuclear weapons in the Strategic Air Command arsenal," Ashland, Nebraska: Strategic Air Command Museum.
4. *The Development of the Strategic Air Command, 1986. The Fortieth Anniversary History*. (Omaha, Nebraska: Offutt Air Force Base, Headquarters Strategic Air Command, Office of the Historian, September 1, 1986), V.
5. *The Development of the Strategic Air Command,* 1986.
6. "B-47 alert procedures," B-47 Stratojet Association.
7. "Activities and accomplishments of the Abilene Chamber of Commerce, 1959 & 1960," Abilene, Texas, Abilene Chamber of Commerce to author, October 2012.
8. Colonel Jenson, Offutt Air Force Base, Headquarters Strategic Air Command, "Strategic Air Command Rotational Movements," Washington, DC: testimony before the United States House of Representatives Sub-Committee on Military Appropriations, March 12, 1952. Courtesy, of the office of United States Senator John Thune, South Dakota via Dindi Robinson, Information Research Specialist, Foreign Affairs, Defense & Trade Section, Knowledge Service Group, Congressional Research Service, Library of Congress, Washington, DC, to author, November 14, 2012.
9. "B-47 alert procedures," The B-47 Stratojet Association, preserving the legacy of the Boeing B-47 Stratojet bomber, (http://b-47.com/).
10. "341st Bombardment Wing (M), SAC, January-April 1958, TDY, Andersen Air Force Base, Guam," courtesy Colonel Sigmund Alexander, USAF (Ret.), President, Boeing B-47 Stratojet Association to author, January 4, 2013.

11. "B-47E, crash, November 4, 1958," The B-47 Stratojet Association, preserving the legacy of the Boeing B-47 Stratojet bomber, (http://b-47.com/).
12. "Fifty- years after Dyess plane crash, soil contains negligible levels of radioactive materials," Courtesy, of the office of United States Senator John Thune, South Dakota via Dindi Robinson, Information Research Specialist, Foreign Affairs, Defense & Trade Section, Knowledge Service Group, Congressional Research Service, Library of Congress, Washington, DC, to author, November 14, 2012.
13. "B-47 deployments to England," The B-47 Stratojet Association, preserving the legacy of the Boeing B-47 Stratojet bomber, (http://b-47.com/).
14. "Alert Through Dispersal," Assistant Chief of Staff, Installations, Headquarters, United States Air Force, Washington, DC, June 6, 1957. Washington, DC: Department of the Air Force, Air Force Declassification Office, declassified June 8, 2010.
15. *The Development of the Strategic Air Command*, 66-74.
16. Ibid., 75-76.
17. "History, 96th Bombardment Wing (Medium), Dyess Air Force Base, Texas, April 1-30, 1960," prepared May, 1961, Dyess Air Force Base, Texas. (IRIS number 004531234, reel number 5-26009-18/N0057), Montgomery, Alabama: Maxwell Air Force Base, Air Force Historical Research Agency, to author, January 30, 2013.
18. "History, 96th Bombardment Wing (Medium), Dyess Air Force Base, Texas, May 1-31, 1961," prepared June, 1960, Dyess Air Force Base, Texas. (IRIS number 004531234, reel number 5-26009-18/N0057), Montgomery, Alabama: Maxwell Air Force Base, Air Force Historical Research Agency, to author, January 30, 2013.
19. "History, 96th Bombardment Wing (Medium), Dyess Air Force Base, Texas, July 1-31, 1961," prepared August, 1961, Dyess Air Force Base, Texas. (IRIS number 004531234, reel number 5-26009-18/N0057), Montgomery, Alabama: Maxwell Air Force Base, Air Force Historical Research Agency, to author, January 30, 2013.
20. "History, 96th Bombardment Wing (Medium), Dyess Air Force Base, Texas, August 1-31, 1961," prepared September, 1961, Dyess Air Force Base, Texas. (IRIS number 004531234, reel number 5-26009-18/N0057), Montgomery, Alabama: Maxwell Air Force Base, Air Force Historical Research Agency, to author, January 30, 2013.
21. "Strategic Air Command operations in the Cuban Missile Crisis," *Historical Study Number 90*, Volume I. Courtesy, Jerome V. Martin, PHD, DAFG, Command Historian, United States Strategic Command, Offutt Air Force Base, Omaha, Nebraska to author, October 29, 2012.
22. "History, 96th Bombardment Wing (Medium), Dyess Air Force Base, Texas, September 1-30, 1961," prepared October, 1961, Dyess Air Force Base, Texas. (IRIS number 004531234, reel number 5-26009-18/N0057), Montgomery, Alabama: Maxwell Air Force Base, Air Force Historical Research Agency, to author, January 30, 2013.
23. "History, 96th Bombardment Wing (Medium), Dyess Air Force Base, Texas, December 1-31, 1961," prepared January, 1962, Dyess Air Force Base, Texas. (IRIS number 004531234, reel number 5-26009-18/N0057), Montgomery, Alabama: Maxwell Air Force Base, Air Force Historical Research Agency, to author, January 30, 2013.
24. Brian Smith, Air Mobility Command, 317th Airlift Group, Historian Office, 7th Bombardment Wing, Dyess Air Force Base, Texas, "Dyess AFB tornado, July 1962," to author, September 15, 2012.
25. *The Development of the Strategic Air Command*, 117.
26. Ibid., 132.

Chapter Four

1. 11th Air Refueling Squadron, Alumni Association, "Squadron History, 1955-1965," October 23, 2012.
2. "Stratofreighter/Stratotanker, Boeing KC-97G aerial refueling tanker," Strategic Air Command Museum, Ashland, Nebraska.
3. 11th Air Refueling Squadron.
4. *The Development of Strategic Air Command*, 66 & 68.
5. 11th Air Refueling Squadron.
6. *The Development of Strategic Air Command.*

7. "Boeing KC-97L Stratofreighter," Abilene, Texas: Dyess Air Force Base Linear Air Park, Dyess Air Park.

Chapter Five

1. San Bernardino Air Material Center, "Semi-annual historical report, August 18, 1960 to June 30, 1961," Norton Air Force Base, California. Montgomery, Alabama: Maxwell Air Force Base, Air Force Historical Research Agency, author research for Squadron Officer's School in resident program presentation, February 1978.
2. Colonel Hugh B. Manson, Commander, Site Activation Task Force, Dyess Air Force Base, Texas. Montgomery, Alabama: Maxwell Air Force Base, Air Force Historical Research Agency, author research for Squadron Officer's School in resident program presentation, February 1978.
3. Air Force Ballistic Missile Division, "Atlas F silo investigation, Dyess Air Force Base, March 16, 1961 to April 4, 1962," Los Angles, California,. Montgomery, Alabama: Maxwell Air Force Base, Air Force Historical Research Agency, author research for Squadron Officer's School in resident program presentation, February 1978.
4. *Abilene Reporter-News (Evening),* May 11, 1960, 2-A.
5. *Abilene Reporter-News (Evening),* May 28, 1960, 1-A.
6. "96th Strategic Aerospace Wing, History of the 578th Strategic Missile Squadron, July 1961, Dyess Air Force Base, Texas." Montgomery, Alabama: Maxwell Air Force Base, Air Force Historical Research Agency, author research for Squadron Officer's School in resident program presentation, March 1978.
7. "Air Force Ballistic Missile Division, Detachment Number 5, Dyess Air Force Base, March 1961 to April 1962, Los Angles, California." Montgomery, Alabama: Maxwell Air Force Base, Air Force Historical Research Agency, author research for Squadron Officer's School in resident program presentation, March 1978.
8. "96th Strategic Aerospace Wing, History of the 578th Strategic Missile Squadron, July 1961, Dyess Air Force Base, Texas."
9. "Atlas launch sites," Alexandria, Virginia: US Army Corps of Engineers, Historian Office, to author, August 2012.
10. "Atlas F missiles at Dyess Air Force Base, Texas," Ashland, Nebraska: Strategic Air Command Museum.
11. "Dyess Air Force Base, SM-65F Atlas missile sites," (http://www.dyess.af.mil).
12. "History of F.E. Warren Air Force Base," Cheyenne, Wyoming: Francis E. Warren Air Force Base, Museum.
13. "Atlas missile silo, terms and definitions of missile crewmen," Association of Air Force Missileers.
14. "Atlas F missile construction," Fort Worth, Texas: US Army Corps of Engineers, Fort Worth District Office, Historian Office.
15. "Atlas F missile construction operations at Dyess Air Force Base," US Army Corps of Engineers, Fort Worth District Office, Historian Office.
16. "Soviet Intercontinental Ballistic Missiles," Montgomery, Alabama: United States Air Force, Air War College, Correspondence Course. Author was a Major assigned to the Defense Intelligence Agency, Alternate National Military Command Center at Fort Ritchie, Maryland, 1984.
17. "Atlas F missiles on Dyess Air Force Base," US Army Corps of Engineers, Fort Worth District Office, Historian Office.
18. *The development of the Strategic Air Command, 1946-1986*, 108-109.
19. David W. Bath, ed., *Air Force Missileers and the Cuban Missile Crisis,* Lucas A. Morgan, A2C, Electrical Power Production Technician, 578th SMS, Breckenridge, Colorado: Association of Air Force Missileers.
20. "United States Armed Forces nuclear Defense Conditions," Omaha, Nebraska: Offutt Air Force Base, Strategic Air Command, Historian Office, September 1990.
21. David W. Bath, ed., *Air Force Missileers and the Cuban Missile Crisis*, Breckenridge, Colorado: Association of Air Force Missileers.
22. Charles Condit, CMSgt. (Ret.), "Operations, 578th SMS," Breckenridge, Colorado: Association of Air Force Missileers.
23. "Underground silo," Abilene, Texas: Atlas Intercontinental Ballistic Missile Historical Society.
24. *The development of the Strategic Air Command, 1946-1986.*

25. "Dyess Air Force Base, SM-65F Atlas missile sites."
26. "Dyess Air Force Base, SM-65F Atlas missile sites."
27. "Atlas D Intercontinental Ballistic Missile."

Chapter Six

1. "C-124 Globemaster II," Dover, Delaware: Dover Air Force Base, Air Mobility Command Museum.
2. "Douglas C-124A Globemaster II, aircraft number 49-0258," Dover, Delaware: Dover Air Force Base, Air Mobility Command Museum.
3. "The 4th Strategic Support Squadron and the C-124C Globemaster II." Compiled by former Lieutenant Merle M. Allen Jr., pilot, 4th SSS, 1954-1957, to Ellsworth Heritage Foundation, South Dakota Air and Space Museum, to author, September 15, 2012.
4. "History, 4th Strategic Support Squadron, Dyess Air Force Base, Texas, June 1-30, 1957." (IRIS number 00432255, reel number 000012677), Montgomery, Alabama: Maxwell Air Force Base, Air Force Historical Research Agency, to author, October 26, 2012.
5. John Watts, "Recollections of C-124Cs at Dyess Air Force Base," to author, December 15, 2012.
6. John Watts, "The C-124 and Strategic Air Command," to author, December 20, 2012.
7. "History, 4th Strategic Support Squadron, Dyess Air Force Base, Texas, June 1-30, 1957."
8. "The 4th Strategic Support Squadron and the C-124C Globemaster II."
9. "History, 4th Strategic Support Squadron, Dyess Air Force Base, Texas, June 1-30, 1957."
10. "History, 4th Strategic Support Squadron, Dyess Air Force Base, Texas, April 1-30, 1959," prepared June 10, 1959, Dyess Air Force Base, Texas. (IRIS number 00432277, reel number 000012678/KD671), Montgomery, Alabama: Maxwell Air Force Base, Montgomery, Alabama: Air Force Historical Research Agency, to author, January 22, 2013.
11. "History, 4th Strategic Support Squadron, Dyess Air Force Base, Texas, May 1-31, 1959," prepared June 10, 1959, Dyess Air Force Base, Texas. (IRIS number 00432277, reel number 000012678/KD671), Montgomery, Alabama: Maxwell Air Force Base, Air Force Historical Research Agency, to author, January 22, 2013.
12. "History, 4th Strategic Support Squadron, Dyess Air Force Base, Texas, July 1-310, 1959," prepared September 5, 1959, Dyess Air Force Base, Texas. (IRIS number 00432277, reel number 000012678/KD671), Montgomery, Alabama: Maxwell Air Force Base, Air Force Historical Research Agency, to author, January 22, 2013.
13. "History, 4th Strategic Support Squadron, Dyess Air Force Base, Texas, August 1-31, 1959," prepared October 10, 1959, Dyess Air Force Base, Texas. (IRIS number 00432277, reel number 000012678/KD671), Montgomery, Alabama: Maxwell Air Force Base, Air Force Historical Research Agency, to author, January 22, 2013.
14. "The 4th Strategic Support Squadron and The C-124C Globemaster II."

Chapter Seven

1. "Nike Missile Sites," Carlisle Barracks, Pennsylvania: United States Institute for Military History, United States Army War College Library.
2. "Nike-Hercules Site at Ellsworth Air Force Base, South Dakota." Ellsworth Air Force Base, 28th Bomb Wing Historian.
3. "Burleson Papers," Bulletin, Department of the Army, Chief of Legislative Liaison to interested member of Congress, July 31, 1959." Abilene, Texas: Richardson Library, Hardin-Simmons University.
4. "5th Missile Battalion History, Dyess Air Force Base, Texas," Montgomery, Alabama: Maxwell Air Force Base, Air Force Historical Research Agency.
5. "Nike-Hercules Site at Ellsworth Air Force Base, South Dakota," Ellsworth Air Force Base, 28th Bomb Wing Historian.
6. "Nike," (http://www.techbastard.com/missile/nike/dyess-tx.php).
7. "Nike Hercules Surface to Air Missile technical information," South Dakota Air and Space Museum, Ellsworth Air Force Base, South Dakota.
8. "Dyess Air Force Base Defense Area," Carlisle Barracks, Pennsylvania: United States Army

Military History Institute Library, author research August 1982 for Air Force War College Non-resident Program research thesis.

9. "Nike-Hercules Surface to Air Missile technical information."

10. "Description of a typical Nike-Hercules missile site," Carlisle Barracks, Pennsylvania: United States Army Military History Institute Library, author research August 1982 for Air Force War College Non-resident Program research thesis.

11. "W-31 nuclear warhead," Albuquerque, New Mexico: The National Museum of Nuclear Science and History.

Chapter Eight

1. Dan Harrington, Deputy Command Historian, United States Strategic Command, Offutt Air Force Base, Omaha, Nebraska, November 1, 2012, to author.

2. "The history of Castle Air Force Base," Atwater, California: Castle Air Museum.

3. "The story of the B-52 Stratofortress."

4. Harrington

5. Jerome V. Martin, PHD, DAFF, Command Historian, United States Strategic Command Historian, Offutt Air Force Base, Omaha, Nebraska.

6. Harrington

7. Lt. Col. George A. Larson, USAF (Ret.), "Linebacker II," *Military*, June 2003, 6-11 and July 2003, 11-14.

8. "The story of the B-52 Stratofortress."

9. "B-52H," Offutt Air Force Base, Omaha, Nebraska, Strategic Air Command Historian.

10. "The story of the B-52 Stratofortress."

11. "Dyess Air Force Base, 96th Bomb Wing, B-52H Stratofortress."

Chapter Nine

1. "917th Air Refueling Squadron," Omaha, Nebraska: Strategic Air Command, Offutt Air Force Base, Historian Office, 1992.

2. "KC-135A Stratotanker," Dyess Air Force Base, Dyess Linear Air Park.

3. Carl Berger, Ed., The United States Air Force in Southeast Asia, 1961-1973: An illustrated account (Washington, DC: Office of Air Force History, United States Air Force, 1984), 204-205.

4. "96th Bombardment Wing," Strategic Air Command Association.

5. "Tankers at War, Air Refueling in Southeast Asia," *US Air Force Fact Sheet.* 6 "96th Bombardment Wing."

6.. "Gallery of USAF Weapons, Tanker Aircraft," *2011 USAF Almanac*, Air Force Association, *Journal of the Air Force Association, Air Force Magazine,* May 2011.

7. "History of Dyess Air Force Base." Dyess Air Force Base, Base Library.

8. "KC-135A Crash at Dyess AFB," Dyess Air Force Base, Public Affairs.

9, "AMARC history," (http://www.amarcexperience.co/amarchistory.asp).

10. "917th Aerial Refueling Squadron."

11. "Gallery of USAF Weapons, Tanker Aircraft," *2012 USAF Almanac*, Air Force Association, *Journal of the Air Force Association, Air Force Magazine,* May 2012.

Chapter Ten

1. MSgt. William J. Allen, *Abilene Airlifters, A History of Tactical Airlift at Dyess Air Force Base, Texas*, "The 64th Troop Carrier Wing, 8 February 1961-1 January 1963," page 1-3, Dyess Air Force Base, Texas: 7th Bombardment Wing, Office of History, December 31, 1995. Courtesy, Brian Smith, 317th Airlift Group History Office to author, October 19, 2012.

2. Ibid.

3. Allen, 3-24.

4. Allen, 25-31.

5. Allen, 32-59.

6. "Air Combat History," (http://www.acc.af.mil/library/acchistory).

7. Allen, 61-64.

8. "317th Airlift Group," (http://www.dyes.Af.mil/units/317thairliftgroup).

9. "The 64th Troop Carrier Wing, 8 February 1961-1 January 1963."

10. "First C-130J Super Hercules delivered to Dyess Air Force Base," Dyess Air Force Baser, 7th Bomb Wing Public Affairs, April 17, 2010.

11. "Units make history with the Air Force's first Homeland Defense ORI," 123rd Airlift Wing, Kentucky Air National Guard, 123rd Airlift Wing Public Affairs, June 3, 2010.

12. "Deployed C-130 Loadmaster supports Southwest Asia airlift operations," (http://wwwamc.af.mil/news/story), August 21, 2010.
13. "317th Air Group conducts first JPADS training," Dyess Air Force Base, 7th Bomb Wing Public Affairs, February 29, 2012.
14. "317th AG delivers resupply to the joint warfighters," Dyess Air Force Base, 7th Bomb Wing Public Affairs, April 426, 2012.
15. "317th AG makes with 16-ship formation," Dyess Air Force Base, 7th Bomb Wing Public Affairs, July 5, 2012.
16. "The end of an era," Dyess Air Force Base, 7th Bomb Wing Public Affairs, September 27, 2012.
17. "Tail swap enables Afghan mission support and humanitarian effort," Dyess Air Force Base, 7th Bomb Wing Public Affairs, October 11, 2012.
18. "Highlights from the 317th Air Group history from January 2012 to June 2014." Dyess Air Force Base, Texas: Brain Smith (317th Air Group Historian), to author June 30, 2014.

Chapter Eleven

1. "Agreement between the Atomic Energy Commission and military organizations," Montgomery, Alabama: Maxwell Air Force Base, Air Force Historical Research Agency, author (at this time, Captain, United States Air Force) research during attendance at Air Force Squadron Officers School in Residence Course, January to March 1978 for class speech presentation).
2. "Strategic Air Command Mission." Presented to Second Lieutenant George A. Larson, Strategic Air Command, October 1971, Offutt Air Force Base Junior Officers' Council.
3. W.A. Gardner, Sandia Corporation, "Summary of Construction Project at the weapons storage areas," dated March 2, 1955. Montgomery, Alabama: Maxwell Air Force Base, Air Force Historical Research Agency (at this time, Captain, United States Air Force) research during attendance at Air Force Squadron Officers School in Residence Course, January to March 1978 for class speech presentation).
4. I.H. hart, Jr., Atomic Energy Commission to L.J. Paddision, Sandia Corporation, Memorandum, "Technical Monitoring of Nuclear Shipments." Montgomery, Alabama: Maxwell Air Force Base, Air Force Historical Research Agency (at this time, Captain, United States Air Force) research during attendance at Air Force Squadron Officers School in Residence Course, January to March 1978 for class speech presentation).
5. Memorandum (sender unknown-no title page on document), "Sandia Corporation Operations at AEC Storage Sites," dated, October 15, 1955. Montgomery, Alabama: Maxwell Air Force Base, Air Force Historical Research Agency (at this time, Captain, United States Air Force) research during attendance at Air Force Squadron Officers School in Residence Course, January to March 1978 for class speech presentation).
6. Lt. Col. George A. Larson, USAF (Ret.), *Thunder over Dakota, The Complete History of Ellsworth Air Force Base* (Atglen, Pennsylvania: Schiffer Publishing, 2013).
7. "Inventory of Cold War Properties," United States Air Force, Headquarters, Air Mobility Command, Scott Air Force Base, Illinois and US Army Corps of Engineers, Fort Worth District, Fort Worth, Texas, *United States Air Force Mobility Command, Cold War Series, Report of Investigations,* number 5, dated October 1996.
8. "Winston Churchill's Fulton, Missouri Speech," (Speech made at West Minister College at Fulton, Missouri). Independence, Missouri: Harry S. Truman Library and Museum. Author (at the time a Lieutenant Colonel, assigned as Commandant of Cadets, University of Iowa), research, August 15, 1986 (material used for Cold War lecture for Junior Air Force Reserve Officer Training Corps, Air Science [AS] 300 class).
9. "Inventory of Cold War Properties."
10. Inventory of Cold War Properties, Headquarters Air Mobility Command, United States Air Force, Scott Air Force Base, Illinois and U.S. Army Corps of Engineers, Fort Worth District, Fort Worth, Texas, United States Air Force Air Mobility Command, Cold War Series, Report of Investigations, Number 5, October 1996.
11. "Inventory of Cold War Properties."
12. "SAC atomic weapons Storage," Omaha, Nebraska: Offutt Air Force Base, Strategic

Air Command, Historian Office, June 1991.

13. "Atomic storage igloos in England," Royal Air Force Base, Fairford, The Royal Air Force Benevolent Fund Enterprises, to Author, 1992.
14. "History of Dyess Air Force Base, B-1B Operations," Part of B-1 aircraft special collection donated by Assistant Secretary of the Air Force for Acquisitions. Montgomery, Alabama: Maxwell Air Force Base, Air Force Historical Research Agency.
15. "Types of earth-covered magazines," (http://armymunitions/pub.com).
16. "SAC atomic weapons storage."
17. "History of Dyess Air Force Base, B-1B Operations."
18. "The number of US nuclear warheads," Washington, DC.: United States Department of Defense, May 3, 2010.
19. "New Start Treaty warhead numbers," Washington, DC.: United States Department of State, *Fact Sheet,* October 3, 2012.
20. Federation of American Scientists, "US nuclear weapons numbers," (http://www.fas.org).
21. "SAC two-officer policy," Omaha, Nebraska: Offutt Air Force Base, Strategic Air Command, Historian Office, June 1991.
2. The author served as a SAC EWO/SIOP officer, Positive Control Custodian, thermonuclear weaponeer (Air Force and Navy), conventional weaponeer and Wing Combat Operations Officer and Security Officer.
23. Inspector General, United States Department of Defense, "Report Number DODIG-2012-113," dated July 20, 2012 (http://www.dodig.mil/reports/DODIG-2012-113).
24. "Munitions Storage and Handling Facilities," *United States Air Force Munitions Facilities Standards Guide,* Volume I, Dated May 31, 2004. Washington, DC.: Department of Defense, United States Air Force.
25. "The history of Dyess Air Force Base, October 1, 1993," IRIS number 01117439, reel number 47591 and "The history of Dyess Air Force Base, January 1, 1996 to December 31, 1997," IRIS number 01127922, reel number 48655. Montgomery, Alabama: Maxwell Air Force Base, Air Force Historical Research Agency, to author, February 11, 2013.
26. "Careers, Munitions Systems, Enlisted," (http://www.airforce.com/careers/detail.munitions-systems)
27. "Air Force Munitions Squadron Responsibilities," (http://www.usafammo.com).
28. "Conventional munitions bunkers." Carlisle Barracks, Pennsylvania: US Army History Institute, Historical Reference Branch.
29. "Conventional munitions storage areas operations," (http://www.armymunitions.tpub.com).
30. "Dyess Air Force Maintenance Group," (http://www.dyess.af.mil/units/7thmaintenancegroup).
31. "B-1B conventional weapons capabilities," Ellsworth Air Force Base, 29th Bomb Wing Public Affairs.
32. "We don't drop bombs, 7th MUNS wins 4th consecutive Safety Award," Dyess Air Force Base, 7th Bomb Wing Public Affairs.
33. "AMMO pride in end product," Undisclosed located in Southwest Asia, 379th Air Expeditionary Wing Public Affairs.

Chapter Twelve

1. "96th Bomb Wing," www.dyessafb.com.
2. "History of B-1B force distribution," Joint Base Langley-Eustis, Virginia: Air Combat Command, Command History Office.
3. "B-1B nuclear bombing mission profiles," Offutt Air Force Base, Strategic Air Command, Historian Office.
4. "History of Dyess Air Force Base, B-1B operations," Montgomery, Alabama: Maxwell Air Force Base, Air Force Historical Research Agency.
5. "7th Bomb Wing History," *US Air Force Fact Sheet* (http://www.dyess.af.mil/library/factsheets).
6. "History of Dyess Air Force Base, B-1B operations."
7. "B-1B makes impact throughout Southwest Asia," (http://www.af.mil/news/story).
8. "Location, location, location: Dyess B-1Bs temporarily moved to allow for runway construction," (http://www.af.mil/news/story), August 29, 2007.
9. "B-1 adapts, remains effective after 25 years," (http://www.af.mil/news/story), April 26, 2010.

10. "Boeing honors 25 years of B-1 excellence," (http://www.af.mil/news/story), April 29, 2010.
11. "B-1 simulator training system support consolidates," (http://www.dyess.af.mil/news/story), April 21, 2006.
12. "B-1B simulators go from Mario Brothers to Halo," (http://www.af.mil/news/story), April 20, 2011.
13. "Dyess installs last B-1 LCTP upgrade," (http://www.dyess.af.mil/news/story), March 15, 2012.
14. "New upgrades revitalize B-1B Lancers," (http://www.af.mil/news/story), June 2, 2012.
15. "337th TES demonstrates ability to triple B-1B payload," (http://www.dyes.af.mil/news/story), April 4, 2011.
16. "As focus turns to Asia, B-1's role may grow," (http://www.airforcestime.com/news), July 9, 2012.
17 "Continued START compliance," *BUF Bulletin, Newsletter of the B-52 Stratofortress Association*, Winter 2013.
18 "As focus turns to Asia, B-1's role may grow."
19 "7th BW returns from largest B-1 deployment in last decade," (http://www.dyess.af.mil/news/story), July 31, 2012.
17. "Global Strike Challenge 2012: the Operations Group Team members," (http://wwwdyess.af.mil/news/story), September 13, 2012.
18. "Dyess' readiness tested during ORE," (http://www/dyess.af.mil/news/story), October 18, 2012.
19. "ACC IG rates Dyess Excellent," (http://www/dyess.af.mil/news/story), January 18, 2013.
20. "Dyess B-1Bs participates in multi-service exercise," (http://www.dyess.af.mil/news/story), January 30, 2013.
21. "COMACC visits Team Dyess," (http://www.dyess.af/mil/news/story), February 15, 2013.
22. "Dyess maintainers learn new methods of refueling jets," *Patriot*, Ellsworth Air Force Base, 7th Bomb Wing, Public Affairs, March 8, 2013.
23. "B-1s provide close air support during joint training exercise," (http://www.dyess.af/mil/news/story), May 6, 2013.
27 "B-1 test squadron demonstrates anti-ship missile," (http://www.dyess.af/mil/news/story), July 15, 2103.
24. "Deployed Dyess bombers participate in exercise," (http://www.dyess.af/mil/news/story), August 22, 2013.
25. "B-1B provides combat support," (http://www.dyess.af/mil/news/story), December 12, 2013.
26. "Dyess receives first operational IBS-upgraded B-1," (http://www.dyess.af/mil/news/story), January 24, 2014.
27. "B-1B Lancer software upgrade will ensure future warfighting capabilities," (http://www.dyess.af/mil/news/story), April 17, 2014.
28. "Link 16: The B-1B's future link to the battle field," (http://www.dyess.af/mil/news/story), April 9, 2014.
29. "The B-1 is a little bit tired," Lieutenant Colonel Shane Henderson, Chief, Air Combat Command B-1 Weapons Sustainment Team. Joint Base Langley-Eustis, Virginia, Air Combat Command Public Affairs, October 2014.
30. "AF turns to 4-star to resolve nuclear problems," Washington, D.C., Air Force Times, August 10, 2015.

Chapter Thirteen

1. Richard A. Warner, Civilian, United States Air Force Air Combat Command, Bomb Wing/CVM, Dyess Air Force Base, Texas, 7th Bomb Wing, "Dyess Air Force Base Linear Air Park aircraft."
2. "Dyess' Warhawk makes final flight," Dyess Air Force Base, 7th Bomb Wing Public Affairs.
3. Brian P. Smith, Civilian, United States Air Force Air Mobility Command, Dyess Air Force Base, Texas, 317th Airlift Group Historian and Richard A Warner, "Dyess Air Force Base Linear Air Park aircraft."

Appendix I

1. The Development of the Strategic Air Command (The Fortieth Anniversary History) (Omaha, Nebraska: Offutt Air Force Base, Headquarters Strategic Air Command, Officer of the Command Historian, September 1, 1986).
2. Atlas D Intercontinental Ballistic Missile, Ashland, Nebraska: Strategic Air Command Museum and Dayton, Ohio: Wright Patterson Air Force Base, National Museum of the United States.

3. "Nike," (http://www.techbastard.com/missile/nike/dyess- tx.php).
4. "B-52C," Offutt Air Force Base: Omaha, Nebraska, Strategic Air Command Historian.
5. "B-52E," Offutt Air Force Base, Omaha, Nebraska, Strategic Air Command Historian.
6. "Nuclear weapons," Albuquerque, New Mexico: National Museum of Nuclear Science and Technology.
7. "B-52D," Offutt Air Force Base, Omaha, Nebraska, Strategic Air Command Historian.
8. "B-52H," Offutt Air Force Base, Omaha, Nebraska, Strategic Air Command Historian.
9. "Boeing Kc-135A," Offutt Air Force Base, Omaha, Nebraska, Strategic Air Command Historian.
10. "C-130A Hercules," Dyess Air Force Base, 7th Bombardment Wing, Dyess Air Force Base Linear Air Park.
11. "C-310E," U.S. Air Force Fact Sheet, Dayton, Ohio: Wright Patterson Air Force Base, National Museum of the United States Air Force.
12. "C-7A Caribou," Dyess Air Force Base, 7th Bombardment Wing, Dyess Air Force Base Linear Air Park.
13. "C-130H Hercules," Dyess Air Force Base, 317th Airlift Group, 317th Air Group Historian.
14. "C-13J Hercules," Dyess Air Force Base, 317th Airlift Group, 317th Air Group Historian.

Appendix II

1. "B-83," South Dakota Air and Space Museum, Ellsworth Air Force Base, South Dakota.

Appendix III

1. "Boeing AGM-69 and AGM-69B," Dyess Air Force Base, 7th Bomb Wing Public Affairs.

SOURCES

Abilene Reporter-News (Evening), May 11, 1960, 2-A.

Abilene Reporter-News (Evening), Nay 28, 1960, 1-A.

"ACC IG rates Dyess Excellent." (http://www/dyess.af.mil/news/story), January 18, 2013.

"Activities and accomplishments of the Abilene Chamber of Commerce, 1959 & 1960." Abilene, Texas, Abilene Chamber of Commerce to author, October 2012.

"Air Combat History." (http://www.acc.af.mil/library/acchistory)

Air Force Ballistic Missile Division. "Atlas F silo investigation, Dyess Air Force Base, March 16, 1961 to April 4, 1962." Montgomery, Alabama: Maxwell Air Force Base, Air Force Historical Research Agency. Author research for Squadron Officer's School in resident program presentation, February 1978.

"Air Force Ballistic Missile Division, Detachment Number 5, Dyess Air Force Base, March 1961 to April 1962, Los Angles, California." Montgomery, Alabama: Maxwell Air Force Base, Air Force Historical Research Agency.

Author research for Squadron Officer's School in resident program presentation, March 1978.

"Air Force Munitions Squadron Responsibilities." (http://www.usafammo.com).

"Agreement between the Atomic Energy Commission and military organizations." Montgomery, Alabama: Maxwell Air Force Base, Air Force Historical Research Agency. Author (at this time, Captain, United States Air Force) research during attendance at Air Force Squadron Officers School in Residence Course, January to March 1978 for class speech presentation).

Air Material Command Museum. "C-133B Cargomaster." Dover, Delaware: Dover Air Force Base.

"AirNav: KDYS-Dyess Air Force Base." (http://www.airnav.com/airport/KDYS)'

"Alert Through Dispersal." (listed as Tab "B") Assistant Chief of Staff, Installations, Headquarters, United States Air Force, Washington, DC, June 6, 1957. Washington, DC: Department of the Air Force, Air Force Declassification Office, declassified June 8, 2010. (http://www.afdeclassification.com).

"Alert Through Dispersal." (listed as Tab "C") Assistant Chief of Staff, Installations, Headquarters, United States Air Force, Washington, DC, May 21, 1957. Washington, DC: Department of the Air Force, Air Force

Allen, MSgt. William J. *Abilene Airlifters, A History of Tactical Airlift at Dyess Air Force Base, Texas.* "The 64th Troop Carrier Wing, 8 February 1961-1 January 1963." Dyess Air Force Base, Texas: 7th Bombardment Wing, Office of History, December 31, 1995. Courtesy, Brian Smith, 317th Airlift Group History Office to author, October 19, 2012.

"AMARC history." (http://www.amarcexperience.co/amarchistory.asp).

"AMMO pride in end product." Undisclosed located in Southwest Asia, 379th Air Expeditionary Wing Public Affairs.

"As focus turns to Asia, B-1's role may grow." (http://www.airforcestime.com/news), July 9, 2012.

"Atlas F missiles at Dyess Air Force Base, Texas." Ashland, Nebraska: Strategic Air Command Museum.

"Atlas F missile construction." Fort Worth, Texas: US Army Corps of Engineers, Fort Worth District Office, Historian Office.

"Atlas F missile construction operations at Dyess Air Force Base." US Army Corps of Engineers, Fort Worth District Office, Historian Office.

"Atlas F missiles on Dyess Air Force Base," US Army Corps of Engineers, Fort Worth District Office, Historian Office.

"Atlas D Intercontinental Ballistic Missile." Ashland, Nebraska: Strategic Air Command Museum and Dayton, Ohio: Wright Patterson Air Force Base, National Museum of the United States Air Force.

"Atlas missile silo, terms and definitions of missile crewmen." Association of Air Force Missileers.

"Atlas Intercontinental Ballistic Missile." Ashland, Nebraska: Strategic Air Command Museum, author. Research on August 15, 2002.

"Atlas launch sites." Alexandria, Virginia: US Army Corps of Engineers, Historian Office, to author, August 2012. Declassification Office, declassified June 8, 2010. (http://www.Afdeclassification.com).

"Atomic storage igloos in England." Royal Air Force Base, Fairford, The Royal Air Force Benevolent Fund Enterprises, to Author, 1992.

"C-130A Hercules." Dyess Air Force Base, *Dyess Air Force Base Linear Air Park,* 7th Bombardment Wing, Public Affairs.

"Camp Barkeley." Handbook of Texas Online (http://www.tshaonline.org/handbook/articles/gbc02), accessed August 30, 2009. Published by the Texas State Historical Association.

"B-1 adapts, remains effective after 25 years." (http://www.af.mil/news/story), April 26, 2010.

"B-1B conventional weapons capabilities." Ellsworth Air Force Base, 29th Bomb Wing Public Affairs.

"B-1B Lancer." *US Air Force fact Sheet* (http://www.af.mil/information.factsheets).

"B-1B Lancer software upgrade will ensure future warfighting capabilities," (http://www.dyess.af/mil/news/story), April 17, 2014.

"B-1B makes impact throughout Southwest Asia." (http://www.af.mil/news/story).

"B-1B nuclear bombing mission profiles." Offutt Air Force Base, Strategic Air Command, Historian Office.

"B-1s provide close air support during joint training exercise." (http://www.dyess.af/mil/news/story), May 6, 2013.

"B-1B provides combat support." (http://www.dyess.af/mil/news/story), December 12, 2013.

"B-1 simulator training system support consolidates."
(http://www.dyess.af.mil/news/story), April 21, 2006.

"B-1B simulators go from Mario Brothers to Halo." (http://www.af.mil/news/story), April 20, 2011.

"B-1 test squadron demonstrates anti-ship missile." (http://www.dyess.af/mil/news/story), July 15, 2103.

"B-47 alert procedures," The B-47 Stratojet Association, preserving the legacy of the Boeing B-47 Stratojet bomber, (http://b-47.com/).

"B-47E." B-47 Stratojet Association.

"B-47E, crash, November 4, 1958," The B-47 Stratojet Association, preserving the legacy of the Boeing B-47 Stratojet bomber, (http://b-47.com/).

"B-47 deployments to England," The B-47 Stratojet Association, preserving the legacy of the Boeing B-47 Stratojet bomber, (http://b-47.com/).

"B-52C." Offutt Air Force Base, Omaha, Nebraska, Strategic Air Command Historian.

"B-52D." Offutt Air Force Base, Omaha, Nebraska, Strategic Air Command Historian.

"B-52E." Offutt Air Force Base, Omaha, Nebraska, Strategic Air Command Historian.

"B-52H." Offutt Air Force Base, Omaha, Nebraska, Strategic Air Command Historian.

Bath, David W., ed. *Air Force Missileers and the Cuban Missile Crisis*, "Charles Condit, CMSgt. (Ret.), Operations, 578th SMS." Breckenridge, Colorado: Association of Air Force Missileers.

Bath, David W., ed. *Air Force Missileers and the Cuban Missile Crisis*, "Lucas A. Morgan, A2C, Electrical Power Production Technician, 578th SMS." Breckenridge, Colorado: Association of Air Force Missileers.

"Basic specifications of the B-52H." (http://www.stratofortress.org/specifications-b52h.htm).

Berger, Carl, ed. *The United States Air Force in Southeast Asia, 1961-1973: An illustrated account*. Washington, DC: Office of Air Force History, United States Air Force, 1984.

"Boeing honors 25 years of B-1 excellence." (http://www.af.mil/news/story), April 29, 2010.

"Boeing KC-97L Stratofreighter." Abilene, Texas: Dyess Air Force Base Linear Air Park, Dyess Air Park.

"Boeing KC-135A Stratotanker." Offutt Air Force Base, Omaha, Nebraska, Strategic Air Command Historian.

"Burleson Papers." Bulletin, Department of the Army, Chief of Legislative Liaison to interested member of Congress, July 31, 1959. Abilene, Texas: Richardson Library, Hardin-Simmons University.

"C-7A Caribou." Dyess Air Force Base, *Dyess Air Force Base Linear Air Park*, 7th Bombardment Wing, Public Affairs.

"C-124 Globemaster II." Dover, Delaware: Dover Air Force Base, Air Mobility Command Museum.

"C-130." *US Air Force Fact Sheet*. (http://www.af.mil/information/factsheets).

"C-130J Super Hercules." (http://www.dyes.af.mil/library/factsheets).

"Careers, Munitions Systems, Enlisted." (http://www.airforce.com/careers/detail.munitions-systems/).

"COMACC visits Team Dyess." (http://www.dyess.af/mil/news/story), February 15, 2013.

"Continued START compliance." *BUF Bulletin, Newsletter of the B-52 Stratofortress Association*, Winter 2013.

"Conventional munitions bunkers." Carlisle Barracks, Pennsylvania: US Army History Institute, Historical Reference Branch.

"Conventional munitions storage areas operations." (http://www.armymunitions.tpub.com).

Craven, Wesley Frank and James Lea Cate, ed. *The Army Air Forces in World War II*, Volume One, *Plans and Early Operations, January 1939 to August 1942*. Washington, DC: Office of Air Force History, US Government Printing Office, 1983.

"Curtis P-40E Warhawk." Dayton, Ohio: Wright-Patterson Air Force Base, National Museum of the United States Air Force.

"Deployed Dyess bombers participate in exercise." (http://www.dyess.af/mil/news/story), August 22, 2013.

"Description of a typical Nike-Hercules missile site." Carlisle Barracks, Pennsylvania: United States Army Military History Institute Library, author research August 1982 for Air Force War College Non-resident Program research thesis.

"Development of the Atlas ICBM." Convair Division of General Dynamics Corporation, Missile Papers.

Montgomery, Alabama: Air Force Historical Research Agency, author research for Squadron Officer's School in resident program presentation, March 1978.

"Deployed C-130 Loadmaster supports Southwest Asia airlift operations." (http://wwwamc.af.mil/news/story), August 21, 2010.

"Douglas A-24." Dayton, Ohio: Wright-Patterson Air Force Base, National Museum of the United States Air Force.

"Douglas A-26 Invader." Dayton, Ohio: Wright-Patterson Air Force Base, National Museum of the United States Air Force.

"Dyess Air Force Base." (http://www.dyes.af.mil/units/index.asp)

"Dyess Air Force Base, 96th Bomb Wing, B-52H Stratofortress." (http://www.dyess.af.mil).

"Dyess Air Force Base, SM-65F Atlas missile sites." (http://www.dyess.af.mil).

"Dyess Air Force Base, Texas." *The Military Standard-Air Force Bases,* (http://www.techbastard.com.afb/tx/dyess.php).

"Dyess Air Force Base Defense Area." Carlisle Barracks, Pennsylvania: United States Army Military History Institute Library, author research August 1982 for Air Force War College Non-resident Program research thesis.

"Dyess Air Force Maintenance Group." (http://www.dyess.af.mil/units/7thmaintenancegroup).

"Dyess History." *US Air Force Fact Sheet*. (http://www.dyess.af.mil/library/factsheets).

"Dyess installs last B-1 LCTP upgrade," (http://www.dyess.af.mil/news/story), March 15, 2012.

"Dyess maintainers learn new methods of refueling jets," *Patriot*, Ellsworth Air Force Base, 7th Bomb Wing, PublicAffairs, March 8, 2013.

"Dyess B-1Bs participates in multi-service exercise." (http://www.dyess.af.mil/news/story), January 30, 2013.

"Dyess' readiness tested during ORE." (http://www.dyess.af.mil/news/story), October 18, 2012.

"Dyess receives first operational IBS-upgraded B-1." (http://www.dyess.af/mil/news/story), January 24, 2014.
"Dyess' Warhawk makes final flight." Dyess Air Force Base, 7th Bomb Wing Public Affairs.
11th Air Refueling Squadron, Alumni Association. "Squadron History,1955-1965." (http://www.facebook.com/pages/11thairrefueling-squadron-alumni-association/1266), October 23, 2012.
Federation of American Scientists. "US nuclear weapons numbers," (http://www.fas.org).
"Fifty- years after Dyess plane crash, soil contains negligible levels of radioactive materials." Courtesy, of the office of United States Senator John Thune, South Dakota via Dindi Robinson, Information Research Specialist, Foreign Affairs, Defense & Trade Section, Knowledge Service Group, Congressional Research Service, Library of Congress, Washington, DC, to author, November 14, 2012.
"5th Missile Battalion History, Dyess Air Force Base, Texas." Montgomery, Alabama: Maxwell Air Force Base, Air Force Historical Research Agency.
"First C-130J Super Hercules delivered to Dyess Air Force Base." Dyess Air Force Baser, 7th Bomb Wing Public Affairs, April 17, 2010.
"Gallery of USAF Weapons, Tanker Aircraft." *2011 USAF Almanac*, Air Force Association, *Journal of the Air Force Association, Air Force Magazine*, May 2011.
Gardner, W.A. Sandia Corporation, "Summary of Construction Project at the weapons storage areas," dated March 2, 1955. Montgomery, Alabama: Maxwell Air Force Base, Air Force Historical Research Agency (at this time, Captain, United States Air Force) research during attendance at Air Force Squadron Officers School in Residence Course, January to March 1978 for class speech presentation).
"Global Strike Challenge 2012: the Operations Group Team members." (http://wwwdyess.af.mil/news/story), September 13, 2012.
Harrington, Dan. Deputy Command Historian, United States Strategic Command, Offutt Air Force Base, Omaha, Nebraska, November 1, 2012, to author.
Hart, Jr. I.H. Atomic Energy Commission to L.J. Paddision, Sandia Corporation, Memorandum, "Technical Monitoring of Nuclear Shipments." Montgomery, Alabama: Maxwell Air Force Base, Air Force Historical Research Agency (at this time, Captain, United States Air Force) research during attendance at Air Force Squadron Officers School in Residence Course, January to March 1978 for class speech presentation).
Hatcher, John H. "Camp Barkeley." *Texas Military History*, volume 3, number 4, winter 1963, 219-220. Courtesy Hardin-Simmons University, Richardson Library, Austin, Texas, November 9, 2012.
"Highlights from the 317th Air Group history from January 2012 to June 2014." Dyess Air Force Base, Texas: Brain Smith (317th Air Group Historian), to author June 30, 2014.
Krammer, Arnold P. "German Prisoners of War," Handbook of Texas Online (http://www.tshaonline.org/handbook/ articles/gbc02), accessed October 18, 2012. Published by the Texas State Historical Association.
"History, 96th Bombardment Wing (Medium), Dyess Air Force Base, Texas, April 1-30, 1960." Prepared May, 1961, Dyess Air Force Base, Texas. (IRIS number 004531234, reel number 5-26009-18/N0057), Montgomery, Alabama: Maxwell Air Force Base, Air Force Historical Research Agency, to author, January 30, 2013.
"History, 96th Bombardment Wing (Medium), Dyess Air Force Base, Texas, May 1-31, 1961." Prepared June, 1960, "History of Dyess Air Force Base." (http;//www.dyess.af.mil/library/factsheet).
"History of Dyess Air Force Base, B-1B Operations." Part of B-1 aircraft special collection donated by Assistant Secretary of the Air Force for Acquisitions. Montgomery, Alabama: Maxwell Air Force Base, Air Force Historical Research Agency.
"History of F.E. Warren Air Force Base." Cheyenne, Wyoming: Francis E. Warren Air Force Base, Museum.
Dyess Air Force Base, Texas. (IRIS number 004531234, reel number 5-26009-18/N0057), Montgomery, Alabama: Maxwell Air Force Base, Air Force Historical Research Agency, to author, January 30, 2013.
"History, 4th Strategic Support Squadron, Dyess Air Force Base, Texas, June 1-30, 1957."

(IRIS number 00432255, reel number 000012677), Montgomery, Alabama: Maxwell Air Force Base, Air Force Historical Research Agency, to author, October 26, 2012.

"History, 4th Strategic Support Squadron, Dyess Air Force Base, Texas, April 1-30, 1959." Prepared June 10, 1959,

Dyess Air Force Base, Texas. (IRIS number 00432277, reel number 000012678/KD671), Montgomery, Alabama: Maxwell Air Force Base, Montgomery, Alabama: Air Force Historical Research Agency, to author, January 22, 2013.

"History, 4th Strategic Support Squadron, Dyess Air Force Base, Texas, May 1-31, 1959." Prepared June 10, 1959, Dyess Air Force Base, Texas. (IRIS number 00432277, reel number 000012678/KD671), Montgomery, Alabama: Maxwell Air Force Base, Air Force Historical Research Agency, to author, January 22, 2013.

"History, 4th Strategic Support Squadron, Dyess Air Force Base, Texas, July 1-310, 1959." prepared September 5, 1959, Dyess Air Force Base, Texas. (IRIS number 00432277, reel number 000012678/KD671), Montgomery, Alabama: Maxwell Air Force Base, Air Force Historical Research Agency, to author, January 22, 2013.

"History, 4th Strategic Support Squadron, Dyess Air Force Base, Texas, August 1-31, 1959." Prepared October 10, 1959, Dyess Air Force Base, Texas. (IRIS number 00432277, reel number 000012678/KD671), Montgomery, Alabama: Maxwell Air Force Base, Air Force Historical Research Agency, to author, January 22, 2013.

"History, 96th Bombardment Wing (Medium), Dyess Air Force Base, Texas, July 1-31, 1961." Prepared August, 1961, Dyess Air Force Base, Texas. (IRIS number 004531234, reel number 5-26009-18/N0057), Montgomery, Alabama: Maxwell Air Force Base, Air Force Historical Research Agency, to author, January 30, 2013.

"History, 96th Bombardment Wing (Medium), Dyess Air Force Base, Texas, August 1-31, 1961." Prepared September, 1961, Dyess Air Force Base, Texas. (IRIS number 004531234, reel number 5-26009-18/N0057), Montgomery, Alabama: Maxwell Air Force Base, Air Force Historical Research Agency, to author, January 30, 2013.

"History, 96th Bombardment Wing (Medium), Dyess Air Force Base, Texas, September 1-30, 1961." Prepared October, 1961, Dyess Air Force Base, Texas. (IRIS number 004531234, reel number 5-26009-18/N0057), Montgomery, Alabama: Maxwell Air Force Base, Air Force Historical Research Agency, to author, January 30, 2013.

"History, 96th Bombardment Wing (Medium), Dyess Air Force Base, Texas, December 1-31, 1961." Prepared January, 1962, Dyess Air Force Base, Texas. (IRIS number 004531234, reel number 5-26009-18/N0057), Montgomery, Alabama: Maxwell Air Force Base, Air Force Historical Research Agency, to author, January 30, 2013.

"History of B-1B force distribution." Joint Base Langley-Eustis, Virginia: Air Combat Command, Command History Office.

"History of Dyess Air Force Base, B-1B operations." Montgomery, Alabama: Maxwell Air Force Base, Air Force Historical Research Agency.

"Housing options at Dyess AFB." (http://www.housing.af.mil/dyess/govhousingoption/index.asp).

Inspector General, United States Department of Defense, "Report Number DODIG-2012-113." dated July 20, 2012 (http://www.dodig.mil/reports/DODIG-2012-113)

"Installation overview—Dyess Air Force Base, Texas."

"Inventory of Cold War Properties." United States Air Force, Headquarters, Air Mobility Command, Scott Air Force

Base, Illinois and US Army Corps of Engineers, Fort Worth District, Fort Worth, Texas, *United States Air Force Mobility Command, Cold War Series, Report of Investigations*, number 5, dated October 1996.

Jenson, Colonel. Offutt Air Force Base, Headquarters Strategic Air Command, "Strategic Air Command Rotational Movements." Washington, DC: testimony before the United States House of Representatives Sub-Committee on Military Appropriations, March 12, 1952. Courtesy, of the office of United States Senator John Thune, South Dakota via Dindi Robinson, Information Research Specialist, Foreign Affairs, Defense

& Trade Section, Knowledge Service Group, Congressional Research Service, Library of Congress, Washington, DC, to author, November 14, 2012.

"KC-135A Crash at Dyess AFB." Dyess Air Force Base, 7th Bomb Wing, Public Affairs.

"KC-135A Stratotanker." Dyess Air Force Base, Dyess Linear Air Park.

Larson, Lt. Col. George A. USAF, Deputy Commander for Resource Management, Offutt Air Force Base, Nebraska. "History of Capehart Housing, Offutt Air Force Base," October 1989.

Larson, Lt. Col George A, USAF (Ret.), "Linebacker II." *Military*, June 2003, 6-11 and July 2003, 11-14.

Larson, Lt. Col. George A. USAF (Ret.). *Thunder over Dakota, The Complete History of Ellsworth Air Force Base* (Atglen, Pennsylvania: Schiffer Publishing, 2013).

"Link 16: The B-1B's future link to the battle field." (http://www.dyess.af/mil/news/story), April 9, 2014.

"Location, location, location: Dyess B-1Bs temporarily moved to allow for runway construction," (http://www.af.mil/news/story), August 29, 2007.

Manson, Colonel Hugh B., Commander, Site Activation Task Force, Dyess Air Force Base, Texas. Montgomery, Alabama: Maxwell Air Force Base, Air Force Historical Research Agency, author research for Squadron Officer's School in resident program presentation, February 1978.

Memorandum. "Sandia Corporation Engineering Responsibilities concerning New Storage and Assembly Sites," G.P. Kraker to G.A. Landry," dated October 25, 1950. Montgomery, Alabama: Maxwell Air Force Base, Air Force Historical Research Agency (at this time, Captain, United States Air Force) research during attendance at Air Force Squadron Officers School in Residence Course, January to March 1978 for class speech presentation).

Memorandum (sender unknown-no title page on document). "Sandia Corporation Operations at AEC Storage Sites," dated, October 15, 1955. Montgomery, Alabama: Maxwell Air Force Base, Air Force Historical Research Agency (Author, at this time, Captain, United States Air Force) research during attendance at Air Force Squadron Officers School in Residence Course, January to March 1978 for class speech presentation).

Meyers, James M. "Barkley, David Bennes." Handbook of Texas Online (http://www.tshaonline.org/handbook/articles/gbc02), accessed October 5, 2012. Published by the Texas State Historical Association.

Meyers, James M. "Camp Barkeley," Handbook of Texas Online (http://www.tshaonline.org/handbook/articles/gbc02), Accessed October 5, 2012. Published by the Texas State Historical Association.

"Munitions Storage and Handling Facilities." *United States Air Force Munitions Facilities Standards Guide*, Volume I, Dated May 31, 2004. Washington, DC.: Department of Defense, United States Air Force.

"New Start Treaty warhead numbers." Washington, DC.: United States Department of State, *Fact Sheet*, October 3, 2012.

"New upgrades revitalize B-1B Lancers." (http://www.af.mil/news/story), June 2, 2012.

"96th Bomb Wing." Ww.dyessafb.com.

"96th Bombardment Wing." (http://www.strategic-air- command.com/wings/0096bw.htm).

"96th Strategic Aerospace Wing, History of the 578th Strategic Missile Squadron, July 1961, Dyess Air Force Base, Texas." Montgomery, Alabama: Maxwell Air Force Base, Air Force Historical Research Agency, author research for Squadron Officer's School in resident program presentation, March 1978.

"917th Air Refueling Squadron." Omaha, Nebraska: Strategic Air Command, Offutt Air Force Base, Historian Office, 1992.

"Nike." (http://www.techbastard.com/missile/nike/dyess-tx.php)

"Nike-Hercules at Dyess Air Force Base." (e. nuriso@comcast.com to author.

"Nike-Hercules Site at Ellsworth Air Force Base, South Dakota." Ellsworth Air Force Base, 28th Bomb Wing Historian.

"Nike-Hercules Surface to Air Missile technical information." South Dakota Air and Space Museum, Ellsworth Air Force Base, South Dakota.

"Nike Missile Sites." Carlisle Barracks, Pennsylvania: United States Institute for Military History, United States Army War College Library.

"Nuclear weapons." Albuquerque, New Mexico: National Museum of Nuclear Science and Technology.

"Nuclear weapons in the Strategic Air Command arsenal." Ashland, Nebraska: Strategic Air Command Museum.

Odintz, Mark. "TYE, TX." Handbook of Texas Online (http://www.tshaonline.org/handbook/articles/hjt13), accessed September 20, 2012. Published by the Texas State Historical Association.

Procter, Ben H. "World War II," Handbook of Texas Online (http://www.tshaonline.org/handbook/articles/npwni), accessed October 5, 2012. Published by the Texas State Historical Association.

"Republic P-47D Thunderbolt." Dayton, Ohio: Wright-Patterson Air Force Base, National Museum of the United States Air Force.

"Responsibilities for the provision of Zone of Interior atomic weapons storage facilities." Memorandum, dated June 1957. Fort Worth, Texas: National Archives and Records Administration, Fort Worth Federal Records Center to author, October 13, 2012.

"SAC Alert Facilities." (listed as Tab "A") Assistant Chief of Staff, Installations, Headquarters, United States Air Force, Washington, DC, May 8, 1957. Washington, DC: Department of the Air Force, Air Force Declassification Office, declassified June 8, 2010. (http://www.AFdeclassification.com).

"SAC atomic weapons Storage." Omaha, Nebraska: Offutt Air Force Base, Strategic Air Command, Historian Office, June 1991.

"SAC bases: Abilene/Dyess Air Force Base." (http://www.Strategic-Air-Command.com/bases/ Dyess_afb.htm)

"SAC two-officer policy." Omaha, Nebraska: Offutt Air Force Base, Strategic Air Command, Historian Office, June 1991.

San Bernardino Air Material Center. "Semi-annual historical report, August 18, 1960 to June 30, 1961," Norton Air Force Base, California. Montgomery, Alabama: Maxwell Air Force Base, Air Force Historical Research Agency, author research for Squadron Officer's School in resident program presentation, February 1978.

"7th Bomb Wing History." *US Air Force Fact Sheet* (http://www.dyess.af.mil/library/factsheets).

"7th BW returns from largest B-1 deployment in last decade." (http://www.dyess.af.mil/news/story), July 31, 2012.

Smith, Brian. Air Mobility Command, 317th Airlift Group, Historian Office, 7th Bombardment Wing, Dyess Air Force Base, Texas, "Dyess AFB tornado, July 1962," to author, September 15, 2012.

"Soviet Intercontinental Ballistic Missiles." Montgomery, Alabama: United States Air Force, Air War College, Correspondence Course. Author was a Major assigned to the Defense Intelligence Agency, Alternate National Military Command Center at Fort Ritchie, Maryland, 1984.

"Status Report." Assistant Chief of Staff, Installations, Headquarters, United States Air Force, Washington, DC,

June 6, 1957. Washington, DC: Department of the Air Force, Air Force Declassification Office, declassified June 8, 2010. (http://www.Afdeclassification.com).

"Stinson L-5 Sentinel." Dayton, Ohio: Wright-Patterson Air Force Base, National Museum of the United States Air Force.

"Strategic Air Command Mission." Presented to Second Lieutenant George A. Larson, Strategic Air Command, October 1971, Offutt Air Force Base Junior Officers' Council.

"Strategic Air Command operations in the Cuban Missile Crisis," Historical Study Number 90, Volume I. Courtesy, Jerome V. Martin, PHD, DAFG, Command Historian, United States Strategic Command, Offutt Air Force Base, Omaha, Nebraska to author, October 29, 2012.

"Stratofreighter/Stratotanker, Boeing KC-97G aerial refueling tanker." Strategic Air Command Museum, Ashland, Nebraska.

"Summary History of Abilene Army Airfield, 1942-1946." Montgomery, Alabama: Maxwell Air force Base, Air Force Historical Research Agency, to author, November 13, 2012.

Summers, Jr., Colonel Harry G. US Army (Ret.) *Korean War Almanac*. New York: Facts on File, 1990.

"Tail swap enables Afghan mission support and humanitarian effort." Dyess Air Force Base, 7th Bomb Wing Public Affairs, October 11, 2012.

"Tanker at War, Air Refueling in Southeast Asia." *US Air Force Fact Sheet* (http://www.nationalmuseum.af.mil/factsheets).

Texas Historical Commission. "Texas in World War II." Austin, Texas: The State Agency for Historic Preservation, 2012.

"The Army Air Base." Texas Historical Commission, Military Sites Program, History Programs Division, Austin, Texas.

The Development of the Strategic Air Command, 1986. (The Fortieth Anniversary History). Omaha, Nebraska: Offutt Air Force Base, Headquarters Strategic Air Command, Office of the Historian, September 1, 1986.

"The Dyess Story." (http://www.tshaonline.org/daybyday/12-12-004.html), accessed September 20, 2012. Published by the Texas State Historical Association.

"The end of an era." Dyess Air Force Base, 7th Bomb Wing Public Affairs, September 27, 2012.

"The 4th Strategic Support Squadron and the C-124C Globemaster II." Compiled by former Lieutenant Merle M Allen Jr., pilot, 4th SSS, 1954-1957, to Ellsworth Heritage Foundation, South Dakota Air and Space Museum, to author, September 15, 2012.

"The history of Dyess Air Force Base, October 1, 1993," IRIS number 01117439, reel number 47591 and "The history of Dyess Air Force Base, January 1, 1996 to December 31, 1997," IRIS number 01127922, reel number 48655. Montgomery, Alabama: Maxwell Air Force Base, Air Force Historical Research Agency, to author, February 11, 2013.

"The history of Castle Air Force Base." Atwater, California: Castle Air Museum.

"The history of the Strategic Air Command." Offutt Air Force Base, Nebraska: Strategic Air Command, Historian Office.

"The number of US nuclear warheads." Washington, DC.: United States Department of Defense, May 3, 2010.

"The story of the B-52 Stratofortress." (http://www.stratofortress.org/history.htm).

"341st Bombardment Wing (M), SAC, January-April 1958, TDY, Andersen Air Force Base, Guam." Courtesy Colonel Sigmund Alexander, USAF (Ret.), President, Boeing B-47 Stratojet Association to author, January 4, 2013.

"317th Airlift Group."(http://www.dyes.Af.mil/units/317thairliftgroup)

"317th Air Group conducts first JPADS training." Dyess Air Force Base, 7th Bomb Wing Public Affairs, February 29, 2012.

"317th AG delivers resupply to the joint warfighters." Dyess Air Force Base, 7th Bomb Wing Public Affairs, April 26, 2012.

"317th AG makes with 16-ship formation." Dyess Air Force Base, 7th Bomb Wing Public Affairs, July 5, 2012.

Truman, Margret. *Harry S. Truman*. New York: William Morrow & Company, Inc., 1973.

"337th TES demonstrates ability to triple B-1B payload." (http://www.dyes.af.mil/news/story), April 4, 2011.

"12th Armored Division." (http://www.12tharmoredmuseum.com/)

"Types of earth-covered magazines." (http://armymunitions/pub.com).

"Underground silo." Abilene, Texas: Atlas Intercontinental Ballistic Missile Historical Society.

"United States Armed Forces nuclear Defense Conditions." Omaha, Nebraska: Offutt Air Force Base, Strategic Air Command, Historian Office, September 1990.

United States House of Representatives, Military Appropriations Committee, "Operational Support for the United States Air Force, Fiscal Year 1953." Witness, Colonel J.C. Jensen, Directorate of Operations, Deputy Chief of Staff for Operations, March 12, 1952. Courtesy of the office of United States Senator John Thune, South Dakota via Dindi Robinson, Information Research Specialist, Foreign Affairs, Defense & Trade Section, Knowledge Service Group, Congressional Research Service, Library of Congress, Washington, DC, to author, November 14, 2012.

United States House of Representatives, Military Appropriations Committee, "Operational Support for the United States Air Force, Fiscal Year 1953." Witness, Lieutenant Colonel C.M. Turner, Directorate of Installations, Deputy Chief of Staff for Operations, March 12, 1952. Courtesy of the office of United States Senator John Thune, South Dakota via Dindi Robinson, Information Research Specialist, Foreign Affairs, Defense & Trade Section, Knowledge Service Group,

Congressional Research Service, Library of Congress, Washington, DC, to author, November 14, 2012.

United States House of Representatives, Military Appropriations Committee, Mr. Mahon, Chairman, "Request for funds for bases not yet authorized for the United States Air Force, fiscal year 1953," March 12, 1952. Courtesy of the office of United States Senator John Thune, South Dakota via Dindi Robinson, Information Research Specialist, Foreign Affairs, Defense & Trade Section, Knowledge Service Group, Congressional Research Service, Library of Congress, Washington, DC, to author, November 14, 2012.

United States Senate and House of Representatives of the United States of America, "Public Law 534, Title III, Continental United States, Strategic Air Command," Washington, DC, July 14, 1952. Courtesy of the office of United States Senator John Thune, South Dakota via Dindi Robinson, Information Research Specialist, Foreign Affairs, Defense & Trade Section, Knowledge Service Group, Congressional Research Service, Library of Congress, Washington, DC, to author, November 14, 2012.

"Units make history with the Air Force's first Homeland Defense ORI." 123rd Airlift Wing, Kentucky Air National Guard, 123rd Airlift Wing Public Affairs, June 3, 2010.

USAF Factsheet. "Douglas C-124 Globemaster II." Dayton, Ohio: National Museum of the United States Air Force. US Army Corps of Engineers, Engineering Branch, War Construction Section, to Operations Branch, Air Forces Project Section. "Proposed Air Support Command Base, Camp Barkeley, Abilene, Texas," July 3, 1942. Courtesy, US Army Corps of Engineers, Historical Archives Section, Washington, DC.

"W-31 nuclear warhead." Albuquerque, New Mexico: The National Museum of Nuclear Science and History.

Warner, Civilian, United States Air Force Air Combat Command, Bomb Wing/CVM, Dyess Air Force Base, Texas, 7th Bomb Wing, "Dyess Air Force Base Linear Air Park aircraft."

Watts, John. "Recollections of C-124Cs at Dyess Air Force Base," to author, December 15, 2012.

Watts, John. "The C-124 and Strategic Air Command," to author, December 20, 2012.

"We don't drop bombs, 7th MUNS wins 4th consecutive Safety Award." Dyess Air Force Base, 7th Bomb Wing Public Affairs.

"Welcome to Dyess AFB Housing." Dyess Air Force Base, 7th Bomb Wing, Public Affairs.

"Winston Churchill's Fulton, Missouri Speech." (Speech made at West Minister College at Fulton, Missouri).

Independence, Missouri: Harry S. Truman Library and Museum. Author (at the time a Lieutenant Colonel, assigned as Commandant of Cadets, University of Iowa), research, August 15, 1986 (material used for Cold War lecture for Junior Air Force Reserve Officer Training Corps, Air Science (AS) 300 class.

"WW2 US Medical Replacement Training Centers (MRTC)." (http://www.med-dept.com/mrtc.php), "XB-47."